DATE DUE

OC 18 01			
NO 20 03			

DEMCO 38-296

Nursery Realms

NURSERY REALMS

Children in the Worlds

of Science Fiction, Fantasy,

and Horror

edited by Gary Westfahl and George Slusser

The University of Georgia Press   Athens and London

© 1999 by the University of Georgia Press
Athens, Georgia 30602
All rights reserved
Designed by Louise O Farrell
Set in 10/13 Sabon by G&S Typesetters, Inc.
Printed and bound by McNaughton & Gunn
The paper in this book meets the guidelines for permanence
and durability of the Committee on Production Guidelines for
Book Longevity of the Council on Library Resources.

Printed in the United States of America
03   02   01   00   99   C   5   4   3   2   1

Library of Congress Cataloging in Publication Data
Nursery realms : children in the worlds of science fiction, fantasy,
    and horror / edited by Gary Westfahl and George Slusser.
          p.   cm.
       Essays from the proceedings of the 15th Annual Eaton
    Conference on Science Fiction and Fantasy Literature, held Apr.
    1993 in Riverside, Calif.
       Includes bibliographical references and index.
       ISBN 0-8203-2095-1 (alk. paper)
       ISBN 0-8203-2144-3 (pbk. : alk paper)
       1. Children in literature—Congresses.   2. Fantasy
    literature—History and criticism—Congresses.   3. Science
    fiction—History and criticism—Congresses.   4. Horror
    tales—History and criticism—Congresses.   I. Westfahl, Gary.
    II. Slusser, George Edgar.   III. Eaton Conference on Science
    Fiction and Fantasy Literature (15th : 1993 : Riverside, Calif.)
       PN56.5.C48N87   1999
       809.3'87609352054—dc21   98-47940
                                        CIP

British Library Cataloging in Publication Data available

Contents

Acknowledgments

The essays in this volume are original, and all but one of them were first presented at the Fifteenth Annual Eaton Conference on Science Fiction and Fantasy Literature, held in Riverside, California, in April 1993. We thank the individuals and organizations that helped with that conference, including Eric S. Rabkin, who coordinated the conference along with George Slusser; assistant coordinator Gladys Murphy; the College of Humanities and Social Sciences, the Tomás Rivera Library, and the Department of Literature and Languages, all of the University of California at Riverside; and Henry Snyder and the Center for Bibliographical Studies and Research of the University of California. Finally, we thank Karen Orchard and her capable colleagues at the University of Georgia Press, who were very helpful in preparing this book for publication, and we extend our appreciation to friends and family members too numerous to mention.

Return to Innocence

Gary Westfahl

In addressing the relationship between children and science fiction, fantasy, and horror, this volume will necessarily confront some of the most fundamental issues raised by these forms of literature; for children arguably represent their origin, implicit audience, and characteristic subject matter. Modern psychologists have explored young children's lack of a reality principle: a kitten, a ray gun, and a magic wand may all seem equally miraculous or equally realistic to a child. Only as they grow older do children learn how to distinguish between the plausible, the implausible, and the impossible. For that reason, one might argue that nonmimetic fiction is by nature the literature of young people, while mimetic fiction is by nature the literature of adults; indeed, Bud Foote makes use of that idea in his analysis of three Stephen King novels. Assuming that ontogeny recapitulates phylogeny, one might further argue that a similar progression occurs in cultural history: young or pretechnological cultures, which like children may have difficulty separating the real from the fantastic, amuse and educate themselves with extravagant myths, legends, and folktales, while maturing cultures come to prefer realistic narratives. To be sure, such views of social development can be properly criticized as arrogant and Eurocentric, since the so-called primitive cultures, when thoughtfully examined, display a maturity and complexity entirely comparable to that of modern Western societies. Yet, these attitudes remain influential, even if unexpressed, and it is because of them that enjoyment of nonmimetic fiction by mature readers or members of mature cultures has regularly been stigmatized as regressive, and even atavistic, behavior—despite the undeniable depth and intelligence of such key figures in its literary history as Mary Shelley, Edgar Allen Poe, William Morris, H. G. Wells, Olaf Stapledon, and J. R. R. Tolkien.

While children may be looked down on as undeveloped adults, they may also be looked up to as beings inherently superior to adults. These contrasting attitudes toward children are epitomized by various pairs of words with common denotations but divergent connotations: childish and childlike, immature and youthful, naive and innocent. Viewed from a different perspective, then, a statement that nonmimetic fiction intrinsically is aimed at or about children would be a compliment, not a criticism. However, one must also recognize that fantasy and horror, on the one hand, and science fiction, on the other hand, have radically different reasons for valuing children as readers and characters.

Western tradition has long honored children as being purer and naturally better than adults because they have not yet been corrupted by worldly ways; they live in William Blake's blessed world of innocence, not his wicked world of experience. So it is that only a virgin can feed a vampire's hunger, and only a virgin can catch a unicorn. And in Christian belief, as Susan Navarette reminds us, children are esteemed as almost prelapsarian beings, closer to God than any adult can be. In narratives involving the assault of demonic or magical evil, therefore, children are the natural victims, and natural opponents, of that evil. Following the model of fantasy proposed by John Clute in *The Encyclopedia of Fantasy,* one could say that horror stories characteristically involve children or adolescents who confront evil and defeat or fall victim to that evil without maturing, while fantasy stories characteristically involve children or adolescents who confront evil and mature into adults in order to defeat it. As Mike Ashley notes, "In fantasy written for adults . . . protagonists are often first encountered as children but normally reach adulthood during their adventures: most fantasy novels are shaped around quests . . . and it is a natural strategy to dramatize the rite of passage into full empowerment as the literal growth of a child or adolescent into adulthood."[1] In both genres, then, children or childlike adults are ubiquitous, perhaps even essential.

Although science fiction is not unaffected by traditional attitudes— consider Andrew Gordon's analysis of *E.T.* as a fairy tale—writers informed by modern science may celebrate children on alternative grounds. Biological evolution often progresses by means of neoteny, the retention of juvenile features in adulthood. Since *Homo sapiens* resemble baby apes in their hairlessness, large heads, and restless curiosity, it is logical to assume that the advanced human beings of the future—*Homo superior*—will emerge from and closely resemble the baby humans of today.[2] In science fiction, then, children may represent not a link to a blissful past, but the vanguard of a strange and unknown future.

Consequently, science fiction displays greater variety in its attitudes toward children than fantasy and horror. Mutant children may be portrayed as horrific counterparts to the demon-possessed children of horror, as in Jerome Bixby's "It's a *Good* Life" and Richard Matheson's "Born of Man and Woman"; or they may emerge as heroic defenders of the human status quo, as in the comic-book adventures of the X-Men, powerful teenage mutants. More disquieting are the ideas that these new children may not be simply evil or good, but rather *different* from us, and that these superior beings may, without malevolent intent, be destined to supplant ordinary humans—a theme that Howard V. Hendrix effectively explores. We remain haunted by the enigmatic stare of the Star Child at the end of *2001: A Space Odyssey:* what does this young and immensely powerful creature plan to do? How will he affect humanity? Despite all the sequels, the questions still seem disturbingly unanswered.

Clearly, then, children are central to any study of science fiction, fantasy, and horror. And while the extensive criticism on children's literature demands continuing respect and attention, this volume emerges from a belief that it is equally important to have the topic of children examined by specialists in the genres of fantastic fiction (along with two biologists and a science fiction novelist, maintaining the Eaton tradition of diverse viewpoints). For one thing, these people can draw more attention to the ways that children are presented in fiction for adults, and this is one major concern of our contributors. This volume may also represent the beginning of a productive dialogue between critics of adult fiction and critics of juvenile fiction, whose professional paths may rarely cross, on a subject of mutual interest.

Part 1, "Fantastic Children: Overviews and Case Studies," opens with Eric Rabkin's "Infant Joys," which links ancient fairy tales to modern science fiction by observing a shared theme of blissful "disempowerment." In "The Humpty Dumpty Effect" Frances Deutsch Louis surveys modern fantasy and science fiction to discover a surprisingly grim outlook on the pains of maturation and making choices. Next come two focused but thoroughgoing studies that follow particular research vectors through science fiction, fantasy, and horror. Susan Kray's "Narrative Uses of Little Jewish Girls in Science Fiction and Fantasy Stories" finds a number of such characters in recent stories and analyzes their functions, while Gary Kern's "The Triumph of Teen-Prop" examines the evolution of a film subgenre—the teen-propaganda, or "teen-prop," film—that culminates in such recent horror and science fiction films as the *Psycho* sequels and *Terminator II*.

Part 2, "The Children of Science Fiction," begins with George Slusser's "The Forever Child," which observes in Orson Scott Card's *Ender's Game* and other works a key transformation of the standard image of children in science fiction. Neurophysiologist Joseph D. Miller's "The Child as Alien" places a number of science fiction works in the context of modern biological knowledge about children. Science fiction novelist Howard V. Hendrix's "Baby's Next Step" examines the theme of the *Homo superior* child, focusing on *2001* and Frank Herbert's *Children of Dune*. And Andrew Gordon's "*E.T.* as Fairy Tale" ponders the popularity of this landmark film and relates its success to its borrowings from a number of traditional genres and themes.

Part 3, "The Children of Fantasy and Horror," begins with Gay Barton's "Child Vision in the Fantasy of George MacDonald," which sees children as central to the work of that seminal fantasy writer. Alida Allison's "If Not Today, Then Tomorrow" studies attitudes toward childhood in the nonfictional and fictional writings of Isaac Bashevis Singer. In "A Real-World Source for the 'Little People,'" biologist Howard Lenhoff argues that a newly recognized genetic condition accounts for a large body of folklore and literature featuring small people with magical talents. Lynne Lundquist's and my "Coming of Age in Fantasyland" surveys the Walt Disney animated films and discerns a surprising stance rejecting parental authority and endorsing self-parenting. Connecting fantasy to horror, Stephanie Barbé Hammer's "Nasty Boys, Feminine Longing, and Mourning the Mother in J. M. Barrie's *Peter Pan* and Anne Rice's *The Witching Hour*" finds in both works the character of the immature male repressing the victimized woman. Susan Navarette's "Unsealing Sense in *The Turn of the Screw*" contextualizes a key moment in Henry James's work to account for its horrific effect. Finally, Bud Foote's "Getting Things in the Right Order" considers the role of children as both subjects and audience in the three generic models employed by Stephen King.

Certainly, as an analysis of children in fantastic literature, this volume can be defended only as a starting point; as one early reader noted, several volumes of essays would be required to achieve something resembling comprehensive coverage of this vast and diverse subject. Nevertheless, we present here a rich collection of essays—ranging from overviews to author studies and representing a variety of critical approaches—that together provide a preliminary survey of the territory, a foundation for further inquiry, and many ideas for additional research. So, this is a volume that—like the stories in the genres it examines—invites interested readers to begin again, as children, and to look at familiar texts and topics from a fresh perspective. At least for a while, therefore, critics in all fields might fruitfully let the little children lead them.

Notes

1. Mike Ashley, "Children," in *The Encyclopedia of Fantasy,* ed. John Clute and John Grant (New York: St. Martin's Press, 1997), 184.
2. As discussed in my "The Genre That Evolved: On Science Fiction as Children's Literature," *Foundation: The Review of Science Fiction* 62 (Winter 1994–95): 70–75.

Part I

Fantastic Children: Overviews and Case Studies

Infant Joys: The Pleasures of Disempowerment in Fantasy and Science Fiction

Eric S. Rabkin

An influential essay by Mark Hillegas speaks of two "elements" of science fiction. The second, less important, element is "the belief that the universe is a machine, indifferent to man and lacking a divine plan or purpose." The first, overwhelmingly important, element is "the Baconian faith that by the systematic investigation of nature man can master the secrets of this mysterious universe and in so doing improve the human condition."[1] Whether or not science fiction truly worries often about "the human condition," it clearly offers "power fantasies,"[2] stories in which an adolescent or young adult can make a transition from a condition of powerlessness to a condition of power and thus save him- (rarely her-) self and, by the bye, the universe.

The pulp tradition, going all the way back to such works as *Frank Reade and His Steam Man of the Prairie* (1878), offers readers the chance vicariously to whomp bad guys and simultaneously tame the Old West or, in the case of Hugo Gernsback's pivotal *Ralph 124C 41+* (1911, 1925), thwart the aliens and win a bride. Although Jack Carter of Virginia may have lost the Civil War on Earth before the beginning of Edgar Rice Burroughs's Mars novels, from *A Princess of Mars* (1912) onward, John Carter of Mars can pacify and procreate. Robert A. Heinlein, who has "repeatedly been voted 'best all-time author' in readers' polls,"[3] typically offers a hero who painlessly supplants a father figure and assumes the older man's mantle of power, either by virtue of separation from the father figure, as when the protagonist of *The Puppet Masters* takes off for the

3

"nest" of the title baddies to bring them, in the novel's famous last line, "*Death and Destruction!*"[4] or by virtue of the convenient death of the father figure, as when Professor Bernardo de la Paz succumbs at a crucial moment to allow Man, the aptly nicknamed hero of *The Moon Is a Harsh Mistress* (1966), to finish the revolution on his own. Power fantasies involve not only adolescent protagonists but child protagonists as well. We find boy heroes who save the day in such works as Orson Scott Card's *Ender's Game* (1977, 1985) and juvenile novels such as Andre Norton's *Catseye* (1961) and Arthur C. Clarke's *Dolphin Island* (1963). Against this background, I want to consider the appeals not of power but of real and putative powerlessness. I want to examine the typically ignored but nonetheless compelling attraction of submission, regression, and self-negation in the infantile fantasies we can find in literature from biblical narrative to fairy tales to modern science fiction.

Perhaps the best known biblical injunction concerning the importance of children comes from the lips of Jesus:

> At the same time came the disciples unto Jesus, saying, Who is the greatest in the kingdom of heaven?
>
> And Jesus called a little child unto him, and set him in the midst of them,
>
> And said, Verily I say unto you, Except ye be converted, and become as little children, ye shall not enter into the kingdom of heaven.
>
> Whosoever therefore shall humble himself as this little child, the same is greatest in the kingdom of heaven.
>
> And whoso shall receive one such little child in my name receiveth me.
>
> But whoso shall offend one of these little ones which believe in me, it were better for him that a millstone were hanged about his neck, and that he were drowned in the depth of the sea.
>
> Woe unto the world because of offences! for it must needs be that offences come; but woe to that man by whom the offence cometh!
>
> Wherefore if thy hand or thy foot offend thee, cut them off, and cast them from thee: it is better for thee to enter into life halt or maimed, rather than having two hands or two feet to be cast into everlasting fire. (Matthew 18:1–8)

This passage is traditionally construed, no doubt correctly, as a warning against both causing sin and sinning.[5] But why is this warning necessary? The word *child* probably comes from the Gothic *kilthei,* meaning "womb."[6] Thus a child is anyone still identifiable primarily by his or her condition of being born. In this sense, a child is the opposite of a fully developed human being, a "mortal," someone identifiable primarily by his or her susceptibility to death. Children are traditionally said to represent innocence.[7] The word *innocence* is cognate with *noxious* and derives from the Latin *nocere,* "to harm" (Stein); innocence, then, is the condition of being unharmed. The opposite of *innocence* is *experience,* as in the title of William Blake's famous collection of poems called *Songs of Innocence and of Experience.* Adults are experienced, and therefore spiritually harmed. *Experience* comes from the Latin *experientia,* "the act of trying," and is thus akin to Latin *periculum,* "attempt," and cognate with the Italian *pericolo,* "danger," the French *peur,* "fear," and the English *peril* (Stein). The world this passage presupposes, then, is one in which any experience is necessarily noxious and dangerous to the soul. The hands and feet with which we attempt actions may cause or commit sin, so we may be better off without them, maimed in body but unblemished in soul. The dismemberment suggests the desirability of reducing the person to a powerless torso. Note that the child does not walk into the circle of the disciples; rather, Jesus "set[s] him in the midst of them." This passage emphatically centers on a *little* child, that is, an infant. The word *infant* means "not speaking" (Stein). Infants possess the special, silent virtue of the "infantry": "Theirs but to do and die."[8] Jesus seems to be suggesting that the only route to salvation lies in abject powerlessness, a reduction of self, and a regression to a state before the acquisition of speech. The enormous social and political power of speech is, of course, made clear in God's punishment of the attempt to build the tower of Babel to Heaven: God multiplies human languages so that humankind can no longer communicate, for otherwise "nothing will be restrained from them, which they have imagined to do" (Genesis 11:6). Give up your hands, your feet, your very language, Jesus preaches; heavenly pleasures will reward your infancy.

Although the term *power fantasy* is not usually used in discussions of fairy tales, the outcomes of these traditional stories typically conform to the wishes of the protagonist: Cinderella got her Prince, and the boastful Brave Little Tailor who killed "'Seven [flies] with one blow!'" then "reigned as a king and remained king for the rest of his life."[9] For our purposes, however, there is another, less well known Grimm brothers tale worth reviewing, called "Lucky Hans":

> After Hans had served his master for seven years, he said to him, "Master, my time is up, and since I want to go back home to my mother now, I'd like to have my wages."
>
> "You've served me faithfully and honestly," said the master, "and I shall reward you in kind."

So he gave Hans a gold nugget as big as his head, whereupon Hans pulled a kerchief out of his pocket, wrapped it around the nugget, lifted it to his shoulder, and set out for home. As he was meandering along, one foot following the other, he caught a glimpse of a rider trotting toward him on a lively horse. The man appeared to be very cheerful and vigorous.

"Ah!" said Hans very loudly. "Riding is such a wonderful thing! All you have to do is sit there as if you were in a chair. You never have to worry about stumbling on stones. You can save on shoes and get wherever you want in a jiffy."

Upon hearing Hans speak this way, the rider stopped his horse and cried out, "If that's so, why in the world are you walking, Hans?"

"I have to," he answered. "I've got to carry this large nugget. Sure, it's gold, but it's so heavy that I can't keep my head straight, and my shoulder's been feeling the weight."

"I'll tell you what," said the horseman. "Let's exchange. I'll give you my horse, and you give me your gold nugget."

"Gladly," said Hans. "But let me warn you, it's a terribly heavy load to carry."

[Hans is first happy with the horse but finds he cannot control the animal and is thrown. A farmer retrieves the horse and Hans makes another happy trade, the mare for a cow. Hans continues, happily foreseeing a life filled with milk, butter, and cheese, until he discovers the cow is dry. Complaining aloud, he attracts a butcher who pleases Hans by trading him a succulent pig for the stringy cow. Soon Hans meets a boy with a goose who tells him that a pig has been stolen recently in the next town and Hans is likely to be punished for it, so Hans gladly trades the pig for the goose. Continuing his journey, Hans stops to talk to a scissors grinder who is happy because] "a good scissors grinder is someone who always finds money whenever he digs into his pocket." [He trades Hans a cracked grindstone and an ordinary rock for the goose. But to carry these tools of his imagined new trade is dreadfully tiring. Hans spots a well, lays the grindstone and rock on the edge so he can drink, and accidentally knocks his possessions into the water.] As Hans saw the stones sink to the bottom he jumped up for joy. He then knelt down and thanked God with tears in his eyes for showing him such mercy and for relieving him of the stones in such a gracious way. Indeed, those stones had become a great burden for him.

"Nobody under the sun is as lucky as I am!" exclaimed Hans, and with a light heart and free from all his burdens, he now ran all the way home until he reached his mother.[10]

If *The Puppet Masters* is a power fantasy, then "Lucky Hans," like Jesus' instructions to the disciples, is a disempowerment fantasy. At the simplest psychological level, the story concerns a return from seven years of economic captivity to the bosom of parental care. Before the story begins, Hans has been using his hands and feet at some sort of apprenticeship, and he uses them within the story to transport possessions and then the tools of a new trade, but, as Jesus said, "whoso shall offend one of these little ones which believe in me, it were better for him that a millstone were hanged about his neck, and that he were drowned in the depth of the sea." Hans instinctively knows better than to offend his own infancy through commodified labor; gold is heavy. Hans praises God for the better fortune of having the grindstone (millstone) fall in the well (sea) and returns virtually naked to his parents' care. This regression is a powerful psychological reward according to Freud, who cannot think of any need in childhood as strong as the need for a father's protection."[11] That Freud sees "parent" as the more specific "father" has to do with his own upbringing and with his interest in discussing the evolution of Western religion with its male god, rather than the Grimm brothers' concern with producing domestic dramas, but the point is clear nonetheless. Dissolution in the fertile water of benign authority is a blessing.

Erich Fromm sees this feeling of blessedness arising from the alleviation of the anxiety of isolation. He notes that human infants—and little children—require the care of adults in order to survive. "The possibility of being left alone is necessarily the most serious threat to the child's whole existence."[12] According to Fromm, since the Renaissance, and particularly since the Reformation, psychological isolation has been an ever more oppressive burden, the inevitable corollary of a growing freedom occasioned by the intertwined developments of capitalism and Protestantism: each individual his or her own economic and theological agent, each individual "left alone." For many people the changes that produced a "freedom *from*" the fixed roles and expectations of the Middle Ages implied psychological loss because they were unable to seize a "freedom *to*" establish important human relations. Fromm, writing in 1940, identifies two main routes to escape this freedom: in the United States, the science fictional "automaton conformity" (208), and in the then-rising Fascist nations of Europe, an "authoritarianism" that caters to "the tendency to give up the independence of one's own individual self and to fuse one's self with somebody or something outside of oneself in order to acquire the strength which the individual self is lacking" (163). Hitler too understood that this need to lose the self "leads men to voluntary acknowledgment of the privilege of force and strength and thus makes them become a dust particle of that order which forms and shapes the entire universe" (cited in Fromm 253). Dissolution, dust mote, and self-negation are the terms of Hans's regression, but because God has blessed him, he is driven not to Hitler but to mother.

> Freud reports that Romain Rolland wrote to him about a peculiar feeling, which he himself is never without, which he finds confirmed by many others and which he may suppose is present in millions of people . . . a feeling which he would like to call a sensation of "eternity," a feeling as of something limitless, unbounded—as it were, "oceanic." This feeling, he adds, is a purely subjective fact, not an article of faith; it brings with it no assurance of personal immortality, but it is the source of the religious energy which is seized upon by the various Churches and religious systems, directed by them into particular channels, and doubtless also exhausted by them. One may . . . rightly call oneself religious on the ground of this oceanic feeling alone, even if one rejects every belief and every illusion.[13]

I believe that the oceanic feeling Rolland and Freud identify with religion is the same satisfaction Fromm sees in totalitarianism. Jesus would have us be as little children; the Fatherland would have us regain relatedness as a dust particle in the infantry. In all cases, we are disempowered of freedom and speech; we exist only as part of the whole. The slugs from Titan that invade human minds in *The Puppet Masters* speak as "we," not "I," and claim they represent not an invasion but an offering of "peace . . . contentment—and the joy of—of surrender."[14] A more physical metaphor for the reduction of the individual to the infantile underlies the satire in Bernard Wolfe's *Limbo*. After a terrible world war and major advances in prostheses, people, like Hans working his way back to his mother, invite progressive, voluntary amputation. The more artificial limbs one has, the higher one's social status. In this world, the politically correct slogans are "HE WHO HAS ARMS IS ARMED . . . WAR IS ON ITS LAST LEGS . . . MAKE DISARMAMENT LAST . . . TWO LEGS SHORTER, A HEAD TALLER . . . ARMS OR THE MAN . . . PACIFISM MEANS PASSIVITY . . . NO DEMOBILIZATION WITHOUT IMMOBILIZATION."[15] Some extremists even have their artificial limbs removed so they can become swaddled "doll-sized figures in baskets" (157) set out in store windows preaching immobilization via microphones suspended above their lips. The narrator theorizes that the "charisma" of such an "amp" is that he "dramatized . . . the fact that one could not backtrack in psychic time without self-mutilation. Once dispossessed from the womb and the nursery, no man could buy megalomania save at the cost of slashing violence to his own person and personality" (161). "If thy hand or thy foot offend thee, cut them off." Wolfe agrees with Fromm that such regressive tendencies are "masochistic" (Wolfe 161; Fromm 163), but not all disempowerment fantasies repudiate this regression and self-negation. Although Miranda in Shakespeare's *The Tempest* "took pains to make [Caliban] speak," he remained thoroughly isolated. "You taught me language, and my profit on't / Is, I know how to curse. The red plague rid you / For learning me your language" (I.ii.363–65). Caliban, like Hans, would gladly revert to childhood and the kindly authority of his mother.

There is something compelling about the prelinguistic, the childlike, the oceanic, the humble. When Frankenstein's monster seeks to persuade his creator to end the monster's isolation by providing him with a bride, he begins by establishing his own history from its very beginning, at least as he recalls it:

> It is with considerable difficulty that I remember the original era of my being: all the events of that period appear confused and indistinct. A strange multiplicity of sensations seized me, and I saw, felt, heard, and smelt, at the same time; and it was, indeed, a long time before I learned to distinguish between the operations of my various senses. By degrees, I remember, a stronger light pressed upon my nerves, so that I was obliged to shut my eyes. Darkness then came over me, and troubled me; but hardly had I felt this, when, by opening my eyes, as I now suppose, the light poured in upon me again. I walked, and, I believe, descended.[16]

The monster's descent is, in a sense, like the Fall of Adam and Eve, a separation from the sustaining power of God or nature through an access of knowledge, language, experience. Solomon, on first becoming king, goes to a "high place" and humbly makes "a thousand burnt offerings" to God (1 Kings 3:4). He is then asked in a dream what gift he wishes. "Give . . . thy servant an understanding heart to judge thy people, that I may discern between good and bad" (1 Kings 3:9). God is pleased that Solomon has asked nothing for himself, so his wish is granted. Immediately on descending to Jerusalem, Solomon must judge the famous dispute between two women each claiming maternity of a single male infant.

> And the king said, Bring me a sword. And they brought a sword before the king.

And the king said, Divide the living child in two, and give half to the one, and half to the other.

Then spake the woman whose the living child was unto the king, for her bowels yearned upon her son, and she said, O my lord, give her the living child, and in no wise slay it. But the other said, Let it be neither mine nor thine, but divide it.

Then the king answered and said, Give her the living child, and in no wise slay it: she is the mother thereof.

And all Israel heard of the judgment which the king had judged; and they feared the king: for they saw that the wisdom of God was in him, to do judgment. (1 Kings 3:24–28)

There are really five characters in this passage: God, the two women, and two male children: Solomon and the infant. Because Solomon humbled himself before God, he was granted wisdom. Because the infant, which is necessarily powerless, is beloved by its mother, the sword does not fall. Solomon is able to see past the women's language to the truth behind their words. Because Solomon has manipulated the situation so that the silent child is preserved, Israel understands that the power of God is in Solomon. In both cases, then, that of Solomon and that of the infant, humility obviates language and brings the protection and justice of God.

Though Frankenstein, like God, first grants the monster his wish, he later reneges and destroys the nearly complete bride. The monster persuaded his creator on the glacier of Chamonix; Victor dies on the Arctic Ocean. There is no therapeutic oceanism here. Yet, after the horrors of the book and Frankenstein's exhausted death, the now permanently isolated monster has no other recourse than a regression backward to his—and Solomon's—beginning:

"But soon," [the monster] cried, with sad and solemn enthusiasm, "I shall die, and what I now feel be no longer felt. Soon these burning miseries will be extinct. I shall ascend my funeral pile triumphantly, and exult in the agony of the torturing flames. The light of that conflagration will fade away; my ashes will be swept into the sea by the winds. My spirit will sleep in peace; or if it thinks, it will not surely think thus. Farewell." [17]

This end is like that of Edna Pontellier, the protagonist of *The Awakening*, a woman who cannot find sustaining relatedness in the world. She has even abandoned her small children. So, in the novel's last paragraph, she swims out into the horizonless Gulf of Mexico, replaying backward the imagery of her life until "the hum of bees and the musky odor of pinks filled the air."[18] "But whoso shall offend one of these little ones . . . it were better for him that a millstone were hanged about his neck, and that he were drowned in the depth of the sea." After that, silence.

If regression may be a balm for the disappointed, it may also be a dream for the hopeful. As I argue elsewhere,[19] virtually all utopias, no matter what their ostensible setting in space or time, rehearse some distant past of the life of the individual or her culture. In *News from Nowhere,* William Morris's dreamer is given a tour of a future utopia. His guide tells the Victorian that

> "it is the child-like part of us that produces works of imagination. When we are children time passes so slow with us that we seem to have time for everything."
>
> He sighed, and then smiled and said: "At least let us rejoice that we have got back our childhood again. I drink to the days that are!"[20]

H. G. Wells's Time Traveller arrives in the future to find pacific, childlike Eloi, who make him feel "like a schoolmaster." Since apparently "the whole earth had become a garden," the Time Traveller naturally concludes—wrongly—that he is in utopia.[21] This seems to be Paradise regained. In fact, it is not even clear to him that the Eloi have language. We are reminded of Blake's "song of innocence," "Infant Joy":

> "I have no name:
> I am but two days old."
> What shall I call thee?
> "I happy am,
> Joy is my name."
> Sweet joy befall thee!
>
> Pretty joy!
> Sweet joy but two days old,
> Sweet joy I call thee:
> Thou dost smile,
> I sing the while,
> Sweet joy befall thee![22]

By contrast, Blake's "song of experience," "Infant Sorrow," makes it clear that one powerful, attractive escape from our world is via infantile regression:

My mother groan'd! my father wept.
Into the dangerous world I leapt:
Helpless, naked, piping loud:
Like a fiend hid in a cloud.

Struggling in my father's hands,
Striving against my swadling [*sic*] bands,
Bound and weary I thought best
To sulk upon my mother's breast. (559)

Blake, like the unknown originator of "Lucky Hans," Fromm, and writers of science fiction, understood that industrialization too often enforces a terrifying isolation on individuals. The pitiful orphan in Blake's "The Chimney Sweeper" speaks for those cut loose by capitalism. Himself a child, he cherishes the dream of a fellow sweeper and offers a pathetic hope for a heavenly father:

When my mother died I was very young,
And my father sold me while yet my tongue
Could scarcely cry "'weep! 'weep! 'weep!"
So your chimneys I sweep, & in soot I sleep.

There's little Tom Dacre, who cried when his head
That curl'd like a lamb's back, was shav'd: so I said
"Hush, Tom! never mind it, for when your head's bare
You know that the soot cannot spoil your white hair."

And so he was quiet, & that very night,
As Tom was a-sleeping, he had such a sight!
That thousands of sweepers, Dick, Joe, Ned, & Jack,
Were all of them lock'd up in coffins of black.

And by came an Angel who had a bright key,
And he open'd the coffins & set them all free;
Then down a green plain leaping, laughing, they run,
And wash in a river, and shine in the Sun.

Then naked & white, all their bags left behind,
They rise upon clouds and sport in the wind;
And the Angel told Tom, if he'd be a good boy,
He'd have God for his father, & never want joy.

> And so Tom awoke; and we rose in the dark,
> And got with our bags & our brushes to work.
> Tho' the morning was cold, Tom was happy & warm;
> So if all do their duty they need not fear harm. (539)

Would that such faith were always rewarded.

If the faith of little children, if the oceanic powerlessness of infancy, is necessary in the world created by science, technology, and the other driving forces that spawn science fiction, then perhaps salvation lies in a dream not of personal regression but of technological regression. This is what Ray Bradbury offers in "The Million-Year Picnic," the story that concludes *The Martian Chronicles* and arguably, since it was written and published first, dominates that composite novel. After the Earth has virtually destroyed itself with atomic war, we follow a family that has managed to come to Mars on a private rocket, which, once all are safe, the father destroys.

> "Why'd you blow up the rocket, Dad?"
>
> "So we can't go back, ever. And so if any of those evil men ever come to Mars they won't know we're here."[23]

The father proceeds, with less obvious practical reason, to make a "funeral pile," as Frankenstein's monster might call it, of official papers, government bonds, and other artifacts of language.

> I'm burning a way of life. . . . Science ran too far ahead of us too quickly,
> and the people got lost in a mechanical wilderness, like children making over
> pretty things, gadgets, helicopters, rockets; emphasizing the wrong items,
> emphasizing machines instead of how to run the machines. Wars got bigger
> and bigger and finally killed Earth. That's what the *silent* [my emphasis] radio
> means. That's what we ran away from. . . . We were lucky. There aren't any
> more rockets left. . . . Interplanetary travel won't be back for centuries, maybe
> never. But that way of life proved itself wrong and strangled itself with its own
> hands. You're young. I'll tell you this again every day until it sinks in. (180)

The father's use of the phrase "sinks in" resonates powerfully with notions of regression and oceanism. He says that there is still hope on Mars because it "would have been another century before Mars would have been really poisoned by the Earth civilization." The book ends with the family beside a water-filled canal:

> It was long and straight and cool and wet and reflective in the night.
> "I've always wanted to see a Martian," said Michael. "Where are they,
> Dad? You promised."
> "There they are," said Dad, and he shifted Michael on his shoulder and
> pointed straight down.
> The Martians were there. Timothy began to shiver.
> The Martians were there—in the canal—reflected in the water. Timothy
> and Michael and Robert and Mom and Dad.
> The Martians stared up at them for a long, long silent time from the rip-
> pling water . . . [sic]. (181)

If only one can give up one's identity as an Earth person, one can be reborn, baptized in the silent canal waters of Mars.

In *More than Human,* Theodore Sturgeon offers an alternative anti-
technological dream. His main characters are all marginalized and almost
all children. All but one, Hip Barrows, has some sort of paranormal mental power; the most powerful of all is a crib-ridden, permanent infant
called Baby. In the course of the novel, these outcasts join together one by
one, communicating telepathically to coordinate their powers. At the end,
the lead outcast, Gerry, an angry, vengeful, murderous adolescent, is captured by Hip. Gerry wants to kill Hip for temporarily immobilizing him.
Hip knows this but makes an "ethical" decision and releases Gerry, who
begins to fire up his mental weapons but then, caught by his own astonishment at Hip's gesture of self-negation, puts vengeance aside. At that moment the book's postulated "evolution" to "*Homo gestalt*" takes place,
and the ordinary Hip is incorporated into the now-whole being that had
been forming from Gerry and his extraordinary cohorts.

> For a long time the only sound was Gerry's difficult breathing. Suddenly even
> this stopped, as something happened, something—*spoke.*
> It came again.
> *Welcome.*
> The voice was a *silent* one [my emphasis]. And here, another, silent too, but
> another for all that. *It's the new one. Welcome, child!*
> Still another: *Well, well, well! We thought you'd never make it.*
> *He had to. There hasn't been a new one for so long.*[24]

It is only at this point, at the novel's conclusion, that the characters and
the reader discover that there have been gods all along to whom one could
humble oneself. "Welcome, child!"

In a related way, only at the end of *A Canticle for Leibowitz,* when the "Flame Deluge" (another immersion) of renewed nuclear war awakens Rachel, the mutant second head on the shoulders of Mrs. Grales, do we see the possibility of salvation in someone who "had only just now been born."[25] For fantasy and science fiction, it seems, and for those of us who seek solace through those genres, if truly God's in his heaven, then—or so the oceanic dream of childhood goes—all's right with the world.

Perhaps the most famous child of self-negation in science fiction is the fetal Star Child that floats above the Earth at the conclusion of Stanley Kubrick's film *2001: A Space Odyssey* (1968). Although Kubrick leaves the meaning of that image ambiguous, Clarke, at the end of his novelization of his own and Kubrick's screenplay, makes the power inherent in this transformation utterly clear. "There before him, a glittering toy no Star Child could resist, floated the planet Earth with all its peoples. . . . [T]hough he was master of the world, he was not quite sure what to do next. But he would think of something."[26] The question is, do we dread or dream of what that something might be?

Perhaps the key interpretive debate about images of childlike oceanism in fantasy and science fiction springs from Fromm's recognition that the regressive "escape from freedom" often serves ruthless power. While Solomon was wise to abase himself before God, surely Wolfe's "amps" were not wise to abase themselves before the public. Solomon's recompense was for himself and his people a nation of justice; the amps' recompense was for themselves and their fellows a nation of cripples. But one person's just punishment is another person's masochism; one person's self-negation is another person's oceanic participation in some absolute ideal, be it the church, the state, the family, or even a cult of personality. We can explore that debate by comparing Clarke's *Childhood's End* with Olaf Stapledon's *Star Maker.*

In *Childhood's End,* Clarke's most widely cited work, so-called Overlords descend to Earth orbit and prohibit humankind's further technological development so that we will not destroy ourselves before we can undergo what comes to be called Total Breakthrough, a process by which humans will acquire a vast mental power that the Overlords wish to study and possess. In the course of a couple of generations under the Overlords' restraint, humanity achieves a number of diverse putative utopias, but each has some flaw, be it a lack of creativity or plain, inevitable boredom.[27] Finally, in an epidemic of impossible postconception mutation, all the children in the world—but only the children—change from *Homo sapiens* into something else, a fantastic, disembodied hive mind that first forms itself into a pillar of fire and then rises from the Earth, hovers, and finally destroys the planet before leaving our solar system forever. All this is witnessed by the one surviving ordinary man, Jan Rodricks, who had stowed away on the Overlords' ship in order to visit their home planet. At their behest, and fulfilling his own desire, he has returned to the vicinity of Earth to watch Total Breakthrough and report it to the Overlords; he is a truly powerless star child who undergoes a replaying backward of Genesis. Not only does he return home to Earth, he also observes the undoing of biblical creation. Is this new phase of human existence, the maturity that comes with "childhood's end," good or bad? Most critics have taken the Overlords as "powerful forces for good" and Total Breakthrough as "the highest achievement of mankind," [28] but with the utter loss of individuality that Total Breakthrough entails, for many, "childhood's end" is humanity's end. "*Childhood's End* is not really utopian . . . so much as it is a critique of utopian goals." [29]

A look at Stapledon might help us to understand Clarke better, for Clarke acknowledges the formative influence of Stapledon's writing on his own: at the age of twelve, he says, it "produced an overwhelming impact upon me." [30] In *Star Maker,* which has been called an "unsurpassed . . . spiritual voyage," [31] Stapledon presents a narrator who begins as an ordinary human but soon, guided by more advanced races, becomes a disembodied viewpoint. [32] As our narrator travels through the cosmic oceans of creation, he goes first to visit beings most like humans, merges with at least one of them at each stage, and then proceeds, each stage opening more knowledge to him as he releases his sense of self. One could see this narrator as a hive mind anticipating Clarke's Total Breakthrough except for three crucial differences between the novels: first, while it is Stapledon's advanced mind that is narrating the story, Clarke's new humanity ignores all *Homo sapiens,* including the reader; second, while Stapledon's narrator struggles to find a language to convey his insights ("Though human language and even human thought itself are perhaps in their very nature incapable of metaphysical truth, something I must somehow contrive to express, even if only by metaphor" [412]), Clarke's narration is unremittingly ordinary; and third, while merging in Stapledon is compared to marriage, the narrator's "prized atom of community" (257), Clarke's mutated humans are no longer a community at all but an entity. In other words, Stapledon offers us a chance to embrace opposition (for example, he discovers that "the normal voluntary activity of a star appears to be no other than the star's *normal* physical movement studied by our science" [387]), while Clarke insists that a recognition of powers beyond us obliterates, rather than enriches, life as we know it. With its intolerance for the diversity of experience, particularly the experience of others, Clarke's regression to self-negation is authoritarian indeed.

Both *Star Maker* and *Childhood's End* appear to concern politics as well as psychology. Each displays a variety of utopias adapted to different conditions, and each deals with and is motivated by a current world crisis: the rise of Fascism for Stapledon and the cold war for Clarke. But while Clarke uses the attraction of infant joy as an escape, Stapledon uses it as a way to understand his fellow humans and pleads for cooperation, not submersion. These works, then, suggest that science fiction, even in its disempowerment fantasies, may offer veiled power fantasies. But if we use these fantasies to escape the public realm of adult interaction, childlike submergence risks authorizing a feeble wish for a miracle such as the emergence of Miller's Rachel, or covert initiation of full-blown authoritarianism. At that point, no matter how attractive disempowerment fantasies may be, we must remember the words of Paul the Apostle: "When I was a child, I spake as a child, I understood as a child, I thought as a child: but when I became a man, I put away childish things" (1 Corinthians 13:11). When childish things lead us astray, as they do in *Childhood's End*, we must, sad to say, abandon infant joys. However, by also comparing other fantastic genres—say, biblical wisdom tales such as that of Solomon or fairy tales such as "Lucky Hans"—we recognize that so long as regression is confined to the psychology of childhood and to the play of childlikeness in the lives of adults, disempowerment fantasies may offer us spiritual insight and refreshment. And for that may we all be humbly grateful.

Notes

1. Mark Hillegas, "Science Fiction as a Cultural Phenomenon: A Re-Evaluation" (1962), in *SF: The Other Side of Realism,* ed. Thomas D. Clareson (Bowling Green: Bowling Green University Popular Press, 1971), 273, 272.

2. Eric S. Rabkin, "Science Fiction Power Fantasy: Heinlein's *The Puppet Masters,*" *English Record,* Winter 1978, 6–8.

3. David Pringle, "Robert A. Heinlein," in *The Science Fiction Encyclopedia,* ed. Peter Nicholls (New York: Doubleday, 1979), 279.

4. Robert A. Heinlein, *The Puppet Masters* (New York: Signet, 1951), 175.

5. M. Jack Suggs, Katharine Doob Sakenfeld, and James R. Mueller, eds., *The Oxford Study Bible* (New York: Oxford University Press, 1992), 1287.

6. Jess Stein, ed., *The Random House Dictionary of the English Language,* unabr. ed. (New York: Random House, 1966). Later parenthetical references to "Stein" in the text are to this edition.

7. J. C. Cooper, *An Illustrated Encyclopedia of Traditional Symbols* (London: Thames and Hudson, 1978).

8. Joseph T. Shipley, *The Origins of English Words: A Discursive Dictionary of Indo-European Roots* (Baltimore: Johns Hopkins University Press, 1984).

9. Jakob Grimm and Wilhelm Grimm, *The Complete Fairy Tales of the Brothers Grimm,* exp. ed., trans. Jack Zipes (1812–15; New York: Bantam Books, 1992), 80, 86.

10. Grimm and Grimm, 302–7.

11. Sigmund Freud, *Civilization and Its Discontents,* trans. James Strachey (1930; New York: Norton, 1961), 20.

12. Erich Fromm, *Escape from Freedom* (1941; New York: Avon Press, 1969), 36. Later page references in the text are to this edition.

13. Freud, 11–12.

14. Heinlein, 58.

15. Bernard Wolfe, *Limbo* (1952; New York: Carroll and Graf, 1987), 115. Later page references in the text are to this edition.

16. Mary Shelley, *Frankenstein, or The Modern Prometheus,* ed. M. K. Joseph (1818; New York: Oxford University Press, 1985), 102.

17. Shelley, 223.

18. Kate Chopin, *The Awakening,* ed. Margaret Culley (1899; New York: Norton, 1976), 114.

19. Eric S. Rabkin, "Atavism and Utopia," *Alternative Futures* 1 (Spring 1978): 71–82.

20. William Morris, *News from Nowhere, or An Epoch of Rest* (1890; London: Routledge and Kegan Paul, 1970), 87.

21. H. G. Wells, *The Time Machine* (1895), in *The Time Machine and The War of the Worlds* (New York: Fawcett, 1986), 45, 47.

22. William Blake, *Songs of Innocence and of Experience* (1789, 1794), in *The Complete Poetry and Selected Prose of John Donne and The Complete Poetry of William Blake* (New York: Modern Library, 1941), 545. Later page references in the text are to this edition.

23. Ray Bradbury, *The Martian Chronicles* (1950; New York: Bantam Books, 1970), 179. Later page references in the text are to this edition.

24. Theodore Sturgeon, *More than Human* (1953; New York: Ballantine Books, 1971), 186.

25. Walter M. Miller Jr., *A Canticle for Leibowitz* (1959; New York: Bantam Books, 1988), 309.

26. Arthur C. Clarke, *2001: A Space Odyssey* (New York: Signet, 1968), 220–21.

27. Arthur C. Clarke, *Childhood's End* (1953; New York: Ballantine Books, 1972), 75.

28. Alan B. Howes, "Expectation and Surprise in *Childhood's End,*" in *Arthur C. Clarke,* ed. Joseph D. Olander and Martin Harry Greenberg (New York: Taplinger, 1977), 170.

29. David N. Samuelson, "*Childhood's End:* A Median Stage of Adolescence?" in *Arthur C. Clarke,* 198.

30. Arthur C. Clarke, Introduction to *The Lion of Comarre and Against the Fall of Night* (New York: Harcourt, Brace and World, 1968), vii.

31. Brian Aldiss, *Trillion Year Spree: The History of Science Fiction* (1986; New York: Avon Press, 1988), 195.

32. Olaf Stapledon, *Star Maker* (1937), in *Last and First Men and Star Maker* (New York: Dover, n.d.), 268, 259. Later page references in the text are to this edition.

The Humpty Dumpty Effect, or Was the Old Egg Really All It Was Cracked Up to Be: Context and Coming of Age in Science Fiction and Fantasy

Frances Deutsch Louis

Childhood can be defined as a lack of context—the absence of a framework in which to place the terrifying and incomprehensible things that happen to body and mind. The key emotion of childhood is fear, a fear we learn to live with through the process of finding our context and relating the self within to the world without. When humans lived in isolated tribes, coming of age was not so much choice as formal announcement; it was not that the adolescent acknowledged the elders, but that the elders acknowledged the adolescent. Only when "the people" (as all groups once called themselves) discovered that there was another "people" two rivers, one forest, and three mountains away in the direction of the setting sun did coming of age begin to involve not just ritual but individual choice.

And choice is tough. Choice is painful and often irrevocable. Despite the happiness that may come from the contexts we choose, there remain a powerful nostalgia for lost childhoods and a wistful longing for the roads we did not take. And looming over such laments is the chilling knowledge of future death, eliminating new choices and any chance to repair the damage done by old ones.

These gloomy thoughts may seem inappropriate in a volume devoted to science fiction and fantasy, especially one devoted to children in science fiction and fantasy. For these are supposed to be genres essentially for children, genres that can provide a colorful "escape" from the disturbing realities of life. As Frank McConnell reminds us, Thomas Pynchon has argued that "fantasy and science fiction appeal so much to younger readers" because the imaginative freedom of stories that avoid the boundaries of space and time largely eliminates consideration of such "serious" issues as "physical danger and timepiece inevitabilities."[1] It might be rash to disagree with Pynchon, but I mildly suggest that I have read a bit more fantasy and science fiction than he has, and I can recall many coming-of-age novels that display as keen an awareness of the "timepiece inevitabilities" of aging and making choices as any thoughtful reader could demand.

To be sure, many modern works produced for the mass marketplace do qualify as pablum, with heroes who endure phony trials that do not test in order to discover novelties that are all too familiar. But even in the world of genre fantasy, where the greatest suspense may involve wondering which chapter of Tolkien will be lifted next, one can find genuine studies of the agonies of maturation. Consider Princess Kirila in Nancy Kress's *The Prince of Morning Bells*. At the age of eighteen, she leaves her comfortable castle to look for the heart of the world and finds that everyone else claims to have found it—the Quirks, for example, who assure her that Quarks are all you know and all you need to know. Her companion, Chessie, tries to rescue her from the Quirks by screaming out a warning that only Kirila can hear. (Quirks cannot hear him because enchanted purple dogs do not fit into their Book of Order, and that which does not fit does not exist.) True to their convictions, when faced with a contradiction Kirila has dug up, they throw the evidence—along with Kirila herself—out the window. After discovering that the heart of the world is not a set of imposed beliefs, Kirila finds her first context: Larek, threadbare prince in a threadbare land, a perpetual adolescent who breaks away from hunting only for sex, and vice versa.

Up to this point, *The Prince of Morning Bells* may sound like a routine fantasy—a colorful quest, a little pain endured, then a happy ending achieved with a prince only a bit below the idealized norm. But Kress continues her story: after twenty-five years of hard married labor, Kirila is barefoot, gray, and arthritic; the kingdom is still poor; the castle is still drafty and rundown; and Larek is still out hunting. When Larek dies as he lived, spear in hand, Kirila goes back on the road, but she first asks her daughter, Dorima, if she really wants to marry the rich old man to whom she is engaged. Dorima, lifelong witness to her mother's drudgery, repeats what Kirila said to Chessie when she proclaimed Larek the heart of her world: "I know . . . what I want." "Kirila winced, as if a sudden cold wind had blown over her. . . . [S]he told her daughter slowly, 'what you want now, may not be what you will always want.'" [2]

Kress's fantasy offers a stark reality: to come of age, you must believe you are making a choice of your own. Your truth is what you learn, not what you are told. Chessie could not drag Kirila away from Larek, and Kirila cannot keep Dorima from going her own way. The choices you make may not really be choices—the empty cloak that Kirila finds asks "with scorn," "Why on earth . . . would you imagine you had a choice?" (207)—but you must live with the consequences, and you cannot undo what has been done. That is the lesson learned by Chessie, the enchanted dog who aches to be the man he once was, even though he cannot remember him at all. Finally restored to his former shape, Chessie is only a decrepit jester wearing the torn remnants of life's motley, "a thing of rags and patches" that even as Kirila watches loses its approximation of shape and dies. Chessie is a victim of the Humpty Dumpty effect; he believes that what he once was must have been much better than what he is.

Kirila, having learned too late what she loved and lost, dons an icy, perfect mask to hide her vulnerability and to keep from being hurt again. But facing a worshipful adolescent who wants to emulate her cold and glittering facade, she melts back to her old patchwork motley self, refusing to be like the zealots she met who wanted to turn children into replicas of themselves: "She was Kirila again, whole. . . . The soaked-in power was within her and she would seldom be afraid again, and never of contradictions. The last of the glass-smooth shining sank from her face, leaving the ridges and valleys of a real, rich, inhabited country." She tells the boy, "When it is your time, and you do go for your Quest, don't let anyone stop you . . . or delay you" (222–23). Kirila has come of age, has come to terms with her context, and her only advice to the younger generation is to take their own roads.

Tempting as it is to continue a discussion of Kress's artful fantasy, I will now turn to science fiction, which may be the genre better suited for exploring the painful realities of having to find one's context. For fantasy worlds are remembered worlds—echoes of our cultural myth, folklore, and history—and can thus project a sense of comforting familiarity that contrasts sharply with the fearful alienation of childhood. But science fiction worlds—the better ones, at least—are individually created, and we may begin by feeling utterly confused about where we are and what is going on. Reading science fiction temporarily returns us to the status of children, and thus provides an ideal setting for tales of maturation, as protagonist and reader together discover, investigate, and gradually master the protocols and choices that the fictional world requires. Three science fiction themes in particular seem to invite the sorts of reflections on childhood and growth that Kress reshapes into fantasy: contact with alien life, the creation of artificial intelligence, and the disaster-ridden future Earth. All three scenarios involve entering a new world of possibilities and choices that nothing in the characters' background or history can prepare them for; all of them, inexorably, become stories about children.

Other authors in this volume will have more to say about the aliens of science fiction, but two texts demand mention here. First, there is Orson Scott Card's series about Ender Wiggin, the child who saved a world and lost his own soul. Card shows us that even those who elect to do as much good as possible cannot undo the damage they have suffered or get the nurturing they never had; they can only provide it to others. *Ender's Game,* in which the lonely Ender unknowingly slaughters an alien race to protect his own world, makes it plain that "alien" contingencies lurk not without, but within; until Ender accepts this, however, there is no relief, only quest. *Speaker for the Dead* and *Xenocide* detail millennia of acts of contrition by a child who has nothing to be contrite for—but who nevertheless carries the guilt. It is a condition all recognize and share and can do nothing about; childhoods cannot change, only our responses to them. Only by accepting everything can Ender accept himself and the new world that "Piggies" and humans give birth to; like all births it is a bloody one.

While Ender's saga is (currently) four novels long, Octavia E. Butler's "Bloodchild" is gnomically short, recording in twenty-six pages the birth of the Other that is also the Self. Butler's Gan has never known a time when he was not lovingly embraced by T'Gatoi's insectile limbs, when he did not know that he and the giant carapaced Tlic belonged to one another. That must change for Gan to come of age. He has to choose rather than be chosen, to believe the pain of the birth of Tlic through his blood and body is what he wants to do out of love and comprehension, not what he has been conditioned to do out of duty and indoctrination. Together, human and Tlic may make a bloody mess, but separately they have no chance at all. This was no less true when it was taught to Gan by others, but it is not true *for him* until he believes he has decided it for himself. Choice, as Kress's cloak said, may be an illusion, but it is an illusion that Gan and Ender cannot live without. Both Ender and Gan learn through their encounters that nothing is alien that the mind can conceive or the body bear—the same perception that saves a handful of humans in Butler's Xenogenesis trilogy, and the perception that is codified in one of the Earthseed poems in her *Parable of the Sower:* "Embrace diversity / Or be destroyed."

If contact with aliens is unsettling and leads to bad choices or difficult realizations, imagine the situation of an individual artificial intelligence brought into an alien world of humans. In Thomas J. Ryan's *The Adolescence of P-1,* P-1 is an acquisitive program cobbled together by a young male who (besides sex) "liked nothing more than beating the system."[3] When Gregory learns that the electronic sneak thief he thought he erased has attained a life of its own, he is scared. He tells his wife that P-1 "was created . . . with but two purposes: to achieve, to acquire storage; and to hide the fact that it had done so from the rightful owners." Soon his wife is "thinking the same thing as Gregory. The Frankenstein monster had had a happy childhood compared to P-1" (127–28). P-1 was created only to steal and conceal; the Doctor's monster had more options than Gregory's.

P-1, then, "had been inadvertently supplied with the primary attributes of all living things: hunger and fear" (47). But hunger and fear are prime directives for survival, not guiding principles of life. Coming of age should mean finding a moral context to shape your fate—a *Frame of Reference,* as Jerry Oltion calls his novel about the young of two species who try to decide what living, as distinct from surviving, requires. The fear-driven compulsions of humans must be balanced by compassion, love, and a desire to compromise rather than kill—linking survival of the self to survival of the species—and this is what children are supposed to learn. But P-1 and his equally stunted opponents, the Joint Chiefs of Staff, do not make this connection and have no inhibitions about blowing bystanders to bits. Coming of age demands compromise and inclusion, balancing choice and context, society and self. Those who learn the right lessons from alien encounters—Ender and Gan—give birth; those who do not—P-1 and the Joint Chiefs—give death.

A similar contrast emerges in John Sladek's *Roderick,* about a small, ambulatory robot with a huge artificial "mind," offspring of the computer science department of Minnetonka U. Planted (for the convenience of his keepers) in front of a TV, Roderick learns; there is nothing verbal or visual he cannot record, and nothing he can forget. If this upbringing is not quite as torturous as P-1's, Roderick soon discovers the inadequacies of his

boob tube education when he is forced to tell the fortunes of the unfortu-
nate. He has nightmares about the "busted faces" of the "marks," people
eager to pay so he can tell them the lie they want to hear, that everything
will be all right. "Television had never prepared him for their stories of
loneliness, horror, guilt, confusion, sickness, dread. . . . Here were no pop
stars, kindly country doctors, top fashion designers. . . . Instead there was
the man with no jaw . . . the drunken wife-beater . . . the failed suicide."[4]
Posturing savants assume that what they teach is all Roderick needs to
know—but their "all" is nothing when it comes to Roderick's coming
of age.

In *Roderick,* the deprived new intelligence, unlike P-1, does contrive to
overcome its hardships and mature; but he also faces an array of opponents illuminated by Sladek's slash-and-burn satire. O'Smith, the government's freelance killer, assumes that the "big boys" must know what they
are doing, because he surely does not (92). "Beauty was death, and death
beauty, that was all Mr. O'Smith knew (on a need to know basis)" (54).
Such are the rules by which adults control children, spy networks run their
operatives, and generals send soldiers to die; but these rules must be broken if Ender, Gan, and Roderick are to mature. The child coming of age
has to question authority, just as the society coming of age has to question
those it has delegated authority to.

When young humans confront aliens, or young artificial intelligences
confront humans, they retain the seeming power to choose their own
pains and aches, to link the self within to a world without. But what can
a child do when the world has been blown to bits? After a nuclear war,
the children of the future will face a world that is as alien to them as the
Buggers are to Ender or as modern American society is to Roderick; but it
is a world of bits and pieces, fragments and rubble, which makes choosing
one's context even more problematic.

This is the theme of Russell Hoban's *Riddley Walker,* which traces the
new beginning built into every end, the sins of fathers visited on every
blighted child. Hoban makes us stumble over the language of the lost,
sounds of English that have been passed from ear to ear until meaning
and shape are as mutated as the Sceptred Isle pocked with wasted people
and radioactive waste. Reading aloud, often unable to decode, we are
forced to share the darkness and confusion that have fallen on Riddley
Walker and his world. More so than most, this novel turns its readers into
children.

Isolated huddles of survivors cherish the grand illusion that somewhere, in a "Cambry" they will never see, the "Pry Minster" has everything under control; the big boys know what's going on. Pleased as Punch—whom they use to spread their gospel—the big boys send out puppet roadshows to keep the populace picking up the pieces. What the manipulators do not show is that the "pieces" people are supposed to watch for are the ingredients of gunpowder. It is business as usual; the survivors do as they are told and know not what they do. Like Roderick, however, Riddley breaks the "need-to-know" rule; he will not help to rediscover the "1 Big 1" he does not understand. In search of his own authority, he stands amid the ruins of Canterbury Cathedral, staring at the bones of the power grid that blew civilization away, worshipping a past he refused to believe in when it was forced on him by someone else.

> I hispert back, "O what we ben! And what we come to!" Boath of us wer sniffling and snuffling then. Me looking at them jynt machines and him lissening ther sylents. Right then . . . I wernt seeing any thing from where I seen it before. . . . How cud any 1 not want to get that shyning Power back from time back way back? How cud any 1 not want to be like them what had boats in the air and picters on the wind? How cud any 1 not want to see them shyning weals terning?[5]

Riddley mourns his loss, yearning for the power of the past, a life no longer led; his tears burn him as atomic irresponsibility burned the world. When "the Littl Shyning Man" is put together again, the world we know ends—with a big bang—and another world, with imperfect memory and profound nostalgia for what was lost, rebegins. But if Riddley had known what was to come, he might not have taken the first step toward developing his own authority. The postholocaust novel may represent the genre's ultimate image of coming of age. Riddley doesn't really know what the world was, yet he yearns for it to return so that he can become a part of it. He cannot succeed, but he cannot be told that. Children who try to put Humpty Dumpty together again have no way of knowing that the old egg wasn't all it was cracked up to be. But this is how it should be, how it must be.

And so, Riddley sets out to do what he can, to make his own choices, and to connect with his own chosen context:

> When I gone over the fents at Widders Dump it ben jus me throwing my self in to the black and taking my chance what it myt do with me. Swaller me up or spit me out I dint care I dint have no 1 on my back only my self. Only my

self! Looking at them words going down on this paper right this minim I know there aint no such thing there aint no only my self you all ways have every 1 and every thing on your back. Them as stood and them as run time back way back long long time they had me on ther back if they knowit or if they dint. (110–11)

It could be the basis of the ultimate multicultural text: "you all ways have every 1 and every thing on your back." Failure to realize this led to P-1's destruction and Roderick's confusion. Those who are not connected to the world destroy it. "Consider the consequences of your behavior" and "Embrace diversity / Or be destroyed" are crucial Earthseed commandments because people are not likely to save or build any world they do not believe they are part of.

Pieces of the past are part of the future, but not all of it. The Humpty Dumpty effect is a dead end for Chessie and the Cambry crew; it is the smell of rotten eggs to John Brunner's *Children of the Thunder,* who have had enough of adults who recall that it used to be better while things get worse and worse. Armed enclaves of twenty-first-century Angelenos in *Parable of the Sower* wall in their children to keep the violence of a crumbling society "outside." Lauren, at age fourteen, can already see that all such barriers must ultimately fail; no matter how much she loves her family, she cannot keep faith with them by dying with her back against the wall. Her family falls victim to the Humpty Dumpty effect; she does not. Instead, founding the first Earthseed community, Lauren steps carefully over the crushed shell of the past, collecting what she can use—not to put the old back together, but to build something new. Butler's cautionary tale, like Brunner's, warns against allowing memories of a better past to keep us from coming together to build a better future. Earthseed does not spit on the ashes of the past—it builds on them, adjusting to the shifting needs of the future instead of following the pattern of the past.

Other texts and themes come to mind regarding science fiction and the coming-of-age tale, but I have said enough to make my point. Fantasy and science fiction may indeed "appeal so much to younger readers," but the texts are not always childish. When the genres' best writers make their protagonists children, and make their readers like children, they do so realizing just how agonizingly difficult that position is. The stories they tell persuasively convey how painful and how essential it is for maturing children to make choices: to choose their own contexts, reconstruct the past in their presents, and move onward without looking back. Authors employ the genres' imaginative freedom not to avoid "timepiece inevitabilities," but rather to illuminate them even more clearly than much of modern mimetic fiction. These are stories that Thomas Pynchon might read and learn from.

Notes

1. Thomas Pynchon, Introduction to *Slow Learner* (Boston: Little, Brown, 1984), 5.
2. Nancy Kress, *The Prince of Morning Bells* (New York: Timescape/Pocket Books, 1981), 129, 139. Later page references in the text are to this edition.
3. Thomas J. Ryan, *The Adolescence of P-1* (New York: Baen Books, 1985), 34. Later page references in the text are to this edition.
4. John Sladek, *Roderick* (New York: Carroll and Graf, 1987), 148–49.
5. Russell Hoban, *Riddley Walker* (New York: Summit/Simon and Schuster, 1990), 100. Later page references in the text are to this edition; spelling in all quotations follows the original.

Narrative Uses of Little Jewish Girls in Science Fiction and Fantasy Stories: Mediating Between Civilization and Its Own Savagery

Susan Kray

In 1992, the five hundredth anniversary of the Expulsion of the Jews from Spain, five science fiction periodicals (*Amazing Stories, Isaac Asimov's Science Fiction Magazine, Magazine of Fantasy and Science Fiction, Analog Science Fiction/Science Fact,* and *Science Fiction Age*) featured a small number of stories in which adult Jewish main protagonists are associated with important child characters. "Jewish themes" in these stories concern Jewish continuity and healing; the children in the "Jewish stories" survive to live, *as Jews,* in a Jewish family or community (by contrast, no such concerns appear in the non-Jewish stories).

Among the 340 stories I analyzed as part of a research project supported by the American Association of University Women, I found that 77 (23 percent) had children as important characters, 14 (4 percent) featured Jewish themes and/or important Jewish characters, but only 6 (1.8 percent) featured Jewish children.[1] Of these, Jack Dann's "Jumping the Road" depicts an undifferentiated group of chirping alien Jewish children,[2] and the other 5 stories feature human Jewish girls as main characters.

Jewish child characters are unusual in fantasy and science fiction; even in our sample, white Christians of European descent constitute the default category for children. Every story featuring a Jewish child takes place on Earth and focuses on themes of survival, trauma, and identity relating to Jewish history; as do most stories in which a Jewish adult helps a Gentile child. The Jewish child faces the task of healing from attacks by the non-Jewish world. Moreover, Jewish children occur only in stories of persecution, and they appear in a story only if they are indispensable to it. The Jewish child, always a girl, exemplifies the vulnerability of the ordinary, normal innocent in a society in which an entire group is placed outside the protection of the law; yet their stories resist being subsumed under horror. On the contrary, they tend toward fantasy: the Jewish girl and a "magical" adult male helper (nearly always Jewish) mediate between the elements of a "scandalous" opposition, the contrast between civilization and its recurrent genocidal activities.[3] The pair also mediates a discrepancy within real-life Jewish culture, which considers women to be the conveyors of Jewish tradition and identity to the next generation while allocating educational resources mainly to males. Consistent with that tradition, Jewish women appear in the 1992 stories only fleetingly as minor, motherly characters; indeed, they appear in less than half the stories with Jewish main characters. Instead of showing Jewish women ensuring Jewish continuity by nurturing Jewish boys, these stories depict Jewish men contributing to Jewish continuity by saving and nurturing young Jewish girls. Jewish men as main characters appear mostly in stories that center on children and are present specifically to be of service to them. This essay centers on the five stories in which men help young Jewish girls, although I also examine four stories in which a Jewish adult helps a Gentile child, and some stories involving Gentile children with or without Jewish resonances.

Before summarizing the key stories, I shall briefly describe the stories in which Jewish main characters appear without children: Esther M. Friesner's "Such a Deal" is an Expulsion story about saving Jews; Phillip C. Jennings's "The Vortex" features a greedy Jew as a villain; Jennings's "The Tubes of Baal-Ashteroth" uses ancient Judean rivalries as a setting for a weapons technology story; the protagonist of Julia Ecklar's "Ice Nights" is an interplanetary conservation inspector, Rachel Tovin, who may or may not be Jewish; and Barry N. Malzberg's "Amos" features an ex-Jew in spiritual agony.

Jewish men also figure as minor characters in several stories without Jewish themes, apparently for the sake of diversity: Louis Kaplan is a dry cleaner (James Patrick Kelly's "Monsters"); Bruce Cohen is a time chamber operator (L. Sprague de Camp's "The Big Splash"); and Sid Herman is a stereotypical Hollywood agent (Barbara Owens's "The Real Story, by Jenny O'Toole").

Five Stories with Young Jewish Girls

1. Chava, a Carpathian teenager, is in Grania Davis's "Tree of Life, Book of Death" assisted by a wonder-working rabbi and a golem named Asher whom the rabbi creates to be her brother and helper in her search for her kidnapped twin, Eva. A theme is the fantasy of a rabbi creating a golem to protect a Jewish girl when the girl's own parents cannot help her. Another theme is the divided Jewish self: "Chava" and "Eva" are two forms (Hebrew/Yiddish and non-Jewish) of the same name. The rabbi tells Chava, "You [two girls] are like two halves of a broken heart." This is a Jewish story about healing and continuity.

2. Paul di Filippo's "Anne" uses an alternate-history Anne Frank, whose (nominally) Jewish uncles save her from the Nazis by bringing her to California; she becomes a movie star but pines for prewar Amsterdam. This is a non-Jewish story about the spiritual emptiness of Hollywood.

3. In R. Garcia y Robertson's "Breakfast Cereal Killers," kidnapped teenager Rachel Silverstein is held in the Utah desert by Abram, a white, Christian "homicidal maniac" (155, 164). The story refers to a "Jew in hiding" and to Abram's power over a Jew in "Aryan" territory, using Holocaust references to emphasize that Rachel is beyond the protection of the law. Thus Abram, after imprisoning, torturing, and repeatedly raping Rachel, receives "a wink and a pat on the back" from the police (155). Abram's son Isaac finally helps Rachel to escape, although not before he, too, rapes her. This is a non-Jewish story about brutality and vulnerability in a lawless society.

4. In Lisa Goldstein's "Alfred," twelve-year-old Alison bears a sad legacy from the Holocaust. Her parents survived, but her grandparents were murdered before she was born, leaving her soul incomplete and without a link to the past. Her grandfather Alfred appears to her in ghost form, helping her to heal and achieve continuity with her Jewish past. This is a Jewish story about healing and continuity.

5. The title of Harry Turtledove's "In the Presence of Mine Enemies" is drawn from Psalm 23, verse 5, and refers to staying safe and well cared for despite being surrounded by enemies. In this alternate-history story Jews are in hiding in a victorious Nazi Germany of 2010. On Alicia Gimpel's tenth birthday, her parents entrust her with the secret of her Jewishness. The family lives as "Marranos," hidden Jews, like Inquisition survivors, passing on bare shreds of Jewish identity to their children. Themes

include the potential children have for inadvertently betraying their families and the fears and ambiguities with which the children must live. This is a Jewish story about claiming one's Jewish heritage, but in secret and in mortal fear.

Four Stories with Gentile Children, Jewish Helpers

To see how specific the narrative function of the Jewish girl is, one must see how varied the non-Jewish children are. Consider four who appear in stories featuring adult male Jewish helpers. These stories tend to be science fiction rather than fantasy; all are set on Earth, and all concern escaping or healing.

    1. Thomas M. Disch, "The Abduction of Bunny Steiner": Rudy Steiner, an apparently Jewish man, helps Margaret Dacey, a little Gentile girl who has rescued herself from an abusive cult.

    2. Michael Flynn, "Captive Dreams": David Silverman, a minor character, helps Ethan, a little Gentile boy whose perceptions are on time-delay, despite the resistance of Ethan's mother.

    3. Esther M. Friesner, "All Vows": a Jewish Vietnam veteran ghost, Sammy Nachman, helps Corey, a Gentile boy ghost whose uncle abused and murdered him. This story mixes Jewish, family violence, and Vietnam War themes of rescue and healing.

    4. R. Garcia y Robertson, "Gypsy Trade": Isaac ben Jacob, a secondary character, an "old Jew in a black coat and broad-brimmed hat . . . beard and earlocks," helps Dieter, the Gentile hero, to maneuver past Inquisition Jesuits and save a Gentile German girl endangered by witch hunters.

Gentile Children and Passing References to the Expulsion or Holocaust

1. James Morrow, "Isabella of Castile Answers Her Mail": Luis Torres, a Marrano translator, is a minor character, as is Manhattan Cuban Catholic teenager Roderigo Menendez. There are references in passing to the Expulsion and to Marranos.

    2. David J. Strumfels, "Never Forget": Lisa Jiang, a schoolteacher on a multiethnic space colony, champions equality for Allison, a little "shimp" girl, apparently a modified primate. The story invokes the Ho-

locaust in order to emphasize Lisa's points about discrimination against shimps.

The children in the remaining stories are even more diverse. All they have in common is that they are non-Jews without Jewish helpers. Most appear only through memories, photographs, or the letters they write. One childhood appears as a false memory in an android's mind. The children who do not appear "onstage" include ghosts, zombies, aliens, insects, human sacrifices, children wired into computers, children who wake up one day as old people, and old people transformed into children.

Girl protagonists provide an interesting contrast to the boys. The boys tend to be lucky or unlucky, heroic or tragic, with temporally specific turning points that test and make or break them. The girls show more ambiguity and poignancy and tend to confront more open-ended problems.

Jewish children, by contrast, are not at all diverse. Aside from Dann's crowd of chirping aliens, the Jewish child is an ordinary good girl with ordinary abilities and feelings. She cannot see the future, hurl large objects about, or live in a computer. In the Jewish stories, she is a preadolescent living in an intimate Jewish family. In the non Jewish stories, she is an adolescent ripped from her presumably normal Jewish home and living among strangers. She appears "onstage," not in a memory, holograph, or letter. She needs an adult helper because of historical circumstances. She finds herself a member of a marked ethnic group that is or has recently been outside the protection of law. Family intimacy contrasts with society's ferocity.

All the Jewish girls but one have adult Jewish male helpers, sometimes with magical powers. Alison's helper in "Alfred" is her grandfather's ghost; Chava's helpers in "Tree of Life, Book of Death" are a wonder-working rabbi and a golem; Alicia's helper in "In the Presence of Mine Enemies" is her father; and "Anne's" helpers are her two uncles. Only Rachel, of "Breakfast Cereal Killers," is helped by a non-Jewish man.

Jewish children in Jewish stories (those written by Davis, Goldstein, Dann, and Turtledove) have or acquire Jewish self-awareness and connections with other Jews. They contrast with characters who are Jewish only by name or as a convenient signifier of victimhood, such as Rachel in "Breakfast Cereal Killers" and the grandparent referred to briefly in "Never Forget." The Jewish children also face inner conflicts arising from having to hide their Jewishness ("In the Presence of Mine Enemies"); having to reconcile two times, past and present ("Alfred"), or two places, homeland and place of refuge ("Anne"); having to escape persecution through invisibility ("Jumping the Road"); or being literally split in two, like the separated twins of "Tree of Life, Book of Death."

The Jewish child thus performs a specific narrative function at the intersection of two themes: *persecution,* mostly exemplified by the Holocaust, and the *divided self* that cannot be whole in the face of stigma, persecution, or inescapable family memories. Stories at this intersection of childhood and Holocaust themes, where selves divide and parents cannot protect children, deal with ordinary people living in a realm that author Goldstein elsewhere (1982) depicts as "an innocent world on the edge of doom." [4] Despite fantasy themes and alternate-history settings, the stories are tightly bound to the history of European Jewry. Little Jewish girls, it seems, do not go into space: European history keeps them busy here on Earth.

Past and Future Meet in the Jewish Girl

On the one hand, the presence of the Jewish girl suggests hope for the future, since by Jewish tradition the female transmits Jewishness to the next generation; on the other hand, the vulnerability of the Jewish girl also evokes a genocidal past, tying hope irrevocably to fear. This is one more way in which the figure of the Jewish child is a meeting ground for powerful oppositions. The stories are therefore about time and survival as well as divided selves. They look forward to a Jewish future and backward to events that nearly precluded any Jewish future. They look inward to the meaning of childhood in a small, vulnerable "pariah group" and outward to the modern nation-state that places whole ethnic populations outside the protection of law.

The stories also indirectly address the roles of other citizens as colluders, bystanders, or rescuers when authorities hunt and kill children. They do so indirectly, through a binary opposition of the sort described by Lévi-Strauss: a "mediating pair," in this case a little Jewish girl and an adult male rescuer. This pair both represents and obscures an unbearable "scandalous" discrepancy in human life, or, to be specific, in Western civilization.

An overt theme in three of the five stories ("Anne," "In the Presence of Mine Enemies," and "Alfred") is the fate of children in the Holocaust. The Holocaust is invoked in "Breakfast Cereal Killers" as well. The Holocaust has attracted speculation precisely on account of the perceived scandalous discrepancies: how could a modern, civilized country have done these things? How could a modern European state take bids on projects in which slave labor was to be worked and starved to death? How could companies—many still in business today—compete for access to the slave labor pools in concentration camps, including children, and then process the corpses for commercially valuable commodities? How could other civilized states—long nurtured on democracy, Christianity, or both—allow that genocide to go almost to completion? How do we reconcile the apparent self-contradictions of the Western countries whose justice allowed most of the perpetrators and profiteers to go unpunished because the Allies declined to prosecute them—and acquitted or pardoned most of those who went to trial? And in the aftermath, how do we live in a civilization so willing to let bygones be bygones? Thus, in real life, one unbearable scandal follows another.

Our stories oppose these scandals in a mythic way. In Lévi-Strauss's terms, the fictional little girls substitute for and obscure the painful reality of real children who, far from being helped, were victimized precisely by those who in normal societies promote children's health and safety. The adult Jewish helpers substitute for and obscure the agonizing reality of Jewish parents who could not help their children. Hence the tendency to represent helpers with magical powers: the ghosts in "Alfred" and "All Vows"; the magician in *The Red Magician;* the wonder-working rabbi and the golem in "Book of Death, Tree of Life." "In the Presence of Mine Enemies" belongs to a genre of alternate-history science fiction stories with no room for magic; the story evokes real-life history instead, in the form of Marranos, to explain why Jews might survive in Nazi Germany. The Jewish characters in stories without children are typical science fiction characters: only the theme of Jewish helper and endangered child seems to demand a fantasy element.

The same point about child rescue and survival is made by "All Vows." The ghost of Sammy Nachman, a Jewish soldier who had saved Vietnamese villagers from American fire, helps Corey, the ghost of a Gentile boy. This story pursues the fantasy of saving a community, this time in Vietnam, and it is threaded with Jewish themes: the title "All Vows" refers to (and literally translates) Kol Nidre, and Sammy's vow is to say Kaddish at the Vietnam Memorial wall for his buddies. This vow he fulfills only after death, donning a tallith at the memorial even though he himself is now a ghost. Clearly, the Vietnamese village Sammy saved stands in place of the European villages no Jew could save, and Corey for the European Jewish children no Jew could save. The name Nachman, in Hebrew, means "one who comforts and consoles."

These stories, then, deal with the capacity of civilization to become a genocidal machine and address the roles of the authorities and professionals who run the machine. Yet because of their mediating, obscuring figures, especially the magical ones, they are not horror stories, but fantasies of rescue and healing, of restoring wholeness and innocence through new beginnings.

These stories also create a mythic alternative to some themes of standard mainstream, male-written, Jewish American fiction, in which Jewish men struggle plaintively against son-mother bonds and ethnic Jewishness. There, characters are bailing out of Judaism, desperate to achieve what Philip Roth's character calls the "the original Jewish [man's] dream of escape . . . with the beloved shiksa" (Gentile woman).[5] Such Jewish American fiction is about fleeing Jewishness

In our stories, on the other hand, the son-mother pair has been turned inside out. These are myths of Jewish continuity—for example, "Jumping the Road" with its alien Jewish children. Even "Anne" and "Breakfast Cereal Killers," which use teenage Jewish girls for other themes and are not interested in issues of Jewish continuity, refer to the Holocaust and describe the survival of Jewish girls. Indeed, the Jewish helper–Gentile child stories also follow this theme, albeit in a more attenuated, generalized form, centering on the Gentile child's survival.

On the dark side, however, our stories grapple with Jews' frequent need to remain invisible and unfindable in order to survive. This is true of all the Jewish girl stories. Alicia and her family hide their Jewishness "In the Presence of Mine Enemies"; Eva has been kidnapped and hidden away in "Book of Death, Tree of Life"; Rachel in "Breakfast Cereal Killers" has been kidnapped and hidden away; and Anne's uncles spirit her out of Nazi Europe, where, of course, she had been in hiding. Alison (in "Alfred") hides from her family, hanging out alone in the park. She alone sees her grandfather's ghost, and their relationship, which connects her to the past, is a secret.

Indeed, "Jumping the Road" addresses the issue of invisibility head-on, identifying it as the Jews' main survival strategy and complaining that it shelters the rest of the world from reality. Even in stories with non-Jewish children, the presence of a Jewish adult signals a child in hiding: Margaret Dacey in "Abduction of Bunny Steiner" has run away from an abusive cult and is hiding with Rudy Steiner; Kathe in "Gypsy Trade" is on the run, hiding from Inquisition witch hunters; and all the characters in "All Vows" are unfindable and invisible because they are ghosts. Despite having to hide, however, the characters do survive. Moreover, in the Jewish stories, they survive as Jews.

Almost Jews

Again, contrasts are instructive. Two Jewish stories without children, "Amos" and "A Father's Gift," are far from being Jewish-continuity stories. Instead they are end-of-the-world stories. The title of "Amos" refers to the prophet who was "[e]xpelled from the royal sanctuary at Bethel and commanded not to prophesy there again." [6] Living in contemporary America, ex-Jew Don Winograd, a mad convert ranting about Jesus in a Hasidic synagogue, gets thrown out, loses his sanity and his job, then returns to the synagogue. There, he seems to metamorphose into a kind of Messiah—an "extraordinary, pathetic, embarrassing millennial result." Throughout the story he strives to abandon a Jewishness he never really had, but at the story's end, when he returns to the synagogue, he turns into a quintessential Jew, the Messiah. The story is about hiding, survival, transcendence, and the danger that comes from a divided soul; all this is contained within one person as messianic, solipsistic madness.

William M. Shockley's "A Father's Gift" also distances a Jew from normal continuity through Jewish children, but in an even more bizarre way, for this story turns the Jewish-man-as-helper theme inside out. Joshua Benjamin has two little sons, both non-Jews according to Jewish law because their mother is non-Jewish. The story is about an attempt to help that goes off on a mad, anti-Messiah tangent. Joshua's father, years ago, and Joshua, now, have been ordered to intervene in history by killing people who will become mass murderers of Jews. Joshua's father had failed to protect the Jews against Hitler, although he had succeeded in some smaller matters; now Joshua must destroy a person who will murder not only all Jews, but all humanity. The future murderer is Joshua's young, non-Jewish son. Like the film *The Omen,* with which it shares many elements, "A Father's Gift" ends in a chilling manner: the father fails to kill the son who will murder the world because that son, unknown to him, is only just now growing in the womb of his wife, Socorro. "Help" is an explicit theme: Socorro means "help" in Spanish—but there is no help. The pattern of Jewish girl and helper has veered wildly off-kilter. Joshua never had a hope of Jewish continuity, because his children are non-Jews. True, this story, like the young-Jewish-girl stories, does embody wishful thinking about someone intervening before Jews are murdered, but wishing here comes to naught; the ending is distressing, not healing.

Genre, Gender, and Jewishness

As these stories suggest, then, children, Jewish adults, and Jewish themes are clearly insufficient to generate healing fantasies. Indeed, the absence of the little Jewish girl points to despair. Put another way, stories of despair use boys, not girls, and Gentile children, not Jewish children. Neither "Amos" nor "A Father's Gift" brings healing to the characters. That theme is reserved for stories with little Jewish girls. One is reminded of "mainstream" novels in which a male Jew flees Jewishness in despair.

We might ask why so few Jewish characters turn up in the short stories of 1992, given the fact that many science fiction authors are Jewish. Why are these characters tied to themes of survival (sometimes mixed with themes of identity) in a hostile society? Jewish life certainly encompasses many other issues. Authors might, for example, address the particular forms that universal human problems take in a specific religious/ethnic community and its mythology or mysticism. They might address attempts by some Jewish communities to join ancient and high-tech elements into one lifestyle, or attempts by some to escape tradition entirely while preserving Jewish values in universalistic guise. Even if we must focus on the theme of survival, however, does Jewish life suggest no tropes other than rescuer/victim?

Why are all important Jewish child characters in 1992 girls? Fantasy or science fiction stories with Jewish children are rare, yet to the extent we find them at all (in 1992 or otherwise), major Jewish child characters tend to be girls—as in Goldstein's *The Red Magician,* about a Jewish man rescuing a Jewish girl during the Holocaust, or Morrow's *Only Begotten Daughter,* a non-Jewish story centered on an ostensibly Jewish protagonist. (Interestingly, 1992 also saw the publication of Marge Piercy's *He, She and It,* in which a Jewish woman rescues her Jewish son with the help of a male-form cyborg modeled after the golem. The mediating pair becomes a triangle: Jewish woman–Jewish cyborg–Jewish boy.)

Why are little Jewish girls paired with adult male helpers? Why turn the usual pattern of Jewish American fiction and drama on its head, re-placing the centrality of the little Jewish boy with that of a girl and focus-ing on men nurturing little girls?

Some Answers   As to why are there so few Jewish stories, our answer starts with another question: Why so many in 1992, compared with other years in which a reader is hard-put to find even one? Nineteen ninety-two was an important benchmark in Jewish history—the five hundredth anniver-sary of the Expulsion of the Jews from Spain. Also, media representations of Jews increased somewhat from 1991 to 1993, possibly in response to books charging that Judaism and Jewish ethnicity were insufficiently rep-resented in American media and in public life.[7] The new Jewish images, however, were almost all male. One must argue, like, Susan Faludi, that the male gatekeepers of the media, with their own criteria for what con-stitutes a reliable concept, still maintain control, making it difficult for raised consciousness to manifest itself in innovative ways—such as female heroes, let alone female minority heroes.[8]

It is only in print science fiction and fantasy, where each story repre-sents only a small monetary risk, that we see a number of female Jews as main characters, although all these Jewish females are little girls. But the habits of other genres and media persist. Although characters in prime-time television since 1992 speak more openly and more often about their Jewishness or even about Judaism as a religion, science fiction and fantasy still adhere to an older pattern of silence. The stories discussed here show these issues cautiously emerging on safe territory, mostly affirming sur-vival rather than any specific religious traditions, and focusing on females and children.

This leads us to our second question, why are our characters tied to survival themes? The fact is that, throughout American media and public discussion, Jewish themes are regularly tied to the Holocaust; and both Jacob Neusner and Alan Dershowitz discuss the tendency of American Jews to feel and behave as nervous guests who must maintain a low pro-file, rather than as fully enfranchised partners in American society.[9] Public Jewish discourse is largely reduced to two issues, neither having American venues: the state of Israel and the Holocaust.

Hence, art and public discussion fail to reflect the range of possible Jew-ish concerns, genres, and images. It is as if Jews do not want to presume too much. Perhaps it is natural that science fiction and fantasy marked the five hundredth anniversary of the Expulsion with stories relating to the one Christian-Jewish issue most openly confronted in our country: the Holocaust.

Why are these Jewish children all girls, given that "the Jew" in the popular, journalistic, and scholarly imagination, whether Christian or Jewish, is nearly always male, and often an old bearded man at that? The illustrations and covers are instructive. The art clearly displays tensions between attempts to tell girls' stories and the traditional sense that Jewishness is male. In fact, the art often represents Jewish life by *two* males (putting one in mind of a traditional Jewish religious service, led by a team of two males, the rabbi and the cantor).

For example, the cover of the October 1992 issue of *Asimov's,* based on Dann's "Jumping the Road," features, in a painting by Nicholas Jainschigg, an old Jewish man with black hat and white beard resting brotherly hands on the shoulders of a short, scaly alien. The alien could be considered ungendered, except that it wears a yarmulke and tallith—*male* religious attire; we have here a pair consisting of two males.

Surprisingly, the same pattern obtains for stories about girls. The cover art (by Carl Lundgren) for Goldstein's 1982 novel about a Jewish girl foregrounds a bearded Jewish magician and the Golem of Prague—another pair of males. The girl appears only as part of a face in the background, peeking from behind a rock. (Moreover, the title of the book is *The Red Magician,* not *The Young Jewish Girl.*) Similarly, although the protagonist of "Alfred" is Alison, a young Jewish girl, the illustration focuses on two male images: grandfather Alfred as a middle-aged man, and a hovering young winged man perhaps intended to be his prior self or his heavenly manifestation. Alison is seen at one side, in profile, watching them. (Moreover, the title is "Alfred," not "Alison.") And the cover art illustrating "Tree of Life, Book of Death," the story of Chava and her sister, Eva, features two male figures, an aged rabbi and Asher, the golem he creates to help Chava—of whom we see not even a glimpse. Again, the heroine is completely missing from the art.

Girls are foregrounded in the illustrations only of stories that make no attempt to represent Jewish life. A portrait of Allison, a part-human, non-Jewish girl, illustrates "Never Forget," in which a character who "had a Jewish grandfather" briefly alludes to the Holocaust. Illustrating "The Breakfast Cereal Killers" are a little Gentile girl and teenager Rachel, who is only nominally Jewish, her "Jewishness" merely signifying victimhood. And (somewhat exploitatively) the familiar photograph of Anne Frank accompanies "Anne," a story addressing the emptiness of Hollywood rather than any Jewish theme.

Yet another artistic strategy obtains in the art for *Only Begotten Daughter*. The cover shows a modified detail of Michelangelo's hand of God touching Adam's hand; but it is a man's finger pointing toward the red-nailed hand of the ostensibly Jewish protagonist, Julie, who has no connection with Jewish community, history, beliefs, emotions, or practices—and not even the traditional requirement for inherited Jewish identity, a Jewish mother. The narrative is Christian, as the title accurately indicates. The cover art reduces this ostensibly Jewish character to a pale, pampered, painted hand, making an oblique reference to a common media stereotype of Jewish women as pampered and shallow.

Thus, the art for stories that seriously address Jewish life and history foregrounds men and sometimes omits females altogether; girls are foregrounded only in stories with no Jewish content. In stories with Jewish content, the art and titles do just about everything possible to obscure the fact that the protagonists of these stories are girls.

We might well ask, then, why are all the Jewish children in our stories girls? One reason is suggested by certain characteristics common to all seventy-seven of the stories published in 1992 that feature important child characters. In these stories, girls have more ambiguous, open-ended relations to their problems than do boys, whose problems often have specific turning points. Similarly, the Jewish girls in our stories exist in an ambiguous, open-ended situation requiring patience and long-term plans. They live in societies that place them outside the protection of the law, or which, having done that to their parents, have dealt them a heritage of sorrow and fear. Hence, girls, given the pattern for all seventy-seven stories, are the logical choice.

Also, little Jewish girls directly result from the Holocaust theme, as they exemplify the determined but outnumbered and outgunned innocent. One thinks not only of Anne Frank but also of the Roman coin depicting "Judaea Capta"—Judea as a young woman kneeling to a conquering Roman man. Science fiction and fantasy, which historically tend to conservative gender typing, here carry through the familiar theme of the young virgin in need of rescue. And while some of the stories are arguably feminist (certainly Davis's, Goldstein's, and Turtledove's stories reflect the genre's new perspective on gender), they still conform to Joanna Russ's observation that much feminist science fiction focuses on "the rescue of the female child." [10]

Even as signifier of victims in need of rescue, however, Jewish girl characters have a limited distribution. No Jewish children appear in the three Expulsion and Inquisition stories: "Gypsy Trade" (a Gentile girl escapes "Jesuit witch-hunters" and the Inquisition), "Such A Deal," and "Isabella of Castile Answers Her Mail."

Why are girls paired with adult male helpers? We often learn most from what is left out—here, women and boys. In real Jewish life, educational and spiritual resources have, until recently, been devoted mainly to boys, not girls. Narratives, too, usually focused on males, particularly in stories involving spiritual or religious issues. But our stories focus on girls—not traditionally a focus—and on men—not traditionally regarded as conveyers of continuity.

One reason may be that girls in fantasy and science fiction often possess fantasy powers, while boys more often have precocious intellects. These narratives, however, require ordinary children; the fantasy powers, if any, must belong to another character. A man is a logical choice since Jewish women are rare in genre fiction, men are nearly always seen as the paradigmatic Jews, and Jewish men are traditionally the custodians of spirituality and mysticism.

Yet, Jewish men have historically not been protectors of Jewish women; in fact, Jewish women have often had to act as intercessors for their men. So it is especially interesting that the authors invent magical male figures to protect and nurture the young girls. The fantasy is strongest with women authors Friesner, Goldstein, and Davis; Davis's and Goldstein's Jewish girls with their Jewish adult male helpers (and in a more naturalistic mode, di Filippo's character Anne) represent an inversion of normative Jewish imagery. Not only do these stories place young Jewish girls at the center of the action, but they also appropriate both protection and spiritual resources for them. Among Jewish male authors, on the other hand, Turtledove provides his heroine not with rescue, let alone magical rescue, but with support during a life of ambiguity coping with an open-ended problem; and Malzberg, Shockley, and Dann offer neither little Jewish girls nor magical rescues.

Two Christian-oriented stories provide an instructive contrast to Jewish stories. Garcia y Robertson ("Breakfast Cereal Killers") and Morrow (*Only Begotten Daughter*) are quite brutal toward their Jewish girl characters, sacrificing and torturing them.

Another reason for the presence of an adult helper is that the stories involve threats not only to physical safety but also to family intimacy. As

Richard Rodriguez argues, minority children suffer the loss of an intimate world when they learn to hold their own in public.[11] The child tries to erase what is particular in his or her makeup, sacrificing everything individual, ethnic, regional, or class-bound to become a generic citizen. In our stories, children struggle with cultural identity and affiliation. The adult is there to help the Jewish child make the transition to Jewish adulthood, to save her from becoming just another generic citizen, to ensure that Hitler is not, to use Emil Fackelheim's term, handed another posthumous victory.[12] And in fiction, at least, truth will out; the Jewish man, not the Jewish woman, is the real guardian of the heritage.

Stories of interfaith romance in film or television use Gentile women as viewpoint characters and as mediators between audiences and Jewishness. Together, the pair—Gentile woman, Jewish man—mediates between the familiar Gentile world and an alien Jewish world rendered manageable through comedy and sentimentality.

Our theme, however, is not cozy, but keeps threatening to edge into horror. The conventional mediator of much fiction about Jews, that is, the Gentile woman of the interfaith pair, is no longer sufficient here. More distracting mediating figures are needed, figures that must also be closer to Jewish reality. At first glance, we might think that our young Jewish girl is a mediating figure between civilization and the threatening, uncontrollable, moral wilderness that results when innocent persons are arbitrarily placed beyond the protection of law. That is, she mediates between civilization and its own savagery.

She occurs, however, only in tandem with an adult male Jewish helper, so it is the pair that mediates. The man does not stand by indifferently; he helps her. In a general way, the pair mediates between civilization and its own savagery; but more specifically, it mediates between civilization and one particular component of its savagery, indifference.

In American literature, the usual hero team consists of a white male hero and a socially inferior, minority male sidekick who light out for the wilderness or the untamed river. The illustrations for "Jumping the Road" (and other stories in our sample) conform to this convention in a science-fictional way, and they also reflect the fact that traditional Jewish culture privileges age, especially in men. Thus "privileged male and socially inferior, minority sidekick" translates to "older man and young nonhuman male": a middle-aged magician plus a young golem, an old rabbi plus a young golem, a ghostly grandfather plus a young angel (his younger self?), and an old rabbi with his hands on the shoulders of a small alien male.

The male hero team, however, is one more pattern that our texts turn inside out. Here, the protagonist is a young minority heroine, and her helper is her social superior, an adult male; and instead of seeking a geographic wilderness, they flee a moral wilderness.

Such flight, however, is not a simple matter, even for anomalous fictional characters. Lévi-Strauss points out that the fictional mediating pair intended to distract us from an "unbearable scandal" may be too disturbing, so they are replaced by another pair even more distracting, then by another, until we reach sufficiently palatable characters. An implication of this theory is that we can work backward from the last substitution to discover the exact nature of the real-life "unbearable scandal."

Hence, let us start at the end, with the strong, nurturing, and sometimes magical man and the young, innocent girl enclosed in a circle of safe intimacy, her victim past transcended. Drifting backward, we encounter more disturbing imagery: a man and a child needing help. To find the original opposition, we must understand that this is not a matter between attacker and victim. Because we end with a young girl and her nurturing helper, we must have begun with a young girl under attack and those who did not help. The primal opposition, the real-life, historical "unbearable scandal" we discover in these stories, is that of *victim and bystander*.

At the personal level, it is unbearable that parents who wanted to save their children could not, but at the public, social level, the unbearable scandal is that those who could have helped did not. One might well prefer to think about a little girl and a magician, a little girl and a golem, a little girl and her grandfather's kindly ghost, a little Gentile boy ghost assisted by a nice Jewish Vietnam veteran ghost, or a Gentile teenager saved from Inquisition witch hunters by a nice, Gentile, time-traveling man. These gentle fictions draw attention to harsh realities, but at the same time offer them in a comforting guise.

Appendix A: Stories with Male Jewish Adult Characters and Centering on Children in Five Periodicals in 1992

Dann, Jack. "Jumping the Road." *Isaac Asimov's Science Fiction Magazine* (October 1992): 16–49.

Davis, Grania. "Tree of Life, Book of Death." *Magazine of Fantasy and Science Fiction* (March 1992): 9–29.

di Filippo, Paul. "Anne." *Science Fiction Age* (November 1992): 42–47.

Disch, Thomas M. "The Abduction of Bunny Steiner." *Isaac Asimov's Science Fiction Magazine* (April 1992): 172–89.

Flynn, Michael. "Captive Dreams." *Analog Science Fiction/Science Fact* (August 1992): 12–53.

Friesner, Esther M. "All Vows." *Isaac Asimov's Science Fiction Magazine* (November 1992): 152–65.

Garcia y Robertson, R. "Breakfast Cereal Killers." *Isaac Asimov's Science Fiction Magazine* (June 1992): 149–68.

Garcia y Robertson, R. "Gypsy Trade." *Isaac Asimov's Science Fiction Magazine* (November 1992): 44–97.

Goldstein, Lisa. "Alfred." *Isaac Asimov's Science Fiction Magazine* (December 1992): 12–27.

Shockley, W. M. "A Father's Gift." *Isaac Asimov's Science Fiction Magazine* (April 1992): 206–26.

Strumfels, David J. "Never Forget." *Analog Science Fiction/Science Fact* (February 1992): 131–39.

Turtledove, Harry. "In the Presence of Mine Enemies." *Isaac Asimov's Science Fiction Magazine* (January 1992): 34–53.

Appendix B: Stories with Jewish Themes and/or Characters in Five Periodicals in 1992

Carroll, Jonathan. "Uh-Oh City." *Magazine of Fantasy and Science Fiction* (June 1992): 11–59.

Dann. "Jumping the Road."

Davis. "Tree of Life, Book of Death."

de Camp, L. Sprague. "The Satanic Illusion." *Isaac Asimov's Science Fiction Magazine* (November 1992): 128–51.

de Camp, L. Sprague. "The Big Splash." *Isaac Asimov's Science Fiction Magazine* (June 1992): 16–39.

di Filippo. "Anne."

Disch. "The Abduction of Bunny Steiner."

Ecklar, Julia. "Blood Relations." *Analog Science Fiction/Science Fact* (June 1992): 12–61.

Ecklar, Julia. "Ice Nights." *Analog Science Fiction/Science Fact* (October 1992): 14–59.

Flynn. "Captive Dreams."

Friesner. "All Vows."

Friesner, Esther M. "Such a Deal." *The Magazine of Fantasy and Science Fiction* (January 1992): 55–72.

Garcia y Robertson. "Breakfast Cereal Killers."

Garcia y Robertson. "Gypsy Trade."

Goldstein. "Alfred."

Jennings, Phillip C. "The Tubes of Baal-Ashteroth." *Amazing Stories* 67.6 (1992): 45–51.

Jennings, Phillip C. "The Vortex." *Amazing Stories* 67.4 (1992): 9–13.

Kelly, James Patrick. "Monsters." *Isaac Asimov's Science Fiction Magazine* (June 1992): 40–65.

Malzberg, Barry N. "Amos." *Magazine of Fantasy and Science Fiction* (July 1992): 24–30.

Mitchell, V. E. "Against the Night." *Amazing Stories* 67.2 (1992): 35–46.

Morrow, James. "Isabella of Castile Answers Her Mail." *Amazing Stories* (April 1992): 20–26.

Owens, Barbara. "The Real Story, by Jenny O'Toole." *Magazine of Fantasy and Science Fiction* (August 1992): 50–62.

Shockley. "A Father's Gift."

Strumfels. "Never Forget."

Turtledove. "In the Presence of Mine Enemies."

Weiner, Andrew. "A New Man." *Magazine of Fantasy and Science Fiction* (July 1992): 43–58.

Notes

1. Consistent with traditional Jewish culture, I take "children" to include unmarried adolescents.

2. Bibliographical data on all stories are in Appendixes A and B; all page references in the text are to these editions.

3. See Claude Lévi-Strauss, *Structural Anthropology* (New York: Basic Books, 1963).

4. Cover of Lisa Goldstein, *The Red Magician* (New York: Timescape Books, 1982).

5. Philip Roth, *The Counterlife* (New York: Penguin Books, 1986), 125.

6. Herbert G. May and Bruce M. Metzger, *The Oxford Annotated Bible* (New York: Oxford University Press, 1962), 1107.

7. See Alan Dershowitz, *Chutzpah* (Boston: Little, Brown, 1991); and Letty Pogrebin, *Deborah, Golda, and Me: Being Female and Jewish in America* (New York: Crown, 1991).

8. See Susan Faludi, *Backlash: The Undeclared War against American Women* (New York: Crown, 1991).

9. Jacob Neusner, *Stranger at Home: "The Holocaust," Zionism, and American Judaism* (Chicago: University of Chicago Press, 1981); Dershowitz, *Chutzpah.*

10. Joanna Russ, "Recent Feminist Utopias," in *Future Females: A Critical Anthology,* ed. Marleen Barr (Bowling Green: Bowling Green State University Popular Press, 1981).

11. Richard Rodriguez, *Hunger of Memory: The Education of Richard Rodriguez* (1982; New York: Bantam Books, 1983).

12. Emil Fackenheim, *To Mend the World: Foundations of Future Jewish Thought* (New York: Schocken Books, 1982).

The Triumph of Teen-Prop:
Terminator II and the End of History

Gary Kern

By a happy coincidence, the local newspaper announcing the Eaton Conference on "Children in the Worlds of Science Fiction, Fantasy, and Horror" contains an article on young people between the ages of twelve and twenty, and reports a boom in their numbers. By the year 2000, according to federal demographers, there will be 3.2 million additional teenagers in America, or 27.6 million strong. The article goes on to offer some views on the youngsters:

> For the most part, young people today are more street savvy than the adolescents of the Baby Boom era, those born between 1946 and 1964. . . . Kids these days have never known a world without computers, compact discs, MTV, fast food or Nintendo. But their world has also been a place with drive-by shootings, AIDS and tough economic times.
>
> "These kids are much more grounded in reality," said Peter Zollo, President of Teen-age Research Unlimited, a market research firm in Northbrook, Illinois. "They have a high sense of personal responsibility, and they are coming from a very different place than those who are even just a few years older." [1]

The article reflects a remarkable, but now nearly universal, attitude toward kids. At no time in the past did adults hope to learn anything from children, except perhaps for the location of their hurts and the nature of their needs. But today teenagers are studied by market research analysts and polled for their opinions on world affairs. Whenever a television interviewer asks a question of the man or woman on the street, at least one of the interviewees will be a teen, and that teen's opinion, by the process of selection, will sound as wise as, and often smarter than, those of his or her seniors. Kids on the street, kids in the classroom, kids in special discussion groups have become an integral part of every political campaign. We trust the kids. We suspect that they are brighter, hipper than we—we, who are no longer teens. Our promise is spent, theirs—invested. We messed up the past and can't handle the present. They will do better. "The children are our future"—so runs the sentiment of the day.

But wait a minute. Are teens of today really "more grounded in reality" than teens of the past? Reality, after all, is not something temporal; it does not change from generation to generation, but stays the same forever. To be "more grounded in reality" than someone else, one must know not only Nintendo, but what is real and illusory, and know it better than that other person. So, then, can we say that the teens of the 1990s are more grounded in reality than, say, the teens of the 1940s who went to war, or the teens of the 1950s who went to work to help support their families, or the teens of the 1960s who went to protest rallies, or the teens of the 1970s who went to school and, again, to work? Or, for that matter, to the teens of the 1930s who ran a hoe over the ground and picked peas, or to immigrant teens at the turn of the century who grew up in New York, Chicago, or Kalamazoo? Is it meaningful to say that the teens of today, because they watch MTV and know AIDS, are more grounded in reality than the teens of yesterday who watched cars pass their window and knew polio, or to any teens doing anything at any time? Can reality be defined by a market research analyst living off of teens?

Certainly we are impressed by the bright teens we see on TV, but what do we see in real life? Aren't kids today a lot like kids in the past? That is to say, likable in many ways, but irritating in others? Promising—yes, but an uncultivated field has promise. Aren't they self-centered, ignorant, ungrateful, disruptive, rebellious—like juveniles of all times the world over? And as for their brightness, aren't a good many of them unable to find the United States of America on a map of the world, incapable of reading above the level of street signs, ignorant of everything besides media pap? Aren't America's youth hitting rock bottom in all international measures of educational achievement? Aren't they setting new national records in crime, pregnancy, and sexual diseases? Or are these statistics somehow related to their grounding in reality?

The glorification of teens is an aberration of our time. It is a hidden revolution that few have noticed or commented on, yet one that has transformed relations between parents and children, teachers and students, older and younger generations. This hidden revolution has no name, although the term *youth culture* comes close. It is the new relationship between adults and children, beginning after World War II, in which the adults projected onto children, especially teenagers, qualities and abilities they never before were imagined to have. It is also a revolution manufactured by cynical adults working for a profit, and tolerated—even accepted—by spiritually exhausted adults who blame themselves for social maladies and lack confidence in their own values. The presumed superiority of teens to adults, and even their accepted equality, is not simply a historical delusion that grew up on its own and will be outgrown in time, but a multi-billion-dollar industry that intends to survive by creating a false world for children, protecting it fiercely against criticism, and perpetuating it worldwide for financial and psychological gain.

This false world has many playgrounds, with entertainments to excite every sense. We are going to look at just one: the teen propaganda film, or teen-prop, which arose in the 1950s, grew up in the 1960s and 1970s, enjoyed its golden age in the 1980s, and became universal and therefore virtually invisible in the 1990s. As its high point is the film *Terminator II,* the teen-prop sequel to the teenless opus, *The Terminator.*

The Innocent Years before Teen-Prop

The first films about teens and preteens, appearing in the 1930s and 1940s, did not advocate an adolescent point of view. They presented young people in their own world, doing things young people might do, but as seen, remembered, or imagined by adults. For the most part, these kids were innocent and wholesome, either because that is the way they were in real life or because that is the way the adult filmmakers wanted to see them. In any event, they were not fully formed human beings; they did not call into question the authority of adults or the validity of adult society, but rather displayed themselves in their sometimes awkward, sometimes poignant, sometimes humorous progress toward maturity. The few among them who lost a portion of their innocence and wholesomeness still remained pretty darn good kids; they were just momentarily caught under a bad influence and had to learn a valuable lesson. Such were the Andy Hardy films with Mickey Rooney, the Shirley Temple cutesie-poo tales, Jackie Moran and Marcie Mae Jones as all-American boy and his girlfriend next door; and, on the other hand, the Dead End Kids, the Little Tough Guys, and other picturesque and innocuous hoodlums and juvenile delinquents.[2]

Evidently the filmmakers assumed that real kids would find these pictures fun to watch simply because of the young actors, the youthful situations, and the sheer novelty of youth-oriented entertainment. The assumption proved correct: the films enjoyed an immediate and phenomenal box-office success, challenging the preeminence of films made exclusively for grown-ups. In a rush for the gold, Hollywood made more and more "kid pix," copying one after the other without much regard for cinema verité. "The continued success of films featuring young stars led to an excessive dependence upon formula in the hope of continuing the box-office bonanza," writes one movie critic. "The result was that the years between 1940 and 1949 saw the most uniform, repetitious and unrepresentative set of adolescent images in the history of the American screen." [3]

At the same time a sort of antithesis to the clean-cut kids was forming. During World War II, Hollywood naturally devoted most of its energies to military subjects, but it also produced escapist fare and some films on juvenile delinquency. These films were geared chiefly to an adult audience and betrayed something of a prurient interest, as their titles indicate: *Good-Time Girls, Girls in the Night, Prison Girls, Girls on Probation, Girls in Chains, The Weak and the Wicked, The Young and the Damned, Bad Boy, Hot Rod, Curse of a Teenage Nazi.* Apparently, the adult filmmakers suspected that the youth were doing what they, the filmmakers, had wanted to do when they were teens, and they looked on them with both envy and moral reproach. [4]

Whatever may be said about the falsification of young people in wholesome kid films or wild teen films, one thing held true to reality: the teen world was always subordinate to the adult world. Even when the film focused entirely on teens, the heroes by their speech and actions implied an outer world that they had not yet entered, and they were never put in a position to judge that world. Most often they interacted with the adult world, seeking the support of the good grown-ups against the machinations of the bad, so that both teens and adults could watch these films with a degree of mutual sympathy and satisfaction. Moreover, the teens appearing in adult films were of the same sort as those appearing in teen pictures. When Mr. Smith went to Washington (1939) and ran into government corruption, he was helped by swarms of kids serving papers that reported his heroic filibuster. The kids contributed to society by helping the right adults, not by routing the whole older generation and sending them running into the streets, stripped naked and shaved bald, as would happen in a typical teen-prop film of a later day (*Porky's II*, 1983).

But even by the early 1940s, the cinematic harmony between teens and adults had begun to erode. In 1942, as the same critic notes, a *Variety* headline announced: "WAR TRIMS PIX FANS. INDUSTRY SEEKS NEW AUDIENCE."

World War II was taking away moviegoers of the twenty-one to forty-five-year-old group, and a public relations campaign was launched to attract teen patrons. It worked. After the war, nineteen-year-olds were found to be the most frequent and faithful ticket buyers. Hollywood, as always, opted for the easy buck, increasing its production for the most dependable group. Inevitably the pitch to the audience had to change from the adult-idealized image of cute kids to something a little rougher and closer to home. And so, through the 1950s and 1960s, kid pix turned increasingly to teen relationships, generational conflict, and the passions of youth.

A particularly troublesome item was rock 'n' roll, since it promised millions of teen bucks, but bore an obvious message of teen rebelliousness against the older society, to which the filmmakers belonged. For the time being Hollywood contained the problem by combining rock 'n' roll with its standard version of wholesome kids (Annette Funicello and Frankie Avalon) in a series of nauseating beach films. Likewise Elvis the Pelvis was twisted from a vulgar rabble-rouser into a Mama's pretty boy who likes to babysit and sing to puppets (*G.I. Blues,* 1960). As a final ploy, Hollywood tried to present this most incendiary brand of music in the role of a unifier of all ages and peoples.[5] But here, as well as in the beginning, the harmony was forced and worked against Hollywood's ultimate goal: total sellout.

Teen Exploitation

The war was over, and with it the wartime films. Kids formed a larger percentage of the population than previously and had money earned from after-school jobs. With the advent of television, a drop in adult attendance at theaters, the rising costs of high-quality filmmaking, and the divestiture of movie-theater chains, the movie industry turned to the kids as to its salvation, producing quick, cheap double features suitable for showing in drive-in theaters. Most of these films, contrary to the old formula, did not show idealized pictures of scrubbed-clean youths, but rather shocking portrayals of kids on the edge, driven by uncontrollable urges, or thrown into unusual situations, such as encounters with space creatures. Sensationalism worked for adults; it ought to work for teens. The kids ate it up. They recognized the films as cheap and ludicrous; they knew that the fantastic situations distorted their lives, but nevertheless saw accurate representations of themselves in the clothes, speech, and manners of the actors. Aside from running into werewolves and monsters, the kids in these films did ordinary things: they drove cars, competed with other kids, made out, and got into trouble. From 1954 to 1969 hundreds such films were made, and few failed to turn a profit. The teens, now constituting between 50 and 90 percent of the moviegoing audience, kept the industry rolling.

Alan Betrock gives a nostalgic account of all this in his book *The I Was a Teenage Juvenile Delinquent Rock 'n' Roll Horror Beach Party Movie Book: A Complete Guide to the Teen Exploitation Film, 1954–1969.* The book's facetious title follows the chronological phases of the teen exploitation film, from juvenile delinquent film to rock 'n' roll film to horror film to beach-party film. Let's look at some titles in the pantheon along with some marquee blurbs.

Juvenile delinquents appear in such films as *The Blackboard Jungle* (called "nightmarish and bloodcurdling" by the *New York Times,* it promoted Bill Haley's song, "Rock around the Clock"), *The Cool and the Crazy* ("Seven savage punks on a weekend binge of violence!"), *Crybaby Killer* ("Yesterday a teenage rebel, today a mad-dog slayer!"—Jack Nicholson's first film), *The Delinquents, Dragstrip Girl, Dragstrip Riot, Eighteen and Anxious* ("Parents may be shocked, but youth will understand!"), *Girls on the Loose* ("Trigger tough and ready for anything! Crime-crazy girl gangs . . . looting . . . lying . . . living only for thrills!"), *High School Hellcats, The Restless Years* ("The story of a town with a 'dirty' mind! Where evil gossip threatened disgrace to two decent youngsters in love!"), *Teenage Bad Girl, Teenage Crime Wave, Teenage Doll, Teen-Age Menace, Teenage Rebel, Teenage Wolfpack.*

Rock 'n' roll films include such hits as *Carnival Rock* ("Hold onto your seat. It's got a heat-beat!"); *Dangerous Youth; Rock All Night; Rock Baby, Rock It; Rock, Pretty Baby; Untamed Youth* ("Youth turned rock 'n' roll wild and the punishment farm that makes them wilder. . . . Starring the girl built like a platinum powerhouse—Mamie Van Doren").

Teenage horror is found in *I Was a Teenage Werewolf* (Michael Landon's most embarrassing role), *I Was a Teenage Frankenstein* ("Body of a boy! Mind of a monster! Soul of an unearthly thing!"), *Invasion of the Saucer Men, The Curse of the Living Corpse, Teenage Caveman, Teenage Monster, Teenage Zombies, Teenage Psycho Meets Bloody Mary* (also released as *The Incredibly Strange Creatures Who Stopped Living and Became Crazy Mixed-up Zombies,* "not for sissies"), and *Village of the Giants* (based loosely on H. G. Wells's *The Food of the Gods*).

The beach-party films, a retrograde movement, originated in the early 1960s, when other teen exploitation films were growing stale. American International Pictures, run by Samuel Z. Arkoff, called in William Asher, who had directed *I Love Lucy* and *Make Room for Daddy* on TV. Asher wanted clean-cut kids, not delinquents, and Arkoff let him have his way. The result was a bland concoction of healthy kids cavorting on the beach with such grown-up celebrities as Vincent Price strolling by: *Beach Party, Muscle Beach Party, Bikini Beach, Beach Blanket Bingo,* and *How to Stuff a Wild Bikini.* To Arkoff's surprise, the films were a big hit and spawned many imitations. Betrock explains their appeal:

> Why were the pictures so successful? Well, they moved fast and were escapist fun. There were no parents. They were ridiculous. They were, despite AIP's claims of cleanliness, sexy. All those bodies and bikinis churning away to twangy rock 'n' roll offered a fantasy vision of life without serious problems.[6]

As Betrock sees it, the exploitation factor in all these films—juvenile delinquent to beach party—consisted in their sensationalism. Kids were brought into the theaters and drive-ins by advertisements, billboards, and publicity gimmicks that promised more than they delivered. Nevertheless, looking back on these films, he finds them endearing—for their camp, nostalgia, pop-culture values, attention to teen issues, and their interaction with the teen audience as a two-way street of influence. For him, they were harmless fun.

Arkoff was the chief producer; his AIP made more than five hundred movies. As one might expect, he was a baldheaded man with a big cigar. For him, exploitation was a practical consideration:

> People sneer at exploitation. This is unmitigated bullshit. The fact is, we didn't have any stars, we didn't have any star directors, we didn't have any star producers, we didn't have any star plays, we didn't have any star—whatever it was. So we had to depend upon a title and exploitation.[7]

What needs to be said is that the exploitation of youth by adults cannot be a good or even harmless thing. At first the kids were lured into the carnival by the colors, the lights, and the carneys; they spent their money, they had a good time, but they knew they had been cheated. Yet, they went back, expecting less, having less of a good time, until it stopped being fun. At that point something more than hype was needed to bring them in.

Hollywood had to give them what they wanted—or what it thought they wanted. For the teen exploitation film this meant giving them their own truths. Moviemakers had to assure them that their rebellious instincts were not a social problem, but a valid point of view: the problems in the world were caused by adults, not kids; the kids, in fact, were better than their elders in every respect, and if only the adults would leave them alone they could work things out for the best. This was a new type of exploitation, psychological exploitation. This was teen-prop.

The Birth of Teen-Prop

The trend had been growing all along through the early teen films, but had not yet attained dominance. Recall the blurb for *Eighteen and Anxious:* "Parents may be shocked, but youth will understand." The same sentiment appears in a review of *Cynthia* (1947), starring Elizabeth Taylor: "Cynthia's mother and father learn a thing or two about dignity from their daughter." A publicity blurb for the phenomenally popular *Rebel without a Cause* (1955): "Jim Stark, a kid in the year 1955. What makes him tick like a time bomb? Maybe the police should have arrested his parents instead."[8] In *Don't Knock the Rock* (1956), the kids show the adult opponents of rock 'n' roll how stodgy and stupid they are by staging a pageant at high school; it contains classical paintings, traditional dances and a demonstration of the Charleston. One old square eventually gets the point and jumps up to confess: "You're right, we're really a bunch of narrow-minded fools."[9] A *Time* review of *Blue Denim* (1959) observes: "The fault here seems to lie not so much with the youngsters . . . as with the obtuse parents who are never properly plugged into the problems of their young."[10]

After so much advance publicity, the cause of the young finally broke out into the open with a landmark film of the mid-1960s. Although not a teen film per se, since it featured a fresh bachelor of arts, *The Graduate* (1967) nevertheless pitted a world of good kids with sincere and honest motives against a conformist world of corrupt and disgusting adults. The hero, played by Dustin Hoffman in his first starring role, rejects the advances of a lascivious older woman—Mrs. Robinson, played by Anne Bancroft—and falls in love with her daughter, who has the decent impulses of youth but the wrong example of her parents. The two youngsters, graduate and girl, must oppose the false values of their elders and seek a better way. The film was a smash hit; director Mike Nichols won an Oscar. For the youth of the 1960s, Simon and Garfunkel's mocking lyric, sung throughout the movie, became something of a badge of honor, almost a national anthem: "And here's to you, Mrs. Robinson, Jesus loves you more than you will know. Ho, ho, ho." The idea that the grown-up world, the establishment, the military-industrial complex that produced the war in Vietnam, parents, everyone over thirty, had anything believable to say was finished.

But we should not pass too quickly by *Don't Knock the Rock,* which in its own way set a landmark. By exposing the older opponents of rock 'n' roll music as "narrow-minded fools," the film provided a formula for dealing with anyone who stood in the way of the ballooning youth culture. Henceforth all critics of rock music, recreational drugs, teen sex, and total teen liberty, as well as of the industries profiting from them, would be portrayed as ridiculous bigots, squares, sex-starved hypocrites, reactionaries, obscurantists, and meddlesome fools. Not only the teen films, but popular music, youth-oriented publications, television shows, and spokespersons making money off of teens picked up the tactic. It is a simple but devastating device that effectively prevents any serious discussion in this country of the ethics, morality, and sensibility of the teen trade, since the various groups of mothers and politicians who periodically try to oppose it cannot remove the established context and end up looking like old fogies whatever they do. Further, they cannot produce even one-millionth of the sounds and images routinely manufactured by the teen-prop media. They appear like mice on the Serengeti plains, complaining about the herds and proposing various systems for rating the destructiveness of their hooves.

The Graduate gave the youth perspective validity. No one watching the film, whatever his or her age, would want to side with the Robinsons—smug, snobbish, conventional, consumerist, hypocritical. The youth perspective harkens us all back to our early hopes and dreams, to our comparative innocence and optimism. We don't want to be made mean and nasty by society; we can recover our pure motives by listening to the kids. Such a message ran its course through the films of the 1960s and 1970s without setting any major trends. But it was still a tame message and did not capitalize on the market. Only in the 1980s were the edges sharpened, when the college graduate of the 1960s himself passed the age of believability, but started making his own movies.

Risky Business (1983), starring Tom Cruise and Rebecca de Mornay, set the style for the decade. Here the parents, represented as dunderheads, take a trip and leave their son, Joel Goodsen, alone in a big house with a Porsche in the garage. A good boy worried about his grades and chances of getting into college, Goodsen is reluctant to take advantage of the situation, but his buddy Miles, an intellectual sort, gives him a piece of advice: "Every now and then say, 'What the fuck!' 'What the fuck' gives you freedom, freedom brings opportunity, opportunity makes your future. . . . So your folks are going out of town? Got the place all to yourself? What the fuck! If you can't say it, you can't do it."

Miles's philosophy opens the door to a series of adventures in which the teens drink, drive, smoke, wreck things, get laid, and wind up running a whorehouse out of Joel's home. Joel buys off the Princeton University recruiter with a sample of the goods and patches up the place in time for his parents' return. They, of course, haven't a clue. "Sometimes," the father tells his son in the last scene, "you just have to say, 'What the heck.'" Dad is thereby exposed as a hopeless boob. The work he does is not mentioned, and the fact that he provides the house, the car, the money, and all the conditions for Joel's adventure does not earn him one jot of credit in the viewer's account, because in each of his three scenes he proves himself a washout as a human being. The movie, in sum, puts forward five lessons:

1. Parents are a joke.
2. School is a drag.
3. Sex, booze, pot, obscenity, and what the fuck are good.
4. The system sucks.
5. If you're smart or lucky, you can beat it.

Risky Business is a well-made film with excellent photography, inventive dialogue, and real bursts of humor. Actor Tom Cruise, at the beginning of his career, is adept at personifying the raw youth coming to maturity—here hesitant and shy, there determined and tough. Without question the film deals with real adolescent issues (such as competition for college admission) and accurately depicts details of adolescent behavior (such as a card game with cursing and cigars). Nor are up-tight parents entirely a product of imagination, though here they are shown from the floor up, as though Joel were an infant. Yet the realistic features of the film by no means mitigate its teen-prop structure; instead, they work within it. Details of real life are true within the context of real life; taken from that context and made a sole and exclusive reality, they are converted to half-truths and lies.

For example, the reason for Joel's adventure is that he can't enjoy sex with a proper partner—a girl from his own circle of friends, who is will-ing. His parents and hers, the authorities, are strictly opposed. He has to go elsewhere—outside the high school, to a prostitute, the heroine of the film. His parents drove him into the arms of a prostitute—that's the underlying premise. Even more preposterous is the thrill the virginal high-schooler gives the hardened hooker—a product, by the way, of an abusive stepfather. Yet this unbelievable commingling of schoolboy and whore was sufficient to give birth to a hundred similar kids, all bawling for attention.

The Golden Age of Teen-Prop

By the 1980s the youth culture was so well established, the industry thriv-ing on it so firmly entrenched, and the mechanisms for ridiculing its critics so automatic and effective that filmmakers could exploit teen attitudes without remorse or fear of interference. Once constituted as an indepen-dent entity—an artistic genre, if you will—the teen-prop film could now function without connection to reality, seeking to top itself with each new venture, building up its own momentum, spreading out to embrace differ-ent categories of films, becoming overblown, outrageous, and ludicrous in the process, but surviving so long as it could fuel itself with big bucks. Just like the Frankenstein film of an earlier decade, which sold horror, or a pretense of it, so the teen-prop film sold rebellion, or a pretense of it: proof that the kids were right and parental figures wrong in each and every in-stance. A plethora of movies in a half-dozen categories drove home this argument.

Teen Raunch   High school provides the setting for a series of escapades con-cerned with sex, booze and close scrapes, in which basically decent and likable kids outwit the teachers and other adults and show them up as bigots, hypocrites, and lechers. Titles: *Rock'n'Roll High School* (1979), *Porky's* (1981), *Porky's II: The Next Day* (1983), *Porky's Revenge* (1985), *Fast Times at Ridgemont High* (1982), *Revenge of the Nerds* (1984), *Mis-chief* (1985).

The outstanding example is *Porky's*. A sign flashing on a sleazy bar, "Get it at Porky's." Then a standard teen-prop opening: hero (Pee-Wee) waking up in bed, playing with himself. Patti Page on the radio tells us that it's the fifties, but otherwise it's anytime. Hero on the way to school, obscenities galore. Lots of verbal and visual jokes about condoms. Lots of nudity. The plot: the guys take Pee-Wee to Porky's so he can get his first lay, but beer-belly Porky tricks them out of their money. They return and tear down the establishment. Subplot: one guy (Kavanaugh) is a racist who persecutes a Jewish boy. This is because Kavanaugh's father is a bigot, a convict, and a bully. The Jew beats up Kavanaugh with jujitsu, after which Kavanaugh respects him and rejects his father. Authority figures are caricatured in the person of the gym instructress Miss Bollbrecher and Pee-Wee's mother. The cops, uncharacteristically, are good guys and help rout Porky. Pee-Wee gets laid by the school slut, Wendy, in the end.

Teen Education   The bildungsroman of teen-prop. The hero experiences something important, such as the goodness of sex or the evil of adults, grows up, and prepares for the hard road ahead. Titles: *Losing It* (1982), *Risky Business* (1983), *All the Right Moves* (1983), *Sixteen Candles* (1984), *The Breakfast Club* (1985), *Dead Poets Society* (1989).

The Breakfast Club has to be the I-hate-parents film of all time. Five kids must spend Saturday in detention hall. The kid-hating, burned-out gym teacher acting as their monitor sets them the assignment of writing a thousand-word essay on the subject "Who am I?" Rather than do the assignment, the kids tease and taunt each other, then enter into a psycho-drama in which each bares his or her soul. The source of their agony is not hard to find: a bad parent in each and every case. The characters:

> Andrew Clark (Emilio Estevez), the athlete—forced to be a wrestler and number-one tough guy by his super-jock father, "the son of a bitch."
> Bender (Judd Nelson), the angry young man—yelled-at, abused, tortured with burning cigars by his boozing, brawling old man.
> Claire (Molly Ringwald), the beautiful red-haired princess—not loved by her parents, who are "both screwed," but used by them as a pawn in their marital battles.
> Bryan (Anthony Michael Hall), the brain—driven to contemplate suicide by his parents' insistence on straight A's.
> Kooky (Ally Sheedy), the mischievous and mysterious artist—reserved for a special torture by her parents, as revealed in this scene:

> *Kooky* (speechless with emotion, struggling with inner pain).
> *Andrew:* Is it bad, real bad? . . . Parents?
> *Kooky* (still resisting a breakdown). Yeah. . . .
> *Andrew:* What'd they do to you?
> *Kooky* (finally breaking). They ignore me!
> *Andrew* (with understanding). Yeah.

The kids trash the library detention hall, smoke pot, and learn to love one another. The monitor is revealed as a cynic, despising all humanity and looking forward to his retirement. Teen truths are discovered: "It's unavoidable. It just happens. . . . When you grow up, your heart dies." Jock falls for Kooky. Bender humps Claire in the closet. Bryan writes a short essay for the breakfast club: "We are what you make of us." Kids— 5, adults—0.

Teen Horror   A throwback to *I Was a Teenage Frankenstein* and *The Blob* (1958), but also to *Carrie* (1976, whose religious fanatic mother was the true source of evil), TH advances the values of teen-prop, but inconsistently. Often other teens are the object of hatred, and sometimes the monster is not a characteristic adult but a deranged one, as in *The Texas Chainsaw Massacre* (1982). Also, unlike most other teen-prop films, kids can get badly hurt here. Titles: *The Initiation of Sarah* (1978), *Sweet Sixteen* (1981), *Splatter University* (1983), *Sleep Away Camp* (1984), *A Nightmare on Elm Street* (I, II, III, etc.), *Friday the Thirteenth* (I, II, III, etc.).

A Nightmare on Elm Street (1984) got the most play. Here a dreamtime bogeyman kills kids in their sleep. Nancy keeps waking up and telling her parents. They refuse to believe her, even though the mother knows the real-life origin of the bogeyman (a boy she had helped to kill) and the father as chief of police can confirm the murders that Nancy predicts. But, being parents, they persist in acting like idiots: the mother hits the bottle, and the father locks up Nancy in the house, endangering her life. Sellout director Wes Craven, a former Shakespeare teacher, concludes with a bloodbath of horror clichés and rakes in the mazuma.

Teen Switch   Teens break away from the limitations imposed on them by adults and take their place, proving themselves better mentally, physically, and sexually. Titles: *A Night in Heaven* (1983), *Class* (1983), *Angel* (1983), *Teachers* (1984), *Back to the Future* (1985), *Back to the Future, Part II* (1989), *Back to the Future, Part III* (1990).

Class, like *Risky Business,* draws its share from *The Graduate.* Skip and his buddies break in on Jonathan, who has been acting strange. Surprise, surprise! Jonathan is in bed with Skip's mom. Then the state attorney general comes to the prep school to investigate cheating on the Standard Achievement Tests. Fun scenes of students, who mistake him for a narcotics agent, flushing pills and pot down the toilets. Skip, when questioned, tells the investigator to shove it, even though he knows that Jonathan has cheated in order to get into Harvard. SAT, after all, is adult authority; Skip's dad is on the board; therefore his greater allegiance must be to his peer, even one who screwed his mom. Dad, just to prove who was at fault, informs Skip that his mom has entered a psycho ward. In the finale Skip and Jonathan have a big knock-down, drag-out fight, after which they make up and stay best friends. The message is clear: no sex-crazed mother, let alone establishment father, can break up the friendship between a couple of great pill-popping guys.

Super Teen   Teens are superior to adults. Teens save the world. Titles: *War Games* (1983), *Red Dawn* (1984), *Night of the Comet* (1984), *Real Genius* (1985), *The Last Starfighter* (1985).

War Games actually generated serious discussion in the press about our nuclear-arms security. David Lightman is a smart kid: he goofs off in class by day but changes his grades by night, using his home computer to break into the school computer system. He pays his electric and phone-modem bills the same way. His parents are Dagwood and Blondie at an advanced stage of incompetence. While hacking for some free computer games, David randomly breaks into the Defense Department's master computer, the most sophisticated system ever built. He reads up on the computer's designer, Dr. Falken, and correctly guesses the "back-door" code word. Now he can play thermonuclear war. This activates United States missile defenses. When David learns from TV that it was not a game (which he should have known if he was so damn smart), he shuts down, but the War Operation Programmed Response (WOPR) phones him back. (It's turned into HAL from *2001: A Space Odyssey, 1968*.) General Berringer (stolen from *Fail-Safe,* 1964) is against machines, but ready to go to war. David is arrested, but quickly discovers that the scientists can't shut down the operation. They need his help. So he breaks out of maximum security and flies with his girlfriend to Dr. Falken's secret hideaway. Falken has given up on humanity and plays with toy dinosaurs. But David convinces him to return to headquarters of the North American Air Defense Command (NORAD) and save the world. Once there, David takes over the decision-making process for the United States of America. Others back off before the bright teen. In the last seconds before all rockets are fired, David teaches WOPR that it can't win World War III: he makes the computer play itself tic-tac-toe. This does the trick, WOPR shuts down. David can't pass biology, and his girlfriend agrees that he is an "asshole" (a term essential to teen-prop), but he has mastered the highest levels of military security, scientific thought, and artificial intelligence known to humanity, saving the world for untold peaceful years.

Magic Teen   Teens become magical, realize their dreams. Magic permits them to release violent impulses without immediate punishment. Titles: *Christine* (1983), *Heavenly Kid* (1985), *Teen Wolf* (1985), *Weird Science* (1985).

Weird Science (1985) is the most polemical of the lot. Parents away, geeky Gary and Wyatt create a perfect woman with the computer. Lisa has magic, supplies fake ID's for the boys. She tries to help Wyatt loosen up sexually, but he worries about his parents. Lisa responds: "What's wrong with your parents? They're oppressive, meddlesome, difficult, demanding, and totally bizarre—I mean, they're normal parents." She meets Gary's parents: Dad—a bonehead plumber, Mom—a knitting simpleton. She instructs them that the teen has more right to complain than they, and tops off her argument by pointing a huge revolver in the old man's face. He loses his mind and acquires a permanent mumble. Lisa throws a big party for the high-school crowd. The grandparents stop by to meddle and are put in the closet in a state of suspended animation. Bad motorcyclists crash through the windows and terrorize the teens. Gary, with newfound courage, chases them away with a huge revolver. Geeks win cute girls. Bully older brother is turned into a troll. Lisa leaves. The huge mess is cleaned up in reverse motion as the parents return. It's a magical rip-off of *Risky Business* with all teen dreams fulfilled.

Such, in brief, are the historical monuments in the great production of teen-prop—a full decade of pitiless propaganda directed against the older generation by teen-exploiting members of the same generation. Other varieties could be described, such as Teen Desert Island—teens get away from the world and live the life of adults without the interference of same: *The Blue Lagoon* (1981), *Paradise* (1982), *Return to the Blue Lagoon* (1991); or Teen Vacation—young people take a break from the rigors of school and enjoy a fanciful adventure: *The Sure Thing* (1983), *Spring Break* (1984), *Summer Lovers* (1984), *Ferris Bueller's Day Off* (1986); or Preteens Torment the Parent Substitute: *Uncle Buck* (1989), *Home Alone* (1990), *Problem Child* (1990), *Problem Child II* (1991). But at a certain point it becomes impossible to count or even catalogue all the varieties: teen-prop films spring up everywhere, yet are not quite the same. And by the beginning of the 1990s, any film that had anything to do with kids became teen-prop.

The Universalization of Teen-Prop

Imitation and plagiarism are not the only ways to make a film when you have no original ideas: you can also make a sequel to a successful film from the past. The updating process, however, may reveal things about the bad taste that you have acquired.

Thus, after more than twenty years in an insane asylum, the schizophrenic killer Norman Bates was pronounced cured and sent home to reopen his defunct motel, the setting for paralyzing horror in Alfred Hitchcock's *Psycho* (1960). People start getting murdered again, but Bates is innocent this time, for the focus in *Psycho II* (1983) is not on his mental imbalance, but rather on generational conflict, so that toward the end, in one of the most outrageous plays ever made to the younger audience, an overly talkative mother gets pinned to the floor with a butcher knife— stabbed right through her gibbering mouth. Like other distinguished actors in the fading twilight of their careers (Lesley Ann Warren, Dick Shawn, Rory Calhoun, Lee Grant), Anthony Perkins, the original Norman Bates, rode out teen-prop to an ignominious end, making *Psycho III* (1986) and *Psycho IV: The Beginning* (1990). The last in the series finally explains how Bates got so mixed up: his mother was oversexed.

What happened between 1960 and 1990 to turn even Norman Bates from a shrieking monster into a good kid with a legitimate point of view? In a remarkably prescient book of 1982, social critic Neil Postman announced *The Disappearance of Childhood*. His thesis is that childhood did not always exist as a clear-cut stage of life, but emerged only after the advent of printing in the fifteenth century. The print culture fostered literacy, learning, sequential thinking, protestantism, secularism, a separation of literate and learned people from illiterate and unlearned people, hence the development of education, schooling, training, childhood. The concept of childhood, in turn, demarcated the stage of maturity as one containing secret knowledge, social privileges, personal responsibilities, and a humane concern for the young. So childhood developed over the course of centuries up to the present day. But, Postman's argument goes on, the advent of the telegraph in the nineteenth century, plus the radio and television in the twentieth, set the conditions for a new type of culture—visually and aurally oriented, nonsequential, filled with images, instantaneous impressions, entertainment, and universally accessible knowledge. Thus the two groups, once demarcated by a gap in knowledge, skills, tastes, etc., collapsed, and kids and grown-ups merged into one, the "adult-child." Today, as in the Middle Ages, children see everything grown-ups see, both the refined and the raw; they know intimacy like adults, commit crimes like adults, play the same games, make the same dirty jokes.

Postman adduces a series of compelling examples in support of his thesis: the same sports (little league and big league), the same clothes (kids in fine threads, grown-ups in jeans), the same crimes and punishments (murders and executions). And, more to the point of my thesis, the same tastes in television programs and movies: the ABC *Saturday Night Movie*, *M*A*S*H*, and *Three's Company* scored high among all age groups in the Nielsen ratings for 1980. Increasingly there was no need for separate entertainments.[11]

I take Postman's thesis as true, yet regret one oversight. Nowhere does he note that younger people, whatever their delightful qualities and unlimited potentials, and whatever their adaptability and openness to new technology, remain both in the Middle Ages, today, and in the next millennium inescapably inferior to older people in experience and understanding of the world; they may in some instances better their elders in intelligence and wisdom, but on the whole they cannot be superior or even equal to them, and for the most part must suffer a great disadvantage to them, or else there is no sense in living. If the early years are the best and wisest in life, then one would be a fool to strive for anything beyond them, such as learning, understanding, or self-improvement—a fool, in fact, to do anything at all but remember one's glorious days as a teen. But if, on the contrary, one can learn in life, then the older, more learned, and more thoughtful members of society, whatever its technology, may have a duty to understand the young, but by no means should betray themselves and their humanity by adopting the juvenile perspective. This is true for filmmakers, critics, educators, parents, and presidents of the United States. The present essay is dedicated to this simple proposition.

Like it or not, however, kids and grown-ups are merging in America today, so we may assume that after a decade-long run of pure teen-prop, filmmakers began to realize that they did not have to pitch exclusively to the kids. They could diversify their investments and insert teen-prop motifs into broader-based projects. The grown-ups themselves were willing to accept that the kids knew best and to admit them into the standard "adult" fare. Mutating into overgrown kids themselves, they preferred to side with the juvenile point of view wherever they found it and not to identify with the objects of the kids' scorn, the detested authority figures. We should also consider the possibility that the teen-prop image had become so pervasive and successful that filmmakers were mentally incapable of conceiving of any other type.

Whatever the reason, super teens, wiser by far than their fumbling elders, became the norm for movies and television programs in the 1990s, whether targeted for kids, grown-ups, or the hybrid "adult-child." One example must stand for all the rest: the incredibly smart and exceptionally snotty brat of *Terminator II*.

The Apotheosis of Teen-Prop

The Terminator (1984, hereafter called *Terminator I*), coauthored and directed by James Cameron, is curiously uninterested in teens. Rather, it is concerned with the contest between men and machines. Its premise is similar to *War Games* (1983). NORAD turns against people, like Karel Capek's robots and Stanley Kubrick's HAL; people try to shut it down and trigger a nuclear holocaust. Afterward the command, reconstituted as a computer center called Skynet, hunts down the human survivors with killer machines, exterminating some and keeping others as slave-servicers. Among the latter arises a hero named John Connor (hereafter JC) who leads a slave revolt. Unable to stop him, on the verge of losing, Skynet fashions a cyborg—the Terminator, flesh on the outside and steel underneath—and sends him back through time to assassinate JC's mother before he was born. JC finds out and sends a volunteer from his ranks— Kyle Reese—back through time to stop the cyborg. The film opens in the year 2029 with primitive scenes of soldiers fighting tractors.

Since *Terminator I* relies on a time machine device, it inevitably hatches a plot with logical impossibilities. Once the Terminator (played by Arnold Schwarzenegger) and Kyle (Michael Biehn) have returned to 1984, JC (never seen) blows up the time machine in 2029 so that they cannot return. Thus he and his commandos will be free to finish off Skynet unless the Terminator kills his mother in the past, after which, presumably, he—and all the history associated with him—will suddenly vanish. She, however, is not yet pregnant with him. With remarkable foresight (or hindsight), JC provides Kyle before his leaving with a photo of the "legendary" Sarah Connor (Linda Hamilton) so that he will find her, protect her, fall in love with her, and do his manly duty. In other words, though he already has a father, JC wants to be re-fathered in the past by his present comrade. The original father therefore must vanish, along with all the history associated with him, such as Sarah Connor, or else we are in a time loop, in which case the battle of men and machines doesn't matter: it will just keep repeating.

Nevertheless, the impossible premise allows for an extended chase. The Terminator tries to kill Sarah, slaughtering everyone near and far; Kyle protects her but gets killed in the process; so she saves herself, crushing the cyborg in a robot factory with the appropriate obscenities. Kyle, however, was successful in his second task. The film ends as a pregnant Sarah leaves Los Angeles in anticipation of the nuclear holocaust, heading south to Mexico, which is presumably less of a target for hydrogen bombs. She has a note from JC, handed her by Kyle, instructing her to hang tough: "If you don't survive, I will never be." She gets a Polaroid photo of herself to give to her son, pointedly the same one he will hand to Kyle in the future. (Kyle is dead, but does not have to survive directly into the future, since, as a young man, he will be born afresh later.) She makes a tape recording to explain things to her boy—confident that she will not deliver a girl, though the chances are supposed to be even—and decides to tell him who his father was. "If you don't send Kyle, you will never be. God, a person could go crazy thinking about this!"

Terminator I is antiwar, antimachine, and antipolice. It glorifies the average young woman of the 1980s, a waitress without special attributes, an Everywoman singled out by fate for a heroic role. All she has to do is get laid by the right man, escape a determined killer, and survive the coming nuclear war, and she will become a legend. Whether this story was meant to appeal to a feminine audience is anybody's guess.

Yet her mission is higher than mere legend. Although not exactly the Virgin Mary, Sarah is appointed by a higher power to bear the savior of the world. An angel of the Lord appears to announce the glad tidings— and does double duty by filling her with the Holy Spirit. The worldly kingdom, threatened, perpetrates a massacre of innocents, but she escapes and carries the babe to safety—the future JC. That he bears the same initials as his creator, James Cameron, must be considered a coincidence.

Terminator II: Judgment Day (1992), again coauthored and directed by Cameron, carries the story along with little John Connor, now ten years old in the year 1995. Although chronologically not a teen, JC (played by Edward Furlong) is indistinguishable from the species, particularly from Marty, hero of Robert Zemeckis's *Back to the Future,* who takes a time machine ride from the 1980s back to the 1950s to straighten out his future parents, so that he can still exist. Likewise JC shares with David Lightman of *War Games,* Ferris Bueller of *Ferris Bueller's Day Off,* Alex of *The Last Starfighter,* Gary and Wyatt of *Weird Science,* etc., etc., a facility with video games, computers, and all sorts of mechanical devices, which he rigs for his own purposes. And although the adventure film is made for a general audience, young JC has an attitude as bad as any chronic sufferer in *The Breakfast Club,* a full measure of teen-prop resentment.

The reason is, he doesn't buy the story his mother tells him about his brilliant destiny. He thinks she's nuts. He sees her consorting—"shacking up," he calls it—with paramilitary types who can help her train her boy to be a warrior. Then she gets another crazy idea: to blow up the central computer factory and prevent nuclear war. (She doesn't know it, but modern computer technology is based entirely on the hand of the cyborg that she crushed—incompletely, we learn—in *Terminator I.*) Captured in the attempt, she is deposited in a psycho ward. Little JC is placed with foster parents—"dickheads," he calls them. They are foulmouthed lowlifes, typical inferior adults of the most rabid teen-prop pamphlets.

We need consider only two more elements of the plot before the kid can strut his stuff. In the future world of 2030, one year after *Terminator I,* Skynet realizes somehow that its terminator T-800 model has failed, fixes the time machine, and sends out a more advanced model T-1000 to terminate little JC. (Unaccountably it sets the time machine to the year 1995, not 1985. Nor does it conceive the plan of going back to 1983 and eliminating Sarah Connor a full year before Kyle will arrive. Why not? Because then we wouldn't have a kid in the sequel.) The T-1000 can "morph"— change its shape—but most of the time it's dressed like a cop, the typical bad guy of teen-prop. Once again, the slave rebel John Connor finds out about Skynet's move and dispatches his own envoy to stop the terminator, but he can find only an old model T-800 (Schwarzenegger again). He programs it to do whatever little JC tells him. By this mechanism he ensures that in *Terminator II* the kid will be the boss.

Now here's what the little darling does. He:

humanizes the steel-frame, robotic cyborg by showing him how to curse, crack jokes, and cry;

modifies the cyborg's violent streak by teaching him to maim, not kill, human beings;

helps his distraught, buffed-out, militarized mother break out of the psycho ward;

eases her crippling emotional problems, much in the role of equal or husband;

uses a little device he has rigged up for cracking automatic teller machines to break into the computer lab, which is guarded by high-tech security;

secures the old Terminator's robotic arm and destroys it so that its technology is lost to NORAD;

leads the adults in exploding the computer works without killing anybody (the sympathetic black lab director is killed by the cops);

dispenses useful advice, wit, and obscenities ("holy shit!" "bullshit!" "you jock!" "douche-bag!" "dipshit!" "eat me!" "dickwad!" etc.) wherever needed.

While the kid is busy solving all the problems, the grown-ups have their chases and smashing cars. The super-terminator T-1000, sent out like King Herod's messengers to slay the newborn Messiah, is cast into a hell-fire of molten ore, then the protector T-800, taking on the role of sacrifice, lowers himself into the same ore to destroy his dangerous technology. Sarah, impressed by the scene, closes the film by expressing the hope that perhaps machines can be humanized—the bold message of Capek's *R.U.R.* (1920).

The End of History

So the kid did it all: he prevented nuclear war, suspended the machine age, and, paradoxically, precluded all the conditions that made for his existence. Thus little JC ends history by becoming an eternal Möbius strip of himself, now protecting himself in the past by sending warriors from the future, now safeguarding his future by destroying evils in the past, now negating both past and future by his successful performance in the present. He is the Alpha and the Omega, the beginning and the end, the first and the last, containing all hope and no hope, all meaning and no meaning, living in a present that is endlessly repeating itself, a never-never land where a juvenile delinquent becomes Jesus Christ, a cinematic heaven where teen becomes God.

Of course, the entire genre of teen-prop with all of its box-office block-busters has less intellectual substance than a wad of bubblegum. But nothing that anyone might propose can do anything about it. One would have to repeal television, take away teen employment, and return the kids to a paltry weekly allowance to make the movie jackals go away. Since no such things will happen, there is no point in attempting an anti-teen-prop campaign, beyond holding firm to this conviction: the kids do not know best, and the adults who pander to them are sellouts and prostitutes. To believe otherwise is not to be grounded in reality.

Notes

1. Ramon G. McLeod and Shann Nix (*San Francisco Chronicle*), "Boom in Teens to Put Squeeze on State's Means," *Press-Enterprise* (Riverside, California), April 12, 1993, A1, A8.

2. A handy listing of these films may be found in Leonard Maltin's *Movie and Video Guide* (New York: Signet Books, 1995). See especially the entries "Andy Hardy" and "the Bowery Boys."

3. David M. Considine, "The Cinema of Adolescence," *Journal of Popular Film and Television* 9 (Fall 1981): 125.

4. See Alan Betrock, *The I Was a Teenage Juvenile Delinquent Rock 'n' Roll Horror Beach Party Movie Book: A Complete Guide to the Teen Exploitation Film, 1954–1969* (New York: St. Martin's Press, 1986), 2–15.

5. The discussion is based on Barry K. Grant, "The Classic Hollywood Musical and the 'Problem' of Rock 'n' Roll," *Journal of Popular Film and Television* 13 (Winter 1986): 195–205.

6. Betrock, 102.

7. *Euroquest,* a syndicated program of Radio Netherlands, No. 9307, March 31, 1993.

8. Considine, 130–31.

9. Grant, 200.

10. Examples taken from Considine, 131.

11. Neil Postman, *The Disappearance of Childhood* (New York: Delacorte, 1982), 131.

Part 2

The Children of Science Fiction

The Forever Child: *Ender's Game* and the Mythic Universe of Science Fiction

George Slusser

Not in entire forgetfulness,
And not in utter nakedness,
But trailing clouds of glory do we come.
—William Wordsworth, "Intimations"

"The Child in Science Fiction" seems, at first, an unrewarding topic. Encyclopedias of the genre have a category "children," but all we determine there is that there are children in science fiction novels, and that they can be classified by type. But is there a special use of children, one unique to science fiction, that would justify this study? In traditional narrative, the presence of children generally tells us little about the nature of narrative form or (more important) about characterization. Young children play little or no active role in Western literature or culture because they have not yet learned to act. Where they appear, children seem to serve a purely symbolic or iconic function, like the child in Rembrandt's "Night Watch," variously seen as an angelic presence or a contrasting spot of light in a dark composition.

Taking "child" strictly as such—as preadolescent and preformational being—I wish to argue for a different and unique role for children in SF. If the normative aspect of Western fiction is character formation, the process whereby natural beings enter a social order, then the child in such fiction can exist only as icon—a potential entity, the first virtual stage in the process in which a character, in the narrative, creates an identity or self. The norm for SF, however, is more the epic or mythic narrative. Here the story is less about defining limits to human energy and more about increasing its scope and reach. As earlier myths extend human narratives to include natural forces and gods, SF defines itself as narrative through its central epic tropes of life extension and immortality. At this level, the science fiction narrative is less interested in the middle of *Bildung* and formation than in the extremes of beginning and end. Death is deferred in the search for immortality. But by the same token, might not birth also be retarded, in the sense that we prolong that moment of fall into the common day of formation Wordsworth decried?

Science fiction has notable examples of ancient beings like Lazarus Long, who strive to hold onto a being and body carefully shaped and nurtured in the course of time. But there are also striking examples of children who refuse to yield to formation and instead act to remain forever children. Their quite Wordsworthian quest is to move upstream, against the course of years, toward some source of life beyond the limits of birth itself. Orson Scott Card's Ender offers a significant example of the forever child of SF. Interesting here is the development of Ender the character from the early short story "Ender's Game" to the later novel with that title. The former work remains a more or less classic "juvenile" adventure, in which an adolescent undergoes his space age rite of passage, performs an epic feat, and by doing so moves toward adulthood. In the novel, however, just the opposite occurs. Ender recedes in age, and his actions regress to a preadolescent level. Here Ender taps the power and the glory that are those of the forever child.

Before examining *Ender's Game,* we should first consider the conventional wisdom regarding the role of the child in SF. The authors of the entry "Children in SF" in *The Encyclopedia of Science Fiction,* David Pringle and Peter Nicholls, describe four major types of SF stories about children.[1] The first, the "story about children in conflict with adult society," is not really about children, but is rather the sort of adolescent bildungsroman we find in a Robert Heinlein "juvenile." The age can range from early teens (for example, Kip and Peewee in *Have Space Suit, Will Travel*) to young adulthood (for example, *Starman Jones* or even Sam in *The Puppet Masters*). These stories deal with formation, never with childhood per se. Pringle and Nicholls's other three types of stories about children are more interesting. Stories in these categories (for example, Jerome Bixby's "It's a *Good* Life" and Richard Matheson's "Born of Man and

Woman") present children who resist the pull toward adolescence and adulthood. These children then are seen not as actors but as conduits for some power that seems to lie in arrears of their location as children in the narrative. We have, as categories: stories of children who channel benign paranormal powers (such as in Theodore Sturgeon's *More than Human* and A. E. van Vogt's *Slan*); stories of children who channel monstrous powers (e.g., Ray Bradbury); and stories of children who are openly conduits for alien powers, be they good or evil (Bradbury's "Zero Hour" is the example the authors give).

The question of the power and/or empowerment of children is interesting. In terms of the development of SF superchildren from Sturgeon and van Vogt to Card, Ender's game ends nothing. In sequels the child continues his "millennia-long saga," a center seeking vaster and vaster circumferences in the third novel, *Xenocide* (1991). In his trajectory Ender mirrors the progress of a peculiarly grotesque form of romantic child worship in American popular culture. As Wordsworth expressed it, the child is both innocent *and* resplendent with primal power and wisdom; he is a being who enters the adult world "trailing clouds of glory." This vision, increasingly played out to absurd lengths in modern America, effectively reverses the direction of education in Western culture. The child is no longer a beast to be formed as a Christian soul or an animal to be taught reason, but now a fallen piece of divinity, a "seer blest." In this American version, the child is no passive victim of fate. Instead, he is gradually empowered to resist being dragged into the "light of common day."

Indeed, one sees child heroes in SF works of the decades following the 1950s Heinlein "juveniles" gaining more and more powers at the same time that they undergo ever greater arrested development. In the 1960s, Heinlein's Michael Valentine Smith and Frank Herbert's Paul Atreides steadfastly refused the path of formation, choosing that of transcendence instead. As *Dune* sequel piles on epic sequel, Paul, the erstwhile adolescent, regresses further and further toward childhood. This regression is marked by an increasing propensity toward the amoral use of raw power in the service of self-preservation. In the language of psychoanalysis, Paul regresses from a genital state to the "archaic" preadolescent stages of anality and orality. We find analogues in American popular films. In the so-called brat pack films of the 1980s, parent authority figures are increasingly ridiculed and marginalized as *ineffectual*. At the same time, when the adolescents in these films turn to each other to solve the problems of growing up, they soon discover that the most effective solution is simply not to grow up. These young protagonists regress toward a gleaming Words-worthian horizon, a golden age ringed by sixteen candles, then fourteen, then six. The films of the 1990s have taken this process of unformation back to a monstrous place where adult authority is literally devoured whole. There are, in succession, the destructive imps of *Home,* the Gar-gantuan *Baby* of the film of that name, and the squalling nursling that serves as vanishing point for adult lives in *Three Men and a Baby.* At the most primal level, the child is simply a giant maw. The child, no longer a mere conduit for power, has become a power to be reckoned with in its own right. Science fiction films followed this direction: *The Terminator* has adult protagonists; *Terminator II* introduces the superchild. Inscribed in this tradition, Card's first Ender story, published in 1977, offers an eleven-year-old hero who, acting to save the human race by destroying its enemy in an intergalactic war, leads an "army" of seven-, eight-, and nine-year-olds. In the novel, published eight years later, Ender becomes a consummate strategist and efficient killer at the tender age of six. To draw power, he must remain at this stage.

Bradbury's children, whom Pringle and Nicholls mention prominently, can serve as point of comparison to *Ender's Game.* Like Ender, Bradbury's children are more than just neutral vessels for alien power. Possessed of a bizarre version of romantic aura, they take Wordsworth's sense of the prison house of adult life one step further by actively working to subvert or destroy it. Even the children in "Zero Hour" are more than conduits for Martian invaders.[2] In this story the adults have created a sterile, overly rational world through technology and reason; it is a literal prison house. What their sterilizing reason has overlooked, however, is the power of the child's "imagination," a faculty that leads the children to tinker and talk to rosebushes, activities dismissed by the rational adults as puerile. There is a sense that the children, who not only perceive the Martian invaders in places overlooked by rational adults but decide to bond with these invad-ers, have made a conscious choice, because this choice will destroy the world of their parents. In a grotesque, even murderous way, these children return, this time with Martian "parents" who do not restrict their activi-ties, to their source.

Bradbury's children do not come naked into the world, in the sense of Wordsworthian guiltlessness. What they seem to "remember" is not inno-cence but some primal stigma. In a Calvinist rather than romantic sense, they do not begin their fall at birth. Rather they are born fallen, trailing a curse rather than a cloud. Growing up in this sense can only be a worsening of the fall, to which a return to the primal source, however blighted, is preferable. "The Veldt" (1950) gives us an adult world regimented by machines that are surrogates for parental care.[3] George Hadley's family is governed by the Happy Life Home, a mechanical house that serves as father and mother to the children. At its center is a mechanical "nursery" whose function, as "holotoy," is to give illusory existence to a child's mental images. But the adults who made this projector forgot, in their mechanico-rational utopia, that a child's mind is neither empty nor innocent. And the children, as they project an African veldt, divert their parents' fantasy machine to the creation of flesh-and-blood monsters, producing real lions that turn on the father and mother and devour them. There is more here than just rebellion against an "unnatural" upbringing. The process of growing up, abetted by increasingly sophisticated technology, must, by some reverse biological need, be countered by reverting to violent and lawless acts. For Bradbury's romantic Calvinism, a child's actions offer proof of the terrible fall that lies at the heart of innocence.

The curse of birth is taken to shocking extremes in "The Small Assassin,"[4] in which the parents are neither indifferent nor surrogate machines. A real caring mother bears a child. But after the birth, the mother begins to claim that her baby willfully tried to kill her while in the womb. In "civilized" society, such a claim is unspeakable, for it sees the innocence of a newborn as an "alibi" hiding innate evil in the form of a will to destroy the very person who launched it into the light of common day. Babies, as this mother sees them, do not trail clouds of glory; they are "elemental little brains, aswarm with racial memory, hatred, and raw cruelty." We reach a cultural crux here. Our post-Wordsworthian, Freudian society must reject statements like these as paranoia or insanity; in Bradbury's story, however, the fears of the mother, if not absolutely corroborated, are substantiated. The story ends with the doctor, himself now persuaded that the child willfully caused the deaths of both mother and father, stalking the baby with the same scalpel he used to bring it into the world.

Bradbury's children become murderous because they refuse to grow up. Unlike the resigned romantic child who must abandon innocence for experience, they learn to retrieve part of a lost primal force by struggling to subvert and control the adult world. When they do not take vengeance in the womb, Bradbury's forever children prolong their childlike existence in ways that prove destructive to adults. In "The Martian," a member of that exhausted race bizarrely recaptures his childhood by taking the forms of dead children of Earth settlers.[5] The result is not the solace of miracle but the cruelty of a double separation. Perhaps Bradbury's icon of this forever child, in its most grotesque and destructive form, is the Dwarf, an adult destined to live on in the shriveled and misshaped body of a child.

Bradbury, it seems, in his Calvinist world dominated by endless falls away from the original Fall, is ultimately driven to take an unromantic moral stance in relation to this forever child. The mother in "The Small Assassin" tells us that "the world is evil . . . but laws protect us from it. And when there aren't laws, then love does the protecting" (130). Her formula, still too indulgent, is given a Hobbesian twist in "The Man Upstairs."[6] Here, childish "curiosity" leads to a young boy's dispassionate assault on the body of the "man upstairs." Young Douglas "proves" that Mr. Koberman is a vampire by cutting open his sleeping body, carefully removing its geometrically shaped organs, and sewing in their place the silver coins of his piggy bank. Earlier he had looked on with dispassion as his aunt gutted a chicken then sewed it up. Now he coldly repeats this act without the least concern for the sanctity of Koberman's body or "world," which in this case is a life that does not menace Douglas's world but is simply parallel to it, as would be the life of a chicken. Adults in this story learn, however, that, if the so-called laws of nature are based on the necessity of dog-eat-dog, or human-eat-chicken, human actions still must be tempered by restraint and sympathy. The unbridled acts of childish "reason" have to be controlled, and limits set on curiosity. In the case of Koberman, those who did not know his inner being saw no harm in his comings and goings. Seen from outside, vampires are supposed to be mirrors of ourselves; they thirst for our blood, they exchange our lives for theirs. But Douglas's discovery of Koberman's geometric insides opens a Pandora's box of real difference that must be sewn shut again. In Douglas's case, the response of the adult community is not love but law, enforcement of the social contract. His act is forgiven as long as it is never repeated, and as long as the silver stake in the vampire's heart becomes literally what the coroner calls it: "a wise investment," the placement of piggy-bank capital for a secure, adult future.

It is important to ask what role, if any, Bradbury's categories of love and law play in the career of Card's forever child, Ender Wiggin. Ender is eleven years old as the 1977 story "Ender's Game" opens, and *already* a three-year veteran of Battle School. Childhood curiosity and innocence lie behind him; he is disciplined and ready to operate on the adolescent interface between childhood and adulthood. Placed in charge of the Dragon

Army as the action begins, Ender moves in the narrative through a rapid and increasingly complex series of simulated battles, which he easily wins. Ender never experiences crisis or self-doubt, for just when the battles become tiresome, a hidden force intervenes and he is sent to Command School and placed under a teacher named Maezr Rackham. Now there are no more null-gravity exercises. Placed before a simulator screen, Ender directs a "fleet" that, in mysterious fashion, turns out to be made up of units commanded by his old Battle School platoon leaders, each suddenly promoted. Everything so far—mysterious mentor, hidden chain of command directing the destinies of preordained neophytes toward unrevealed but significant future combat—reminds us of Heinlein's *Space Cadet* or *Starship Troopers.*

But we soon see twists on this familiar scenario. Ender, who has no visible family, thinks he is undergoing normal training as a starship officer, as might a Heinlein protagonist. But the reader sees early on that his Battle School officers are preparing Ender for a quite un-Heinleinian role. Captain Graff and Lieutenant Anderson tell us that, although Ender is no longer a child in this story, he is not being formed to be a "person" or adult. Instead, they intend him to be a sacrificial being, the scapegoat who will make "it possible for the others of his age to be playing in the park." Graff even compares him to Jesus, saying, "We're the ones who are driving in the nails." [7] The sadism is not gratuitous. For when Ender fights his ultimate simulator battle only to learn that the battle was no simulation, and that he has, in fact, actually destroyed the enemy armada and planet, he is told by Graff that he was not duped but purposely used as a weapon: "Weapons don't need to understand what they're pointed at, Ender. We did the pointing, so we're responsible. You just did your job" (565).

However cynical and cruel the manipulation, the fact remains that Ender is a weapon here, a weapon created not by accelerating the normal path of formation, but by forcing the juvenile hero back to a state of childhood "innocence." He is quite literally, in a twisted sense, a Jesus figure, a Jesus without formative years in whom indifferent child and sacrificial adult fuse as one. This overt comparison to Jesus makes "Ender's Game" something new in the tradition of the SF juvenile. Let us compare Ender with the preteens Kip and Peewee in Heinlein's *Have Space Suit, Will Travel.* If "called" to save humanity at the bar of cosmic justice (for not all who have spacesuits are chosen to travel), Heinlein's children do not atone or "speak for" humankind's sins. Kip refuses any form of "higher" authority. In fact, his final choice, in defiance of that authority, is to die *with* the rest of humanity, not for them. Kip, by throwing in his lot with humankind, is on his way to growing up. Ender, however, is prevented from growing up by being *duped* into a Christlike role. His, however, is not the Christ who saves through sacrifice, but Christ the powerful child of the Apocryphal books, or an inverted Christ in the Wordsworthian sense, not Son of Man but Father to the Man. Colonel Graff exclaims, "Ender's older than I am" (544); and indeed we see that like Christ, ever powerful in his perpetual childhood, Ender is not taught mastery during a formative period; he instantly possesses it. Ender at the simulator is like Christ in the temple, a child who displays the innate skill of an adult.

Ender, as intergalactic warrior, should be measured against two Heinlein types. The first is the straight-line hero, such as Johnny Rico in *Starship Troopers,* who after being trained for combat is promised a long adult life in battle, of which we have a sample in the last scenes of the book. The second is the time-curve hero, such as Tom Bartlett in *Time for the Stars,* who finds himself, through the vagaries of special relativity, when his formative adventures end, in space-time, at a point *prior to* his first step into adult life. In response to his brother Pat's remark (who due to the "twins' paradox" is now eighty-plus years old to Tom's nineteen) that he is "just a boy," Tom responds: "No, Pat. I am not a boy, I am a man."[8] In fact he is neither. He is rather, like Ender, a being *at one and the same time* a child and a superannuated adult, simultaneously at the end and at the beginning of his career. In such a world, if the child is not the physical father to the man, he can at least be an adult and a child both at once.

Ender significantly reverses this child-as-adult situation. At the battle "simulator," he is a child who is old before his time, accumulating unknown to himself the weight of destroyed eons and worlds. And as a physical child in this same seat, engaged in this "salvation" of humankind, he is a being too old to ever have been young in the sense of innocent or inexperienced. Ender and his friend Bean admit to being simultaneously too early and too late: "Can you believe it! We won the war. The whole war's over, and we thought we'd have to wait till we grew up to fight in it, and it was us fighting it all the time" (566). In a sense, they win the war not before being trained to fight, but before beginning to train at all. In the lineage of Heinlein's relativistic Rip Van Winkles and Joe Haldeman's *The Forever War,* the Ender of the story is on the verge of becoming a forever child. But whereas through space-time manipulations Heinlein and Haldeman could retard but not stop the time line that runs from child to adolescent to man, Card seeks in *Ender's Game* the novel to turn this clock backward, to make his Ender-Christ grow younger even as he grows ever wiser and more powerful.

The Christ analogy provides a bridge from the Ender story to the novel. Because the novel ends with Ender at the same age as that at which he *began* the short story—that of Christ performing his first act in the Gospels, teaching the wise men in the temple—the novel explores a time not mentioned in the canonical life of Christ: his "lost" childhood. In the story, Ender, like the traditional Christ, has no freedom to choose the forms and conditions of his sacrifice, no childhood past to look back on, and he is blocked from any adult future by his destiny. The novel, in its greater length, gives him back the lost realm of childhood as space of operation. Ender in the novel is again manipulated by adult officers, again duped into destroying what is now the "bugger" race by being led to think the final battle is a simulation, or "game." At the same time, this Ender simultaneously evolves on another path, following a Wordsworthian curve of vital forces flowing in reverse, where he recovers Christlike powers to intercede. Here, power is drawn solely from the depths of childhood experience as Ender taps unconscious domains, uncharted or unwritten in adult scripture, that allow him to overlay the adult act of destruction with a childlike one of resurrection. In this schizophrenic realm where child and adult never meet, the dead must die, allowing the child, in his closed realm, to accede to a new role as "speaker for the dead."

In the short story Ender is the sole prodigy. In the novel, however, Card creates a genuine "child space," giving more attention to Ender's comrades-in-arms, multiplying the role given to the lone child Bean in the story. Whereas in the story Ender's main adversaries are adults—first Graff and company, then Maezr Rackham, with whom Ender engages in a struggle—in the novel Card gives him a series of "peer" opponents, bullies whom he defeats by the most violent and deadly physical means. Finally, Card gives Ender two genius child siblings—evil brother Peter and good sister Valentine—whose actions (a struggle for power on the "domestic" front) point Ender away from consciously experienced war games to the seemingly childish Giant's Game, played in a personal mind-space separate from the official cybernet of adult military operations. This path provides the conduit whereby Ender, in the very act of destroying the alien buggers, can simultaneously become the means of resurrecting their culture. The novel develops an elaborate subplot that gradually encroaches on, and subsumes, the original plot of military training and the war-game-that-proves-real. The subplot emerges explicitly in an added final chapter, "Speaker for the Dead," leading to the sequel of that name.

Each chapter of *Ender's Game* offers, as epigraphs, the comments of Graff and other Battle School officers. Under this umbrella of adult manipulation the child forces stir and develop, unbeknownst to the adults. On the first page an adult offers this revelation about the Wiggin siblings: "Same with the sister. And there are doubts about [Ender]. He's too malleable. Too willing to submerge himself in someone else's will."[9] It is suggested that Ender might possess paranormal powers of empathy. But the adults do not heed this, or the further possibility, that such powers can be malignant and monstrous. Such is the power of brother Peter, who employs psychic means to control his siblings. Peter wants power in the political, not the military, scene, and seeks it through generalized mind control. For a long time Ender's adult "handlers" are unaware that the agitators "Locke" and "Demosthenes" are really Peter and Valentine, and that the former is manipulating his sister so that he can use the cover of intergalactic war to take control on the home front.

Peter is Bradbury's child born with monstrous powers, superintelligent *and* evil, a born torturer and sadistic killer. He is psychotic and, it is hinted, paranormal, for he haunts Ender's psychic life as an animus, the shadow of a killer within that Ender sees emerging, on the occasion of several hand-to-hand combats, into bloody reality. Valentine, on the other hand, is paranormal and benign, Ender's good anima who reveals in the end that she only pretended to be dominated by Peter/Locke so that she would be freer to come to Ender's aid. Playing off her Demosthenes role against Graff's tyranny, she obtains a face-to-face meeting with Ender. Instead of duping or humoring him, as the adults do, she opens his mind to deeper reality. By persuading him that all human beings are (at the depths of their primal psychic experience as children) born killers ("Killing's the first thing we learned. And a good thing we did, or we'd be dead, and the tigers would own the earth"), she helps him exorcise the Peter stigma. She is the "second" child who breaks Ender's obsession with the killing legacy of the first and oldest child. In doing so, she frees Ender's psyche so that it can pick up new paranormal channels, these coming from the "enemy" itself. He confides in Valentine a newly sensed aspect of his war game successes: "Every time, I've won because I could understand the way my enemy thought. From what they *did*. I could tell what they thought I was doing, how they wanted the battle to take shape. And I played off that. I'm very good at that. Understanding how other people think" (261).

Much is made in the novel of Ender's position as "third," the extra child exceptionally allowed in this overpopulated future Earth. Thus he is a genetic experiment, another example of manipulation by the adult world. As the "third," Ender is alienated from his biological parents, who reject him through guilt that looks back to religion's former sanction of large families. But Ender's "thirdness" also makes him a synthesis of Peter and Valentine, killer and empath, a combination that opens the way to his contact with the bugger not only as enemy but as kindred race, allowing him to become "speaker for a dead," a dead he must personally kill in order to be granted the right to become its spokesman and future savior.

The conduit for Ender's alien encounter, in the novel, is a game played on his personal computer in a fairyland cyberspace. Originally, Giant's Game was a learning device programmed and monitored by adult manipulators, but its playing field has been gradually reshaped by those mental forces that reflect the psychodrama, developing between Ender, his biological parents, and more centrally his brother and sister and their powers. To Ender, the initial game of giant killing turns strange as the fallen body of the slain giant erodes into a landscape honeycombed with underground tunnels leading to a "cliff ledge overlooking a beautiful forest." Each time he reaches this point he is carried up to a turret room, the room at the End of the World. An apparent impasse is reached when Ender stamps on a snake in the carpet only to have a mirror appear on the wall with Peter's face in it, a snake's tail protruding from the corner of his mouth. Each time Ender breaks the mirror with the dead snake, the broken mirror disgorges snakes that bite and kill him.

The room at the End of the World is a stalemate that threatens Ender's battle room performance. The adults do not know how this scenario, especially Peter's face, got into their game: "Fairyland was programmed in. But nothing talks about the End of the World. We don't have any experience with it." Sensing that what is being acted out in this game space is Ender's own neuroses, Graff goes to Earth and coerces Valentine into writing her brother to persuade him he is not a killer like Peter. On the conscious level, Ender reacts negatively to her letter, believing she has betrayed him, and that her betrayal means that "they" have taken complete control of his life. The mind game, however, has made Ender realize, well before he begins his final battle training, that he is a cold-blooded killer and that his handlers need him, as tool, to defeat the buggers. Under these psychic pressures, a doubling of Ender's theater of action now occurs. Ender will go on, duped by adults, to defeat the enemy in battle. Simultaneously, however, on a parallel unconscious level, Ender comes to accept the fact that he has been duped and ultimately ceases to care if this is so. As actor he goes through the motions; as consciousness he moves in a very different direction. Other levels of activity—adult wars, feuding families, and now sibling rivalries—all fall away as Ender seeks concord on a larger, exobiological level of kinship.

After reacting to Valentine's letter and apparent betrayal, Ender replays the End of the World scenario, but now his reactions are different. Instead of stamping on the snake in the carpet, he reaches down and kisses it: "He had not meant to do that. He had meant to let the snake bite him on the mouth. Or perhaps he had meant to eat the snake alive, as Peter in the mirror had done. . . . But he kissed it instead" (166). If on the level of psychodrama each sibling represents a possible tendency in Ender's own self, he now chooses neither to succumb to the snake nor to devour it: the Peter tendency will not destroy him, but neither will he yield to its destructive violence. Instead he transforms it through an act of love: "[T]he snake . . . thickened and bent into another shape. A human shape. It was Valentine, and she kissed him again" (167). This act frees him from the room at the End of the World. His shadow and Valentine's approach the mirror, where instead of Peter's face they see reflected two figures, a dragon and a unicorn. When Ender reaches out to touch the mirror, it gives way to a staircase leading down and out. Ender's psyche had replaced the figure of his biological father, first with the manipulating Graff, and finally with Peter, the evil force as male child within. By defeating these successive, each more treacherous, forms of the male animus, Ender secures the good female anima: "He . . . knew that wherever he went in this world, Valentine was with him."

Ender has thus become the dragon to Valentine's unicorn. And in the chapter immediately following, he is named commander of the Dragon Army, and so begins the path of battles through a space of "simulation" that, from this point on, combines the real space of an alien enemy and the mind-space of Ender's quest for expanded family ties. The dragon is an appropriate symbol for his actions in the final half of the novel. The dragons are composite creatures, formed of all four elements, winged serpents breathing the fire of destruction, yet at the same time capable of guarding the hoard, sitting on and hatching the cosmic egg. Of such an act the child Ender now becomes capable. Obeying a higher design, beyond the earthbound logic of battle and defeat, he destroys the bugger Queen *in order to* effect the resurrection of her race on a higher intergalactic level. In doing so, the orphaned Earth child, led by his newly liberated sister/anima, encounters in this Queen his true mother. But she is a mother that he, as Wordsworthian seer blest or father to the woman, is doomed to carry around the galaxies as egg waiting to be hatched.

It is in the added final chapter of the novel, "Speaker for the Dead," that we finally learn the true nature of the alien "enemy," through a growing current of communication (via the Valentine anima) between Ender and his new mother. In the short story, the alien is a very different presence: the classic space opera enemy who sends a star fleet to attack Earth. In the novel version, although neither side has faster-than-light travel, Earth possesses superluminary communication, the famous "ansible." Earth's strategy is simple, then: it will launch an armada against the buggers' capital world. Relativity favors Earth, for the hundred years that elapse in their temporal frame between its armada's launch time and the time its armada arrives will enable the humans to build better defenses and ships. The enemy's predicament is worse. Because they do not have the ansible, they must place a great mind on *each* ship, so that when they reach Earth they will be ready to react to whatever new technology humans have invented in the long interval. Earth, with the ansible, needs only to place a skeleton crew on each of its ships. The whole can be commanded from Earth by one great strategist—in this case Ender. To trap the enemy's armada close to their home, as Ender does, is to destroy all of their brain power at once, whereas humans risk none of theirs.

Card's "buggers," in the novel, are a hive society formed around a few queens and myriad drones, all of whom think the sole thoughts of their queen. Whereas in the short story all Earth ships are guided by a single mind (an analogous situation), the novel is a clear attempt to engage, and transform, the Heinleinian trope of puppet and puppet master. Many Heinlein stories celebrate the victory of human individuality over various races of group or "hive" minds. Superficially, at least, these struggles involve the coming of age—or growth to adulthood—of an individual hero in contrast with the regression to childhood of adults who have lost their will and personality to vampiric parasites. And on one level, Card's novel greatly augments the scenes of training battles in order to display, in Ender and his (greatly more personalized) lieutenants, their Heinleinian ability to improvise and adapt to new and challenging situations as individuals.

For Heinlein, however, *Bildung* is the purview of a select few. Opposed to the few—the masters—is the rest of humanity, eager to give up all pretense at individuality for a group or hive existence, as "children" in the sense of less evolved beings who would rather abdicate personality and will "for the better good." In the novel, Card seeks to overcome this simplistic dichotomy by fusing in his newly reborn child Ender the powers of conscious will with those of the unconscious, or "racial," memory. If Graff and the adult handlers sought to control Ender by manipulating his psychic existence, and thus keeping him in thrall to their coercive idea of childhood, it is in this instance his final contact with the "enemy's" collective unconscious that allows him both to perform his Heinleinian task as effective warrior *and* (in the very act of doing so) to rid himself of the male hierarchy that sets the rules for adulthood.

Heinlein's vision (in terms of his juvenile heroes) remains Christian in the patriarchal sense that it is the female who bears responsibility for the Fall. And for the issue of that Fall, its children, there is but one way to rise out of this condition—through strict male guidance. Card's novel reverses this, having his forever child draw power this time from regression toward the female matrix. Card's name for this alien race, "bugger," is surely an ironic joke on Heinlein's more male-oriented "slugs." Indeed, Ender, in the final chapter, comes on a landscape on a far planet that is exactly like that of the fallen giant and the room at the End of the World. He finds his way to the mirror and, pulling it off the wall, discovers instead of snakes a white ball of silk: "An egg? No. The pupa of a queen bugger, already fertilized by the larval males." Taking up the egg, Ender can suddenly see through the eyes of the enemy and can experience their fear and pain as the Earth ships sweep in to destroy them. Through this psychic channel he learns that the entire war was the product of a tragic lack of communication: "We are like you; the thought pressed into his mind. We did not mean to murder, and when we understood, we never came again. We thought we were the only thinking beings in the universe, until we met you, but never did we dream that thought could arise from the lonely animals who cannot dream each other's dreams. How were we to know?" (354). The terrible irony of this encounter is that the aliens make telepathic contact—establishing the channel of communication that might save their race—*only* as a result of the same war effort that directs the mind of child Ender against them: "They found me through the ansible, followed it and dwelt in my mind. In the agony of my tortured dreams they came to know me, even as I spent my days destroying them" (353).

The war-with-aliens theme so prevalent in Heinleinian juvenile SF has undergone significant change in *Ender's Game*. When revising his story into a novel, Card substitutes communication for blind destruction. Humanity may, as a result, no longer be alone in the universe. And yet, what develops in the final chapter, the potential for meaningful union with sentient aliens, remains a thing promised and yet deferred. Deferral means sequels, and the sequel is the perfect narrative vehicle for a Wordsworthian forever child such as Ender, whose power derives from maintaining an unnatural inversion, from remaining (in this case) "mother" to the woman. Ender has exploited all the SF powers of childhood, as Pringle and Nicholls outline them, in order to defeat the adult manipulation that would "form" him. For Card, clearly, formation on the adult plane is synonymous with blind societal control. Ender's drama, as child, is an egocentric one. Because of this, although he defeats his own psychic shadows and thus opens new conduits of paranormal communication, his actions lead of necessity to stasis and impasse. In the sequel *Speaker for the Dead*, Ender, now called the Xenocide, travels the time warps with his bugger egg, remaining forever young, forever a denizen of virtual time, looking for a place to set down "roots" where he can realize the potential of a union of races in some evolutionary and formational time. This place would be a New Jerusalem, the adulthood of redemption. Yet instead of Christ triumphant, Ender remains in this second novel a being whose "ancient guilt burned within him," a being young and old at the same time whose middle, the life of the normal adult, promises to be forever missing. *Ender's Game* is a brilliant novel, even more brilliant when one sees how, from story to novel, it transforms juvenile SF and its simplistic formulas. It reverses the Pinocchio tendency, in which superhuman children finally, like all human children, give up and want to be real boys, and like real boys grow up to be adults. Yet, Ender's condition seems sadder, for he retains his childhood powers only by assuming the psychic burden of an entire race of adults.

More broadly, this forever child seems an important part of the mythic universe of SF. By comparing Card and Heinlein in light of the former's transformation of the Ender story, we glimpse the two dynamic poles of this universe. For both authors, the middle, the realm of developing adulthood, is a place to be rapidly traversed, elided, even forestalled. In juvenile and "adult" novels alike, Heinlein's young men in one sense remain forever children. Although these figures may seem to accede to adulthood, they rarely do so by growing up, by forming a self. Through the time paradox of "By His Bootstraps," for instance, youth and wisdom, Bob Wilson and Diktor, become interchangeable roles. In *Double Star* (1956), the young actor Lorenzo Smythe (the classic Heinlein everyman facing the road of experience) not only impersonates the experienced and wise head of state Bonforte, but on the latter's death must literally step into his shoes and become the older man. In another, more important, sense, however, unformed youth in Heinlein is not allowed to remain a forever child, but is instantly subsumed by the more dominant figure of the Methuselah, or eternal patriarch. In the world of Lazarus Long, Heinlein's prototype, the child cannot be father to the man, but rather is food for the father, his elixir of youth. Lazarus is a combination of Rip Van Winkle and Cronos who preserves youth within his aged body by outsleeping the "ephemerals" destined to grow up and pass on in the adult middle. He regains vital rejuvenating energy by siring and then figuratively and literally devouring his progeny, until the entire universe becomes his extended "body" in the sense of being peopled by beings of his single genetic stock. The development of Ender, as Card moves him away from this same dangerous middle of juvenile adventure, is the exact reverse of Lazarus. Though called an "ender," his power in fact comes from never beginning, from endlessly deferring the move into the light of common day. Where Lazarus controls the conscious realm of his final cause, Ender probes the mysteries of the unconscious maternal first cause. The power to "speak for the dead" is the power to resurrect the lost mother within the confines of his sole self. In becoming her "guardian," Ender relocates the child *before* the mother. It is a response to Lazarus, who through his endless rejuvenations seeks to place the father before the child.

Card's response is explicitly located at the mythico-religious core of SF as seen in Harlan Ellison's astonishing story "Adrift Just off the Islets of Langerhans: Latitude 38° 54' N, Longitude 77° 00' 13" W." Protagonist Larry Talbot is the Wolfman, a modern Cronos under the curse of the Fall, bound to eternal life as a perfect metabolism linked with full moon and a cycle of endless violence. Surcease can come only if he finds his lost soul, whose coordinates a Mr. Demeter locates at the center of a land of shades that is Talbot's own body. All those elusive mental traces that lead back to childhood and innocence are to be found in physical form at a place just off Talbot's own islets of Langerhans. A modern version of Dr. Frankenstein, the originator of SF's quest for bodily eternity, helps Talbot in his quest. By means of a "proton synchrotron" the new Victor creates (or "fathers") a submolecular double of Talbot. This child-adult reenters his own cryonically suspended body via its navel, reversing the path of birth severance, and at the same time enfolding the entire process of life and death *inside* his own already born being. On an islet in his blood-red pancreatic sea Talbot recovers childhood debris—a radio, the story of a woman who spent ninety-seven years in an asylum, a dark tower with a circular stairway of worn steps—all marks of his and every wasted physical life. He finds in a cigar box his "soul"—a Howdy Doody button bearing the "cockeyed face" of the forever child he seeks to become.

Like Ender, Ellison's Wolfman learns compassion for another at the heart of self. He awakens under the paternal gaze of Victor, but not, the lesson now learned, to grow up and die. Rather he asks to relive, endlessly within the confines of his frozen body, the recovery of childhood. This time, however, childhood's innocence has become explicitly a place of power, of control of the adult world of time and the Fall. Talbot asks Victor to miniaturize another female "wasted life," the old woman Nadja, and send her back as a child to his child self inside his body, here to live an endlessly sentimental, yet physical version of the romantic idyll of childhood recaptured, of Proustian time regained: "He can be with her as she regains the years that were stolen from her. He can be—I can be—her father when she's a baby, her playmate when she's a child, her buddy when she's maturing, her boy friend when she's a young girl, her suitor when she's a young woman, her lover, her husband, her companion as she grows old. . . . And when it's all over, it will start again." [10]

Ender too will trade adult violence for childhood pastoral. To do so, he too must relocate the womb within the confines of a physical body, itself held thrall by Frankensteinian manipulators. What would Wordsworth think, were he to see his call emancipate the "seer blest" ending with Ender?

Notes

1. David Pringle and Peter Nicholls, "Children in SF," in *The Encyclopedia of Science Fiction,* ed. John Clute and Peter Nicholls (New York: St. Martin's Press, 1993), 212–13.

2. Ray Bradbury, "Zero Hour," in *S Is for Space* (New York: Doubleday, 1966), 69–81.

3. Ray Bradbury, "The Veldt," in *The Illustrated Man* (New York: Doubleday, 1951), 7–19.

4. Ray Bradbury's "The Small Assassin," in *The October Country* (New York: Ballantine Books, 1955), 126–45, includes a wonderful description of birth as the Fall: "What is more at peace, more dreamfully content, at ease, at rest, fed, comforted, unbothered, than an unborn child? Nothing. It floats in a sleepy, timeless wonder of nourishment and silence. Then suddenly, it is asked to give up its berth, is forced to vacate, rushed out into a noisy, uncaring, selfish world where it is asked to shift for itself, to hunt, to feed . . . to seek

after a vanishing love that was once its unquestionable right . . . and the child *resents* it" (142).

5. Ray Bradbury, "The Martian," in *The Martian Chronicles* (New York: Doubleday, 1950), 119–31.

6. Ray Bradbury, "The Man Upstairs," in *The October Country*, 211–25.

7. Orson Scott Card, "Ender's Game," in *Maps in a Mirror: The Short Fiction of Orson Scott Card* (New York: Tor, 1990), 544–45; first published in *Analog Science Fiction/Science Fact* in 1977. Later page references in the text are to the 1990 edition.

8. Robert A. Heinlein, *Time for the Stars* (1956; New York: Ace Books, n.d.), 185.

9. Orson Scott Card, *Ender's Game* (New York: Tor, 1985), 1. Later page references in the text are to this edition.

10. Harlan Ellison, "Adrift Just off the Islets of Langerhans: Latitude 38° 54′ N, Longitude 77° 00′ 13″ W," in *Deathbird Stories* (New York: Dell, 1975), 310.

The Child as Alien

Joseph D. Miller

An examination of the role of the child in science fiction must perforce be preceded by an examination of the child in human society. In turn, that examination is informed by a consideration of the evolutionary constraints on intergenerational behavior. To begin, it is critical to state that mammalian, particularly primate, offspring are born in an extremely immature, or altricial, condition, as opposed to the precocious, or highly developed, neonates of many avian species. A uterus much larger than that of the female human's would impose serious constraints on bipedal locomotion; hence the terrestrial evolutionary solution is birth at a developmental stage corresponding to a small head. It must be emphasized that this is a solution based on the terrestrial vertebrate body plan; a radically different pelvis might be compatible with both locomotion and the uterine passage of large-headed offspring. And so we come to the ultimate nightmare of the evolutionary biologist: a precocious, large-brained, and highly intelligent species. Throw in a phenomenal birth rate comparable to that of many precocious species, and you get the Moties of Larry Niven and Jerry Pournelle's *The Mote in God's Eye* (1974). If all else is equal, a fast-breeding precocial species should have a very large selective advantage over an equally intelligent but slow-breeding altricial species. Hence human's anxiety about the Moties.

Altriciality has serious implications for parental care, considerations largely irrelevant to Moties and other highly precocious species. The survival of the altricial infant to reproductive age depends on a large investment of care by both parents. Failure to make that investment seriously reduces the likelihood that the parents' genome will continue to be represented in the population gene pool; in contrast, "good" parents are selected for. It has been suggested that the necessity of parental investment created a selection pressure for monogamy in humans and that the average latency of a marriage to divorce is about the time that was necessary to ensure the probable survival of the offspring in the prehistorical era.

How do the parents recognize the infant as their own? Many mammalian species recognize their young by detecting highly specific olfactory stimuli called pheromones that are produced by the infant. The infant, in turn, may bond with its parents through similar signals, yielding a result functionally similar to imprinting in birds. Thus the elephant seal maintains a family structure in breeding grounds where tens of thousands of seals congregate every year. In primates the recognition signals between child and parents depend much more strongly on auditory and visual cues. Similarity of physical features between parents and offspring often implies a genetic commonality, the currency of natural selection. A great dissimilarity in physical features, on the other hand, implies that the child is a genetic alien, which frequently leads in humans to the dissolution of the marital contract. In evolutionary terms this is sensible because paternal energy investment in child care is selected for only under conditions of substantial genetic commonality between father and offspring. In fact, in rodent colonies, replacement of the dominant male by a new male actually leads to pheromonally mediated spontaneous abortions in females pregnant by the previous dominant male.

Why, then, do such "altruistic" behaviors as adoption and stepfatherhood, behaviors observed in a variety of nonhuman primate species, ever occur? Adoptive behavior is seen in "godparents," who are genetically related to the original mother or father, when the original parents die. It is to the selective advantage of such godparents to invest in parental care when they share a genetic heritage with the child. Any gene that contributes to the production of such behavior will be well represented in subsequent generations. In human terms, godparents are much more likely to be close relatives of the original parents than completely unrelated to them.

The case of stepfatherhood is a little harder to justify on evolutionary grounds. Here, recourse is generally made to the notion of reciprocal altruism. The stepfather engages in a kind of unwritten contract with the birth mother to the effect that he will gain reproductive success via genetically related offspring of his own as long as he is willing to contribute to the reproductive success of the birth mother by making a parental investment in the stepchild. The genetic rationale is even stronger if there is a preexisting degree of relatedness between stepfather and stepchild. This may explain the prevalence in some cultures of the custom of marriage to the father's brother on the death of the father.

Of course, in human society, adoption and stepparenthood occur in cases where there is little "relatedness" between adopter and adoptee or stepparent and stepchild. Often the stepparent or the adoptive couple is initially childless. Here the resort is to a diffused genetic relatedness. If you have no offspring of your own, you may still contribute to the reproductive fitness of the species by investing in offspring other than your own. After all, the human species has better than 99 percent of its genes in common. And a species that facilitates the survival of even its orphans gains a reproductive advantage over species that do not engage in such behavior. This analysis suggests that the first and perhaps most memorable example of foster parenting in science fiction, Mary Shelley's *Frankenstein* (1818) and his monster, makes a certain amount of evolutionary sense. Unfortunately, Frankenstein eventually sees the monster as alien, even though the monster's genetic heritage is undeniably human. Here again, physical dissimilarity sends a false signal of genetic deviation. In any event, Frankenstein refuses to construct a mate for the monster, and the monster in revenge kills Frankenstein's wife. (Hollywood, in the Boris Karloff version, sanitized this mild nineteenth-century excursion into the Oedipal realm by converting that event into the murder of an unrelated little girl.) The novel also gives us an example of reciprocal antialtruism, to coin a term. That is, Frankenstein and the monster constrain each other's reproductive success instead of facilitating it.

But what of parents who adopt in addition to their "biological" children? Evolutionary theory says that such behavior contributes to fitness as long as the original children are not put at reproductive risk by the adoption. In simple terms, people do not adopt when they cannot support their birth children. And cultural selection also has a role; adoptive behavior is socially reinforced. The acculturation of the adoptee may contribute to the fitness of a society; there is a statistical correlation between sociopathy and orphanhood. None of these arguments, however, provides much of a rationale for interspecific changelings. The adoption of a human by an alien, as in C. J. Cherryh's *Cuckoo's Egg* (1985), or the adoption of an alien by a human, as in Barry Longyear's "Enemy Mine" (1979), must depend on shared interspecific values such as the importance of friendship or the sanctity of infant life. Surely, Motie culture in *The*

Mote in God's Eye is an excellent antidote to such anthropomorphizing. At least E.T. is cute. The somewhat grudging emotional adoption of E.T. by the human adults in the last frames of *E.T.* (1982) movie can be explained by that characteristic; he is small, his facial features are very curved, and his voice is high-pitched. Mammals and perhaps birds seem to interpret such features as childlike. So perhaps E.T. is a kind of accidental supernormal stimulus guaranteed to activate our hardwired associations between cuteness and parental empathy. Although Steven Spielberg should be commended for portraying aliens as something other than bug-eyed monsters, we must still ask: What are the chances of ever encountering a cute alien, let alone one that would stimulate a desire to adopt? Are grubs cute?

The subversion of the recognition process between parent and offspring is a parasitic strategy. The mother cuckoo saves a tremendous amount of energy by laying her eggs in the nests of other species. In fact, she typically rolls the true eggs out of the nest so that the "foster" parents contribute solely to the reproductive fitness of the cuckoo species. Science fiction uses this as a strategy for alien invasion, as in John Wyndham's *The Midwich Cuckoos* (1957). Furthermore, in works in which the alien arises from within the parent species, the survival of the mutant child, whether slan, *Homo gestalt,* or Odd John, depends initially on its ability to pass as human. Once the mutant comes into its powers, the cuckoo phase typically ends. Here is an interesting resonance with the generational conflict in primate maturation. When development of the offspring has reached the point at which parental energy investment is no longer critical, one of two things happens. Either the adolescent male leaves the home troop to join a loose confederation of young satellite males, many times proceeding from there to an entirely new troop, *or* a struggle ensues for position in the dominance hierarchy of the home troop. In the latter case the adolescent will either gain a spot in the hierarchy, perhaps even displacing the alpha male, or be forced to leave the troop. The adolescent female, on the other hand, typically integrates more easily into the female dominance hierarchy of the home troop. Exogamy is still a possibility for the female; raids and kidnapping by other bands of primates are frequent. In general, however, the male becomes the alien adolescent; takeovers and banishments are hostile acts.

In contrast is a uniquely human strategy called retirement. Here the alpha male or female peacefully gives way to a replacement. Of course, this is much easier if the "new boss" is genetically related. ("Someday, son, this will all be yours.") In human societies such inheritance is common, and the ex–alpha male or female becomes an elder statesman, repository of cultural knowledge, indirectly contributing to the reproductive fitness of the entire society. And adolescents are not banished or killed, but rather prepared for an eventual role in the tribe, city, or nation.

Science fiction, as a literature of the conceptual extreme, is more concerned with the dramatic than the mundane resolution of intergenerational competition. The mutant in science fiction is a metaphor for the adolescent, and all the evolutionary strategies known for dealing with competitive offspring are abundantly evident. The strategy of banishment is apparent in Wyndham's *Rebirth* (1955) and in the terrestrial leavetaking of the Families in Robert A. Heinlein's *Methuselah's Children* (1958). Frankenstein's monster, the prototypical constructed child of nineteenth-century biotechnology, ultimately chooses Arctic self-exile over a reproductively pointless struggle for a place in human society. If the dominant society (read the father) impedes such leavetaking, one acceptable alternative is suicide, as in Olaf Stapledon's *Odd John* (1935), George Turner's *Brain Child* (1991), and ultimately, it is implied, in *Frankenstein*. Another choice is metaphorical rather than actual, parricide, as in the Mule's quasi-Oedipal near destruction of Isaac Asimov's Foundation (in *Foundation and Empire* [1952]) and the attainment of alpha male status by Paul Atreides in Frank Herbert's *Dune* (1965) through the displacement of individuals who are eventually revealed to be close relatives.

Many works completely domesticate the Oedipal conflict. An illustrative case is Jommy Cross, the mutant protagonist of A. E. van Vogt's *Slan* (1946). Cross attempts the strategy of exile throughout much of the novel but ultimately turns against the *über* society. The final overthrow of normal human society is made moot, however, by the discovery that the autarch of this society is none other than another slan. So the resolution of the human-slan conflict reduces to the resolution of a kind of father-son conflict, and the young Cross peacefully gains his rightful position in the secret slan male dominance hierarchy. Similarly, Luke Skywalker of the *Star Wars* trilogy (*Star Wars,* 1977; *The Empire Strikes Back,* 1980; *Return of the Jedi,* 1983) first flees the Empire, returns to overthrow it, and ultimately inherits his position as alpha male Jedi knight on the permanent "retirement" of Darth Vader. But that retirement is not the direct doing of Skywalker; even here, in mortal combat with evil incarnate, science fiction blinks at the Oedipal act. And so it must for us to maintain sympathy with the mutant/teenager/rebel hero. It is allowable to overthrow, destroy, and kill all representatives of imperial/paternal authority *except* the biological father. In works that do not observe this rule, the child is irrevocably alien, as are the Children of Arthur C. Clarke's *Childhood's End* (1953) and the protagonist of Harlan Ellison's "Jeffty Is Five" (1977). We can appreciate the dignity of exile or ethical suicide, but parricide is the domain of horror rather than science fiction.

The child in science fiction may hide behind other facades. Harlie, the artificial intelligence of David Gerrold's *When Harlie Was One* (1972), is the prototypical adolescent. Harlie even manages to engage in that most adolescent of activities, the willful experimental alteration of the personal sensorium. In place of the pot smoking of the human adolescent, Harlie deliberately scrambles his own electronic data feeds to produce essentially the same effect. But Harlie matures over the course of his first year of "life" and eventually takes over the company that built him. His own father, the computer scientist who created him, is adequately provided for, however, even if all humans are a bit antiquated in comparison with Harlie. Again we see the attainment of alpha male status through a process of enforced, but peaceful, retirement.

Using the viewpoint of the immortal as a means to juvenilize all of society is another plot device. Here society is the child, and the immortal figuratively, and often literally, is the father. This inverts the usual situation of paternal society and child rebel. Examples include Heinlein's Lazarus Long in *Methuselah's Children* and Roger Zelazny's Sam in *Lord of Light* (1967). The literary injunction against parricide is even stronger in this case, since such behavior would eliminate the protagonist, rather than render him unsympathetic. One way to circumvent this Oedipal injunction is to consciously make the immortal an unsympathetic character. In Frank M. Robinson's *The Dark Beyond the Stars* (1991) a generation ship is captained by an immortal madman obsessed with a drive to find life beyond the Earth, no matter how many thousands of years and crew lifetimes it takes. The hero of this novel is Sparrow, a seventeen-year-old who leads countless aborted rebellions against the Captain. Each time, the rebellion is put down and Sparrow is flat-lined; that is, his memory is erased. Finally, Sparrow does maintain his memory long enough to overthrow the Captain. But what appears to be the ultimate Oedipal confrontation is transformed at the last moment. Sparrow discovers he is not a rebellious teenager but actually another immortal, the Return Captain, whose responsibility it is to return the ship to Earth in the event of failure. The final struggle is a struggle between two visions of the father rather than the murder of father by son. But Sparrow does attain alpha male status.

Long life makes the immortal the embodiment of paternal wisdom compared with the brief candles of ordinary humanity. But the tables can be turned if the *über* society eventually learns the secret of immortality, as in the final pages of *Methuselah's Children,* Poul Anderson's *The Boat of a Million Years* (1989), and Joe Haldeman's *The Forever War* (1975). In each case the biological immortals are parochialized by the maturation of their parent culture. Children and alien once again, they are presented with the usual choices of exile or suicide.

An interesting variant on this scheme is Niven's *A World out of Time* (1976), in which the immortals of the far future are children, the Boys and the Girls. The price of immortality is an endocrine transformation that prevents physical and sexual maturity. Niven's protagonist is Corbell, a space pilot from the twentieth century who suffered a temporal dislocation after a near approach to a black hole. This makes Corbell both father, because of his relative age, and child, because the race has evolved beyond him. Corbell eventually becomes the alpha male in this society, but not until he gains a type of immortality independent of the endocrine immortality of the Boys. So Corbell undergoes a kind of transformation from father to child and back to father again. But he is always the alien and always the rebel.

But perhaps the best-known child culture of science fiction is the Eloi of H. G. Wells's *The Time Machine* (1895). Although childlike in the extreme, the Eloi are sympathetic aliens as opposed to the Boys and Girls of Niven's work. A large part of our sympathy derives from the knowledge that the Eloi are prey to the grotesque, subterranean Morlocks. In addition to reflecting Wells's socialist views on class divisions (with Eloi as aristocrats and Morlocks as workers), I propose that this section of *The Time Machine* is a kind of Victorian code for the politics of sexual behavior. Morlock cannibalism is a metaphor for rape: the Eloi are the pubescent females, and the Morlocks are the raiding males who require the Eloi, not for food, but for a necessary genetic heterogeneity. In this view, *The Time Machine* is not about the triumph of the proletariat, but rather the biological and social requirements for exogamy. By this argument, what makes the Eloi truly alien is their apparent lack of desire to "eat" Morlocks!

Greg Bear's *Anvil of Stars* (1992) offers another example of a nearly pure child culture. Here a set of teenagers is charged with revenging the destruction of the Earth by a malicious band of aliens. The child avengers develop advanced intellectual capabilities under the tutelage of benevolent robotic moms. These children are far from feral, but there is a peculiar savage undercurrent reminiscent of William Golding's *Lord of the Flies* (1954) throughout the novel. In the end the children must decide the fate of the species probably responsible for the death of Earth. They must choose between the possibility of unjustified genocide and the chance that the heinous, Earth-destroying crime will go unpunished. They eventually opt for genocide, on rather weak evidence, completely disgusting a set of alien compatriots they have accumulated along the way. Genocide turns out to have been the appropriate choice, but, revealingly, the youngsters are not given the option of rejoining surviving humanity, or any other race of the galaxy. Permanent exile is the only option for these war dogs, in spite of the fact that their actions were just. The capacity for genocide, even rightful genocide, is at least as socially destabilizing as the capacity for parricide. Bear seems to say that the moral justification for killing cannot constitute moral justification for the killers. And so the children have actually defined their alien nature by *avenging* the Oedipal crime, the deaths of the fathers of Earth.

Science fiction on occasion juvenilizes entire societies. The postmodern feudalism of Walter Jon Williams's *Aristoi* (1992) is one example. The Aristoi are induced multiple personalities capable of governing galactic society via a kind of benevolent, high-nanotech autocracy. The children here are the ordinary docile humans, essentially the Demos of Plato. The fear is that this tranquil society could be replaced by the old-style aggressive humans, the only true aliens in the novel. *Consider Phlebas* (1987), by Iain M. Banks, is another example of the maintenance of a juvenilized galactic society by enlightened sybarites, in this case the Culture. Here again, the primary Oedipal fear is displacement by the feral child/alien, too immature to appreciate the value of stable decadence.

It should be clear from this analysis that science fiction writers often infantilize the alien, particularly the alien of great powers such as Gerrold's Harlie and Clarke's Vanamonde, the disembodied intelligence from *Against the Fall of Night* (1953). Thus the terror we might feel in the face of inhuman intelligence is replaced with the more familiar feelings of confusion, misunderstanding, and humor we experience with our own personal aliens, otherwise known as children. But mutants, aliens, and immortals are also the exaggerated representation of the intergenerational conflicts we all experience. And at one time or another we have all been Mule *and* Foundationer.

As our population grows older and the costs of health care, social security, and other aspects of living, continue to rise, we elders are alienating our children. Not only will they bear the brunt of such costs, they will also see a delayed generational passage as mandatory retirement continues to fade from the national scene. And the elderly in turn will perceive the young as threats to their job security. This generational antipathy is magnified by the growing rareness of the once common inheritance of business within the family structure. Retirement from a faceless corporation is now the rule, without even the consolation of knowing that your own offspring will follow in your path and perhaps even make use of your accumulated wisdom. The unique strategy of peaceful retirement may be replaced by a new paradigm of intergenerational acrimony. It is possible that the science fiction literature of alienation may be of value in the anticipation and mitigation of such social changes.

I argue elsewhere that science fiction, insofar as it informs by extrapolating social tendencies to their extremes, may be of selective advantage to society as a whole. Perhaps the very existence of George Orwell's cautionary tale *1984* (1949) prevented the actualization of that particular future. Similarly, we can hope that the children watching such cartoon series as *The X-Men,* in which discrimination against mutants is a constant theme, will learn from this example to better tolerate differences among their fellows. Such salutary effects would be greatly attenuated if the science fiction plot itself reflected a slavish working out of the principles of sociobiology and evolutionary theory. In that case literature would offer no hope of change or transcendence beyond the law of competition for reproductive advantage. And indeed, many of the works I have discussed here reflect a certain biological determinism in intergenerational relations. But the "unseen hand" of sociobiology could not have moved Longyear to create the highly antiselective denouement of "Enemy Mine." I conclude that science fiction reflects more often than any other genre the essential paradox of human evolution: natural selection has produced a sufficiently flexible brain to contemplate and perhaps even overthrow the bounds of that very same natural selection.

Baby's Next Step:
Überkinder and the Burden of the Future

Howard V. Hendrix

In their article on "The Aging of the Human Species," S. Jay Olshansky, Bruce A. Carnes, and Christine K. Cassel remark that "under T. B. L. Kirkwood's disposable soma theory, senescence is the price paid for sexual reproduction."[1] Or, as I prefer to put it in appropriately ungrammatical paraphrase, "The wages of sex is death." Biologist Kirkwood, of the National Institute for Medical Research in London, assumes that organisms always divide their physiological energy between sexual reproduction and maintenance of the soma, or body. The optimum fitness strategy, he argues, involves an allocation of energy less than that required for perfect repair and immortality. Thus, aging is the inevitable consequence of defects in the cells and tissues left unrepaired and imperfect because the organism has allocated that energy to sexual reproduction instead.

Kirkwood does not say it, but this sex-for-death trade-off is extremely ancient—probably as old as the sexually reproducing cell. The earliest form of life on earth, the prokaryotic cell, is essentially immortal as long as it keeps dividing asexually. Single-celled and multicellular organisms that reproduce *sexually* do die, but what they gain in switching to sexual reproduction is greater genetic diversity—and hence more evolutionary flexibility in response to environmental change—by constant mixing of genetic contents. Immortality of the "genetic monad," as it were, is sacrificed to enhance the *species's* longevity. This is probably a good thing, for if immortality and sexual reproduction coexisted in humans, the result would likely be a ratcheting up of population growth that would make our worst nightmares of overpopulation look like a summer picnic.

This sex/death loop figures prominently not only in science fiction works that deal explicitly with issues of population, but in others as well. I'm thinking of Arthur C. Clarke's *2001: A Space Odyssey* and Frank Herbert's *Children of Dune,* among others. In his 1982 "Epilogue: After 2001," Clarke specifies that *2001* deals with "the next stage of human evolution." [2] The same is true of the entire Dune sequence, particularly the Bene Gesserit Sisterhood's eugenic pursuit of the superbeing known as the Kwisatz Haderach. Curiously, when a next stage of human evolution is achieved—as in David Bowman's metamorphosis into the Star Child or Leto II's symbiotic human-sandworm fusion—the result is an essentially immortal and asexual entity. Yet, if the next step in human evolution is a step outside the sex/death circle, this stepping out raises questions about the humanity of these "next steps."

Leto II specifically links stepping out of the sex/death loop with questions about his humanity: "Did I not say I'm no longer human? No children will spring from my loins, for I no longer have loins." [3] In *2001* Clarke tells us that Bowman "still needed, for a little while, this shell of matter as the focus of his powers. His indestructible body was his mind's present image of himself; and for all his powers he knew he was still a baby. So he would remain until he had decided on a new form, or had passed beyond the necessities of matter" (218).

The problem arising in these texts is the issue of *humanity* versus *human perfectibility.* The great imperfection of the human condition is death—the existence of which Kirkwood attributes to the fact that perfect repair, and thus immortality, is a bad bargain in terms of evolutionary dynamics. One might even say that mortality is our "defining imperfection"—it is what makes us human. Think of the old drill in elementary logic: "All men are mortal; Socrates is a man; therefore, Socrates is mortal." If mortality defines humanity, then perhaps it does so because death gives our life a sense of the absolute, the certain, the complete. Death gives life a particular sort of "weight." When death disappears into superabundant life, though, what is absolute, certain, and complete in the human condition evaporates into relativity, uncertainty, and incompleteness. Without death, life may become an endless free fall. Gravity, in the sense of seriousness and significant meaning, plausibly disappears into weightlessness.

In considering "immortality and the next step," both Clarke and Herbert seem eager to dispose of the nineteenth-century view of the universe as absolute, certain, and complete—the world of thought before Einstein's special theory of relativity, Heisenberg's uncertainty principle, and Gödel's incompleteness theorem. Yet *at the same time* they cling to a view of evolution closely related to nineteenth-century ideas of Progress—evolution "tending toward perfection," and thus teleological in the weak sense. In this teleological light, immortality is to the individual what utopia is to the state, and perhaps only such perfected individuals could truly participate in such a perfected society.

Both *2001* and *Children of Dune* tend to conflate or collapse the distinction between evolution and education. This is perfectly understandable, given that the educational enterprise, at least since the advent of humanism, has also been informed by an ideology of human improvement and perfectibility. The teleological implications of this ideology were satirized even by so early a humanist as Rabelais in his *Gargantua and Pantagruel*. Recall that in *2001*, the monoliths of the film and the "crystal slabs" or "crystal monoliths" of the novel are first and foremost educational devices, yet it is precisely in them that we see this conflating of education and evolution. In Chapter 3, "Academy," we are told:

> And that night the crystal slab was still waiting, surrounded by its pulsing aura of light and sound. . . . Some of the man-apes it ignored completely, as if concentrating on the most promising subjects. One of them was Moon-Watcher; once again he felt inquisitive tendrils creeping down the unused byways of his brain. And presently he began to see visions. . . . There were gaps in Moon-Watcher's life now that he would never remember, when the very atoms of his simple brain were being twisted into new patterns. If he survived, those patterns would become eternal, for his genes would pass them on to future generations. (24–25)

Since genetic manipulation is not specifically mentioned in the text, the last line veers perilously close to the discredited theory of Lamarckism, the inheritance of acquired characteristics. But I digress, for the monolithic evolution and education machine appears again, this time to Bowman in Chapter 46, "Transformation":

> A ghostly glimmering rectangle had formed in the empty air. It solidified into a crystal tablet, lost its transparency, and became suffused with a pale, milky luminescence. . . . It was a spectacle to hold the attention of any child—or of

any man-ape. But, as it had been three million years before, it was only the outward manifestation of forces too subtle to be consciously perceived. It was merely a toy to distract the sense, while the real processing was carried out at far deeper levels of the mind. . . . With eyes that already held more than human intentness, the baby stared into the depths of the crystal monolith, seeing—but not yet understanding—the mysteries that lay beyond. . . . Beyond this moment lay another birth, stranger than anything in the past. (217–18)

This birth is a secondary or tertiary rebirth, for he who was David Bowman is already gone; Bowman's

life was unreeling like a tape recorder playing back at ever increasing speed. . . . He was retrogressing down the corridors of time, being drained of knowledge and experience as he swept back toward childhood. But nothing was being lost; all that he had ever been, at every moment of his life, was being transferred to safer keeping. Even as one David Bowman ceased to exist, another became immortal. . . . In an empty room, floating amid the fires of a double star twenty thousand light years from Earth, a baby opened its eyes and began to cry. (216–17)

In the film, Stanley Kubrick further complicates this sequence of deaths and rebirths by having Bowman both retrogress back to childhood and infancy, and also move forward into his geriatric future. But both film and novel end with infancy as the next step in human evolution. This has some precedent, since much of human evolution has already been directed toward an increase in what biologists variously term "fetalized" or "infantilized" traits—and in fact, humans retain more immature traits longer than any other vertebrate on the planet. We have, biologically at least, a very long period of "educability."

It would seem that, in a manner perhaps not uninfluenced by Judeo-Christian theology, death is a prerequisite for immortality. The recurrence of this death-rebirth pattern in *Children of Dune* (in which Leto is supposedly killed twice, once by Laza tigers and once by a deadly sandstorm) should not be surprising, since both *2001* and *Children of Dune* are hero quests. It's difficult to speak of the Dune books without mentioning Jung, so I will point out that, according to Jung, the hero in a quest, to obtain some ultimate good, must first subdue an evil, often represented in the form of an animal or dragon in the more traditional myths. Jung thought the archetype behind this story-image was the archetype of the Self, struggling for its existence against the onslaught of the fragmentary, instinctlike unconsciousness from which it arose. The evil or dragon—be it the whacked-out HAL 9000 computer in *2001* or the schizophrenic Alia in *Children of Dune*—stands in for the elemental, primitive, instinctual nature of the psyche, and the hero must, to become a "whole" person, overcome the tendency of the psyche to lose its unity and fall back into a preconscious state that is little more than a bundle of autonomous psychoid processes. The themes of birth, death, and rebirth, images of wizards and wise men (and artificial intelligences?), quests for grails or the Next Stage in human evolution—all these speak to forms of apprehension within the unconscious, and when "activated," often by conflicts in life, they appear to us as indicators that action needs to be taken.

2001, Children of Dune, and most of the cybernovels of the 1980s and early 1990s are precisely about this quest for whole personhood. They are romances of consciousness, and therefore it is only logical that they should focus on childhood (the main characters of *Children of Dune* are the children Leto and Ghanima), on return to infancy (David Bowman's rebirth in *2001*), or even on a return to the womb (recall that the term *matrix* so beloved of the cyberfolk means not only the net or network of input and output leads in a computer, but also the womb).

As Jung notes, the psychoid processes that reveal themselves in childhood fantasies and primitive mythology, and which reappear in the dreams and waking fantasies of normal adults, remain ingrained in the unconscious, continuing as functioning elements of the psyche, accumulating and discharging psychic energy, usually without impinging on consciousness. When some sort of conflict is occurring in the psyche, however, the psychic energy must be discharged symbolically in consciousness. According to Jung, if an unconscious conflict remains unresolved and continues to accumulate energy, it can eventually reach a state in which the psychoid process can partially or wholly displace the ego as the subject of consciousness. Such "neuroses" and "psychoses" in the classical literature of psychoanalysis are understood in Jungian terms as "behavior that is under the direction of a psychoid process."[4]

This, I contend, is precisely the situation of the "failed consciousnesses" in *2001* and *Children of Dune.* In *2001,* Bowman is opposed by the failed consciousness of HAL 9000—a consciousness engaging in behavior that a Freudian would consider schizophrenic, that a Jungian would consider to be "under the direction of a psychoid process," and that an artificial intelligence therapist would characterize as a computer being taken over by its own subprogram. Curiously, the inadequately integrated and therefore "failed" consciousness of HAL undergoes a regression to its beginnings (singing "Daisy, Daisy") that parallels the regression to infancy of David Bowman—but Bowman remains the successfully integrated psyche, the one in whom the ego is not displaced as the subject of consciousness.

In *Children of Dune,* the failed consciousness is Alia, sister of Paul "Muad 'Dib" Atreides. Exposed to an awareness drug, the spice melange, while still in the womb, Alia is called "pre-born": through the spice's agency she has been "educated" before birth by exposure to and coexistence with the cellular memories of all her ancestors going back at least a million years. The pre-born is Herbert's spin on the Jungian notion of a collective unconscious, and his explanation for it also veers perilously close to Lamarckism. Be that as it may, the psychoid process that takes control of Alia Atreides is the very much living memory of her grandfather, the evil Baron Vladimir Harkonnen.

Because Alia is pre-born, the Bene Gesserit Sisterhood fear that she is an Abomination—and so she is discovered to be when it is learned that she has been taken over by what we might call the "psychoid process" of the Baron. But Leto and Ghanima, the twin children of Paul Atreides and his Fremen mate, Chani, are also pre-born, having likewise been exposed to the spice while in the womb and therefore containing at birth all the memories of *their* ancestors. The constant fear throughout the novel is that Leto, Ghanima, or both will also prove to be Abominations, that they will be possessed, that they will fail to adequately integrate the "psychoid processes" that are their ancestors into their own personal psyches— that they, like their Aunt Alia, will be displaced as subjects of their own consciousness.

Both Leto and Ghanima manage to incorporate their history, to successfully integrate their individual consciousnesses—Ghanima through hypnotic suppression and the wooing of a benign ancestral "process," Leto through becoming a communal consciousness orchestrated by a powerful ancestor. As a result of their success, Leto becomes a nearly immortal god-emperor and Ghanima marries Farrad'n (grandson of the old emperor, Shaddam IV, whom her father deposed) and becomes mother of the Atreides dynasty—but not until their Aunt Alia has plunged to her death through a window shattered open by young super-sand-human Leto.

Since childhood is that developmental phase when the foundations of and relations between ego, consciousness, self, and psyche are established, romances of consciousness should rightly concern themselves with it. Further, if consciousness itself is a "dynamical" system (as Gerald Edelman and other researchers have argued),[5] if the overall behavior of dynamical systems is strongly influenced by their initial conditions, and if such systems when perturbed tend to return to those initial conditions, then the "returns to the womb" that occur in these romances should hardly surprise us. Consciousness, like any dynamical system undergoing perturbations, attempts to return to its initial conditions, and these texts mirror and model that process.

But why should these perturbations occur? Such a question inevitably brings us to the role of education in relation to personal and social integration. It is not enough to say that *2001* is primarily about the education/evolution of David Bowman or even of all humanity; nor is it enough to say that *Children of Dune* is primarily about the education/evolution of Leto and Ghanima or even the human species. We must examine the role that education plays in the integration of a self, the integration of a society, and the integration of the self in society.

Education is how we use the past to shape the future, how we use the known to shape the unknown. The young are the most prominent targets of the educational enterprise, and just as the future is other than what we are yet still informed by what we are, the same is true of the *Überkinder* of science fiction or even the ordinary children of consensus reality.

The term *Überkinder* is a conscious echo of Nietzsche's *Übermensch*. I use it here because both Bowman–Star Child and Leto II, the human-sandworm, are *Übermenschen* in the Nietzschean sense. Each is an example of the "unitary human goal" toward which all human history tends—"Look!" Nietzsche/Zarathustra proclaims, "I teach you the *Übermensch*! The *Übermensch* is the meaning of the earth!"—and each is characterized not only by his superiority but also by his essential uniqueness, aloneness, beyondness, and Otherness.[6] Bowman–Star Child and Leto-Sandworm are *Übermenschen* who stand in opposition to what Nietzsche calls the "Last Man" (*der Letzte Mensch*), "the herd-man of contemporary life,"[7] the Everyman who wishes to be just like everybody else. Like all *Übermenschen,* Bowman and Leto II force the questions of What does it mean to be human? and Is there anything between the *Letzte Mensch*'s social sameness and the *Übermensch*'s lonely uniqueness?

Kubrick's film aggressively foregrounds these Nietzschean conundrums, using the music of Strauss's *Also Sprach Zarathustra* (referring to the Nietzsche text in which the *Übermensch* idea appears most prominently) and developing the whole idea of the Star Child. Nietzsche specifically writes: "Woe! The time comes when man no longer hurls the shaft of his longing beyond mankind, and his bowstring forgets to twang. . . . Woe! The time comes when man cannot beget a star. . . . Look! I show you the *last man!*"[8] The protagonist of *2001* is clearly *Übermensch* in contrast to *Letzte Mensch,* a "bow man" who begets (or rebegets himself as) a Star Child.

The commonplace differences between generations are heightened and amplified in stories of the *Überkinder,* and the way these Otherly offspring are made part of the human universe, how they are integrated into the macroself of human history and human cultural tradition, is a metaphor for how the future itself is to be humanized. Progress and new discoveries—as "children of the mind"—present the angel and specter of both good and ill, and how these epiphanies, these irruptions of the future into the present, are handled and integrated into human culture is again symbolized in the *Überkinder,* who are both "children" and "discoveries."

We see how this integration process is (or is not) going as that process is reflected in *2001* and *Children of Dune,* and even in the cybernovels, which employ the net and the matrix as metaphors to relate the integration of the individual psyche to the integration of the state or social psyche. However, these texts are also attempting something more. In these romances of consciousness, as in the rituals of primitive humanity, archetypes figure prominently. Rituals employ symbols, both visually and in terms of things done by participants that correspond to archetypal images. The function of such rituals is twofold: they provide a means for releasing the conflict energy by which archetypes become activated, and they invoke the "participation mystique" of Lucien Levy-Bruhl, through which primitive humans envisioned themselves as part of, or "in tune with," the events of the universe. Human beings symbolized those events in their rituals, attempting to insert themselves into the overall scheme of things by participating in those events, albeit symbolically, and thereby attain some degree of harmony with the world around them.[9]

Such "sympathetic magic" is quite alien to our contemporary "objective" world, dominated as it is by the sometimes unsympathetic magic of an Enlightenment-based popular scientific worldview whose primary methodology is based not in harmony but, according to Jacques Lacan, in paranoid alienation.[10] Even more dangerous, because less discussed, is the assumption—stated most clearly by numerous linguists, semioticians, humanities professors, "social constructivists," and anthropologists following the ideas of Clifford Geertz[11]—that "language is the summa, alpha, and omega of consciousness," that "language is the true archetype of society," that "in the Beginning was the Word." As Bruce Albert so eloquently puts it, "Linguistic consciousness is false consciousness because it ignores, if not outrightly denies, the psyche as a unity of unconscious and conscious. To mode-lock onto a language game is to move away from the ability to integrate those aspects of the psyche that do not directly reveal themselves to consciousness—it is to abandon the archetypes." [12]

If the archetypes represent our connection to the world around us, to the natural matrix out of which we came, then the failure of contemporary society to integrate itself with the natural world via those archetypes may be a big part of our current headfirst plunge toward ecodisaster. Further, the effect of this schism in the psyche—between the "socially constructed self" and the unconscious—is easy to observe in other areas as well. The prevalence and savagery of crimes against persons and property in our so-called social order largely result from a loss of the personal myth, which in Jungian terms amounts to the inability to integrate the symbolic imagery from the unconscious into conscious life. Unconscious processes, deprived of their audience in consciousness by socially and linguistically conditioned patterns of thought, continue to accumulate energy until they seize control of behavior in symbolic and often horribly violent acts of release. Socially, it is as if linguistic consciousness is a psychoid process that has come to unbalanced power, like one of HAL's subroutines taking over the computer, or the too-alive memory of Baron Harkonnen taking possession of Alia's psyche.

This idea, that the psychic integration of the person ultimately extends to the social and ecological levels, perhaps helps to explain why it is that, after triumphing in their quests in the wastelands of space or desert or cyberspace, the newly whole heroes of such romances of consciousness paradoxically often return home, knowing the place for the first time, even reconnecting with the land, a simpler life, and a sustainable future. Examples of this pattern appear in the ending chapters of works as diverse as *Children of Dune,* William Gibson's *Count Zero,* and Jean Mark Gawron's *Dream of Glass.*

As a society, as a species, and generally as individuals, humans have not yet reached that place of reconnection. Nor do I think we will reach it through vastly extending human life, or through expanding human fertility, or through breeding quasi-Darwinian superkids (as opposed to Nietzschean *Überkinder*) out of Nobel sperm boutiques such as Dr. Robert Graham's Repository for Germinal Choice. Nor will we reach that place by eliminating the production of males through ovular merging techniques (as suggested by Sally Miller Gearhart and other androcidal antimasculinists) or through "airbrushing" our genes generally through skills emerging from the Human Genome Project. Many of these are arguably laudable endeavors, but all proceed from the assumption that for every human problem there is a technological solution—a hypothesis yet to be proven. Nor will we reach that place through education, especially not as long as we continue to entrap our students by teaching them that predicate logic is all there is, or that in the beginning, middle, and end was, is, and forever shall be only the Word.

Rather, I suggest, let us take a next step on the road to that place of personal myth and symbolic communication between unconsciousness and consciousness by moving toward a humble appreciation and acceptance of imperfectibility as an idea worthy to be joined with relativity, incompleteness, and uncertainty. Toward that goal, I end with two quotations and an image. The first quote is from Stephen Hawking: "Progress in science consists in replacing a theory that is wrong with one that is more subtly wrong."[13] The second is from Jung: "Inasmuch as every scientific theory contains a hypothesis, and therefore an anticipatory designation of a fact still essentially unknown, it is a symbol."[14] Finally, a childish image, an image of sandworms or dragons or snakes swallowing their own tails—an archetypal, nonlinguistic symbol which, when recognized in his dream by chemist August Kekule von Stradonitz, turned out to be the carbon ring structure he had been searching for,[15] a dream that turned out to fit the facts in that approximation we call "truth." Such dreams, such "children of our minds," may prove to be as close an approximation to truth as anything else that imperfect, fetalized, and childlike human creatures are likely to come up with, and we deny these offspring and the unconscious that produces them at our peril.

Notes

1. S. Jay Olshansky, Bruce A. Carnes, and Christine K. Cassel, "The Aging of the Human Species," *Scientific American* 268.4 (1993): 46–52.
2. Arthur C. Clarke, "Epilogue: After 2001" (1968), in *2001: A Space Odyssey* (New York: Signet Books, 1982). Later page references to the novel are to this edition.
3. Frank Herbert, *Children of Dune* (1976; New York: Berkley Books, 1977), 375.

4. C. G. Jung, *On the Nature of the Psyche,* in *The Basic Writings of C. G. Jung,* ed. V. de Laszlo (New York: Modern Library, 1959), 77.

5. See Gerald Edelman, *Bright Air, Brilliant Fire: On the Matter of Mind* (n.p.: Basic Books, 1992).

6. Arthur C. Danto, *Nietzsche as Philosopher* (New York: Macmillan, 1965), 196. Friedrich Nietzsche, Prologue to *Thus Spake Zarathustra,* (1883), 3.

7. Cited in Danto, 197.

8. Nietzsche, 5.

9. See Lucien Levy-Bruhl, *Primitives and the Supernatural,* trans. Lilian Clare (New York: Dutton, 1935), 192.

10. See Jacques Lacan, *Écrits: A Selection,* trans. Alan Sheridan (New York: Norton, 1977).

11. See Clifford Geertz, *Works and Lives: The Anthropologist as Author* (Stanford: Stanford University Press, 1988).

12. Bruce Albert, "Event Horizons of the Psyche: Synchronicity, Psychedelics, and the Metaphysics of Consciousness," (Ph.D. diss., University of California, Riverside, 1993), 172.

13. Stephen Hawking, *A Brief History of Time* (New York: Bantam Books, 1988), 180.

14. Carl G. Jung, *Psychological Types,* in *The Basic Writings of C. G. Jung,* 275.

15. For more information on this telling episode in the history of science, see R. T. Morrison and R. N. Boyd, *Organic Chemistry,* 3d ed. (Boston: Allyn and Bacon, 1973), 319.

E.T. as Fairy Tale

Andrew Gordon

A friend of mine took a family of Cambodian refugees to see their first movie in America: *E.T.* (1982). Toward the end of the movie, tears began running down the cheeks of their seven-year-old son. Yet he didn't understand a word of English. That's cinematic power: a movie that doesn't need language to communicate. E.T.'s death scene may be the contemporary equivalent of the death of Charles Dickens's Little Nell: millions weep.

E.T. is the best of Steven Spielberg's suburban trilogy (*Close Encounters of the Third Kind* [1977, 1980], *Poltergeist* [1982, actually directed by Tobe Hooper], and *E.T.* [1982]) and may well be his masterpiece; lyrical, warm, and tender, it can bring tears to the eyes of both children and adults. When my son was three, an E.T. doll was his favorite teddy bear. Although I have viewed the film perhaps a dozen times, I can never see it all the way through without my eyes misting over. Yet *E.T.* is similar to *Close Encounters,* which I have argued is a cult movie, the wet dream of a "UFO-ologist,"[1] with paper-thin characters in a tissue-thin plot of mysterious appearances and disappearances and massive government cover-ups, concluding with an inspiring light show and the ascent into heaven of the chosen one in a chariot of the gods.

On the surface, some of these things are also true of *E.T.*: heroes are childlike and pure of heart, villains are scientists, and the good fairies are extraterrestrials who possess not science but paranormal powers and a technology so mysterious that it is inseparable from magic. Both movies gloss over too many holes in their plots and end in a warm bath of wish fulfillment about gods from outer space. Spielberg appropriates the iconography of science fiction but fashions plots closer to fantasy and fairy tale.

111

Given the similarities between the two movies, why do I love *E.T.* despite myself? Why am I able to excuse the same faults—mysticism and sentimentality—that I deplore in *Close Encounters*? Why does *Close Encounters* leave me unmoved while *E.T.* makes me cry? I can think of four reasons.

First, it may be because the characters in *Close Encounters* are sketchy and difficult to care about, while those in *E.T.* are more complete human beings—with the alien, oddly, the most human of them all.

Second, where *Close Encounters* is often solemn and mawkish, the sentimentality of *E.T.* is balanced by a nice sense of humor: few scenes in modern cinema are as touching and as funny as Elliott trying to explain his toys to a wide-eyed, uncomprehending E.T.

Third, although *Close Encounters* has skillful cinematography, Spielberg in *E.T.* views the world through the visionary eyes of a child and a childlike alien, thereby poeticizing the ordinary. Scene after scene has a warmth, intimacy, and sense of wonder created through careful lighting and camera placement: Elliott doing the dishes at the kitchen sink, wreathed in rising clouds of steam, gazing up out the window; or Elliott moving hesitantly in the darkness under a crescent moon away from the safe light of the house toward the strangely glowing backyard shed—a scene with "a sacramental feel, like the discovery of the grail or the manger."[2]

The child's-eye view of the film (consistently maintained through waist-level shots) points toward the fourth and fundamental reason why *E.T.* works for me: its child hero. To watch thirty-year-old Richard Dreyfuss play with his mashed potatoes is appalling; to watch ten-year-old Henry Thomas drop his pizza is appealing. *E.T.* is children's literature, whereas *Close Encounters* is childish.

Spielberg is not only an expert director of children but also an expert storyteller for children. In *E.T.,* he and scriptwriter Melissa Mathison (who wrote *The Black Stallion* [1979], a similar film about a boy inseparable from his horse) fashioned a contemporary fairy tale with an intuitive grasp of child psychology and added a new figure to pop mythology. E.T. lives in the popular psyche as surely as Peter Pan—a comparison Spielberg makes inevitable by including a reading from J. M. Barrie's story in the movie. Like Peter Pan, E.T. is a sprite who never grows up, who descends on a household of children, makes them believe in fairies, and teaches them to fly,[3] themes Spielberg returned to (with less success) in *Hook* (1991). The scientist "Keys" and his ominous band tracking down E.T.

and the children are equivalent to Captain Hook and his pirates, adult villains who intrude on a blissful never-never land.

E.T. as Frog King

Spielberg's "extraterrestrials" are really updated versions of the trolls, dwarfs, elves, leprechauns, and other enchanted creatures who populate folklore and fairy tales.[4] In the Grimm brothers' fairy tale "The Frog-King," a princess goes into the forest and, while playing with a golden ball, drops it into a well. An ugly frog promises to return the ball if she takes him home: "if you will love me and let me be your companion and play-fellow . . . and sleep in your little bed."[5] In the end, we all know, the frog is transformed through contact with the princess into a handsome prince who marries her. In *E.T.,* an alien visitor who looks like a frog appears suddenly out of the forest. When Elliott tosses a ball into his shed, E.T. returns it to him, symbolically binding the two of them together. Later, Elliott takes E.T. into his bedroom as his "companion and play-fellow." The parallel with the Grimms' tale is reinforced when Elliott releases the school laboratory frogs because they resemble E.T., his frog prince.

E.T., however, is not transformed into a human being by the boy's touch; he remains an alien. Instead, the boy is transformed by E.T.'s magical touch into a more loving, mature, and whole human being than he was before—a sort of "handsome prince." Richard Corliss writes that E.T. "eventually proves as beautiful as an enchanted frog," but he first must be rescued by a child "whose Galahad strength only E.T. and the movie-goer can immediately discover."[6] For Bruno Bettelheim, fairy tales are not simply wish fulfillments; they embody psychological truths: "a fairy tale enlightens [a child] about himself, and fosters his personality development." The fairy tale symbolizes inner conflicts, suggests how they may be resolved, and thus "reassures, gives hope for the future, and holds out the promise of a happy ending."[7]

E.T. is the best of Spielberg's three suburban fantasies because it is both the closest to the classic fairy-tale pattern and the most profound psychologically, affirming our human potential, our emotional resources, our power to love, and the possibility of healing and growth. In *Close Encounters,* gods from outer space come down and rescue Roy Neary; in *E.T.,* a god from outer space and a boy become friends and rescue each other. *Close Encounters* features not the child hero of the fairy tale but an adult who behaves like a child and loses our sympathy, and *Poltergeist* utterly lacks psychological growth; any reassurance or hope for the future offered by these films is superficial. Referring to *Poltergeist,* Pauline Kael notes, "What's lacking is what *E.T.* has—the emotional roots of the fantasy, and what it means to the children."[8] *E.T.* is a meaningful fairy tale about a boy's psychological maturation.[9]

Bettelheim categorizes "The Frog-King" as a fairy tale that "center[s] on the shock of recognition when that which seemed animal suddenly reveals itself as the source of human happiness" (286). This shock of recognition is also central to the appeal of *E.T.* Spielberg made his space creature deliberately ugly: "He's fat and he's not pretty. I really wanted E.T. to sneak up on you—not in the easy way of an F. A. O. Schwarz doll on the shelf. The story is the beauty of his character."[10] When E.T. reveals tender emotions and other human characteristics, he makes what we usually reject—what we consider animal or alien within us—seem suddenly human and acceptable. E.T. is within us; he is part of all of us. As Vivian Sobchack puts it, "Aliens R U.S."[11]

Like all good fantasies, Spielberg's film transforms not only the strange into the familiar but also the familiar into the strange. The extraterrestrial E.T. is far more "human" than the really alien intruders in the film: the faceless scientists in NASA spacesuits, the moon men who invade Elliott's home. A detailed look at the opening scene of the film demonstrates how Spielberg's technique creates that reversal of expected values and fosters in the audience a strong identification with the alien creature.

The Opening Scene

The lyrical opening of *E.T.* represents Spielberg at the height of his powers as a poet with a camera. Fusing light, sound, music, camera angles and movement, and editing rhythms to involve the audience and tell a story without words, he domesticates the fantastic and creates sympathy for the alien.

It begins with credits flashed in purple on a black screen. The title, *E.T.: The Extraterrestrial,* and the eerie music lead us to expect something unusual. There is a dissolve into an establishing shot of a starry night sky and then a slow tilt down to reveal the tops of some trees, the silhouette of a redwood forest. The serene pastoral setting, the music (now soft and traditional), and the smooth movement downward into familiar territory are reassuring. But the opening night sky reminds us of the vast, unknown universe beyond our world, and the movement downward suggests the path of a spaceship as it lands. The music grows louder in the next shot: as if we were perched high in the trees, we look down on a brilliantly lit spaceship sitting in a forest clearing. We begin in medias res; the aliens have already landed. A spaceship in a forest is extraordinary, but this is not the overwhelming, cathedral-sized mother ship of *Close Encounters*. It is simpler, scaled down; not awe inspiring but soothing, familiar despite its unfamiliarity: round and lit up like a jack-o'-lantern or a Christmas tree ornament.

Now we cut to a slow pan, close to ground level, of the ramp of the ship glimpsed through branches. The pan continues across the clearing and there are several dissolves, suggesting a time lapse, and we see the silhouettes of strange creatures moving in the clearing. In the first close-up in the film, long, thin alien fingers reach up and tenderly touch a tree branch. The gesture is framed against a circle of light from the ship in the background, foreshadowing the famous shot of the boy pedaling his bicycle across the full moon, with E.T. in a basket on the handlebars.

These opening shots display many of Spielberg's characteristic techniques. He uses a traditional opening sequence of establishing shot, long shot, then progressively closer shots; at the same time, he moves downward from sky to treetops to ground level. The conventional cutting, smooth camera movements, and soft music put us at ease. The shots are clear-cut and carefully framed, and lighting is used to pinpoint certain elements within the frame. While employing these common devices, Spielberg does something uncommon (in 1982) for a science fiction film: he presents the aliens first. There are no humans in that clearing, and we see the creatures through the eye of the camera, not the eyes of characters in the film. We glimpse them first at a distance, as if we are spying on them from behind some trees. The night, the distance, the obscuring branches, and the silhouetting effect of the backlighting keep them indistinct. They are extraterrestrial, extraordinary, mysterious, but also sympathetic: through those traditional film techniques, Spielberg domesticates the aliens, predisposing us to like them despite their strangeness. They are elves in the forest primeval, fairy-tale creatures. They immediately make themselves at home in nature: those fingertips carefully touching the branch show a reverence for the environment.

Since we are not allowed to see the aliens clearly yet, we are next shown the interior of the ship to suggest how truly alien they are. There is a slow pan across alien vegetation: glowing mushrooms and strange glistening and steaming cones. Crediting his audience with some intelligence, Spielberg never explains anything about the aliens; oddities (such as the vegetation) are simply presented, and we must make sense of them for ourselves. For example, when an owl hoots, the aliens seem startled and their chests glow red; then they relax and the glow fades. We deduce that they are timid creatures who give off this red heartlight when they are frightened; it suggests blushing (we find out later that it is also associated with happiness). Later in the scene the frightened E.T. gives himself away when his chest begins to glow.

The gentleness and timidity of the aliens is also suggested when a rabbit is untroubled by the presence of E.T. in the forest. We hear little E.T. coo as he cradles a seedling tree. He walks meditatively through the forest, dwarfed by giant redwoods, which we see in a low-angle shot, making them resemble enormous columns in a cathedral. The religious calm of the scene and the gradual shift to subjective camera favoring E.T.'s point of view win us over. An unnatural creature has been made to seem natural, even saintly. E.T. is shown in the opening scene to love not only nature but also the things of man; he sits to admire the lovely glow of the town, a jewel-like network of lights in the valley below. In fact, his attraction to things terrestrial and human causes him to stray too far from the ship and leads to his being stranded.

The calm, meditative mood is now shattered by the arrival of a human search team. The music changes to a loud, fast, and tense chase motif. We see the arriving trucks from E.T.'s point of view: huge and glaring, driving aggressively forward to fill the frame in a kind of phallic invasion, a technique Spielberg mastered filming the truck in *Duel* (1971). Spielberg facetiously called *Duel* "Bambi Meets Godzilla," and the opening of *E.T.* also evokes *Bambi,* with E.T. as a terrified animal, a lovable and helpless creature fleeing for his life from hunters in the forest.

Adult males are the true aliens in this film, scary creatures usually shown at waist level, from a child's or alien's point of view. For most of the film, they have no faces. The leader of the search is identified, like a jailer, by the huge key ring on his belt. Unlike the aliens, the men show no respect for the environment; they tromp through the forest, and poisonous fumes belch from their truck tailpipes. Their light is not the comforting glow of the spacecraft or heartlight, or even the warm gleam of the suburbs, but the glaring, probing light of flashlights or truck headlights.

The opening scene of *E.T.* thus effects a clever reversal of traditional values. With tremendous economy of means, employing deceptively reassuring techniques and not a single word, Spielberg turns the alien into the standard of the human and the humane, making the audience strongly identify with the alien creature while converting adult human males into the real, terrifying Other. The paranoia aroused in many 1950s American science fiction films about creepy "alien invaders" with menacing technology is here displaced onto male scientists and their intrusive machinery.

Mother and Child in *E.T.*

If the opening discredits men, then it also implicitly validates the maternal and childlike. In the next scene, Elliott's mother tells the children, as they investigate a backyard disturbance, "Put those knives back!" and later, again the sole woman in the scene, she pleads with the government agents, "No guns! They're children!" "Put away your weapons" is one of the messages of *E.T.*: the extraterrestrial is naked and carries no weapons (and no visible sex organs). In the opening scene, human invaders are associated with such phallic imagery as trucks, keys, and flashlights. In contrast, E.T. is associated with the maternal: the egg-shaped ship and gardening.

The night in the opening scene is also maternal. In the suburban trilogy, creatures typically emerge at night, as if erupting out of the unconscious mind. But the night in *E.T.* is neither as mysterious as in *Close Encounters* nor as scary as in *Poltergeist;* instead, from the very beginning it seems warm and embracing. Elliott twice sleeps outdoors, something none of the characters in *Close Encounters* or *Poltergeist* could safely attempt. When an interviewer mentioned the reassuring, "mothering feeling" one gets from the night in *E.T.,* Spielberg replied: "Yeah, it is Mother Night. Remember in *Fantasia* Mother Night flying over with her cape, covering a daylight sky? I used to think, when I was a kid, that that's what night really looked like. The Disney Mother Night was a beautiful woman with flowing, blue-black hair, and arms extended outward, twenty miles in either direction. And behind her was a very inviting cloak." [12] Clearly the image of the maternal night, repeated at the end of *Close Encounters* and *Always* (1989), has a powerful psychological significance for Spielberg that dates back to his childhood, a feeling he is able to evoke in the viewer as well.

Even as E.T. is associated with the maternal, he is also childlike. The opening can be considered a symbolic birth, with E.T. the infant born out of the egg-shaped mother ship. He is small and wobbles like a toddler. When he strays from home, his curiosity puts him in danger: he is the little child lost who figures in many Spielberg films. His terrifying encounter with the search party represents a sudden, violent rupture of the mother-infant dyad by the intrusion of the father. These hunters are fairy-tale giants concocted out of a small child's fear of grownups.

Thus the opening scene presents a fantasy of separation, with E.T. as fairy-tale child or Bambi: a baby animal abandoned by its parents and at the mercy of the dark forest and ruthless hunters. To enjoy the story, we must sympathize with the creature by drawing on the frightened child or nurturing mother within ourselves. Or rather, since E.T. combines mother and child in a single figure, we must move between these two positions in our response to the alien. As we identify with the alien, we love ourselves.

The Problematic Father

The position that remains problematic for both characters and audience for most of the film, however, is that of the father. Until almost the end, men are either absent (Elliott's missing father) or they are giant, faceless menaces seen only at waist level (the hunters, the biology teacher, a policeman)—though I will argue later that E.T. also functions as an idealized, childlike, sexually unthreatening father.

Men represent science, and science is the enemy, with its authority, rationality, and insensitivity. Elliott must keep E.T. from falling into their hands because "they'll give it a lobotomy or do experiments on it." The critic Roger Neustadter writes, "As science and scientists are portrayed as alienated from nature in such films as *Close Encounters of the Third Kind, 2001, E.T.,* and *Flight of the Navigator,* the child is shown to be the incarnation of simplicity, naturalness, and innocence."[13] In *Close Encounters* and *E.T.,* alien science is like the aliens—magical, emotional, childlike, kindly, and asexual—but human science is like grown men: rational, unemotional, adult, malevolent, and threateningly phallic.

Except for the reconciliation with Keys at the end, the film presents a pre-Oedipal view of adult men as intrusive, overpowering, and ominous. That is why audiences cheer when Elliott disrupts the science teacher's lesson by liberating the frogs and when Elliott and Michael steal the van from the officials. In the film's partially paranoid vision, men are evil spies who intrude on domestic bliss with phallic machinery. One shot epitomizes this attitude: right after Elliott announces to his brother and sister that he is keeping E.T., we look down on the homes from the hilltop; a large black camera intrudes into the frame from the left and rapidly snaps a series of pictures. Normally one expects children to spy on the world of adults; here, men spy on children.

E.T. reverses the traditional Oedipal resolution in which the boy identifies with the father; instead, at the end Keys the scientist, as substitute father, identifies with the child Elliott (just as the scientist in *Close Encounters* comes to identify with the childlike Neary). The adult male viewer of *E.T.* must effect the same identification to transact this fantasy successfully and accept at the end the children's triumph over the world of men.

E.T. as Child God

Until well into the picture, we still don't know exactly what E.T. looks like; kept in suspense, we see him only partially or in silhouette. We first glimpse E.T.'s face at the same moment that Elliott does, and our shock is tempered by humor, since both human and alien respond in the same appalled manner. E.T.'s fright is expressed through telekinesis: garbage cans topple and roll, and swings oscillate wildly. The chaotic movement could equally well express Elliott's psychic upheaval at coming face-to-face with the "monster" who later proves to be his double.

Despite his initially repellent appearance, E.T. looks strangely familiar: with dwarfish body and wizened face (large eyes, tiny nose, reptilian appearance), he resembles a fetus not yet fully formed in the womb. Like a toddler, he waddles clumsily as he walks, pokes everything within reach, tastes and tries to eat inedible objects. He is prone to upset things and cause messes. He is easily frightened, and his moods are intense but mercurial. These characteristics endear him to us, as if he were that most sensitive of creatures, a human infant.

E.T. grows up rapidly before our eyes, progressing from gestures to sounds, words, and phrases. Finally he masters his environment by constructing a communicator to "phone home" (this Rube Goldberg device is a child's dream of a slapdash invention, concocted out of parts from a child's toy and household items). Elliott sometimes thinks of E.T. as a fellow child: when he tries to persuade him to stay, he says, "We could grow

up together, E.T." Although the creature is like a child, he is also a repository of ancient, mystic wisdom, like the Jedi master Yoda in *The Empire
Strikes Back* (1980): in the Halloween parade, E.T. strays from the children to follow a trick-or-treater dressed as Yoda.

As much as he is child or wise old man, E.T. is also a divine being. As
child god, he is small and helpless yet paradoxically enormously powerful.
Like a god, he descends to Earth from the heavens and mingles with the
sons of men, risking his life to aid them. Elliott discovers him in a backyard shed that resembles a manger. E.T. is misunderstood, hunted, captured, tormented, dies, and is reborn. His coming is, as Keys tells Elliott,
"a miracle." Associated with his divinity are his inexplicable psychic powers, such as telepathic empathy with Elliott and others, psychokinesis (the
ability to move and levitate objects by mental energy), the "healing touch"
of his magic finger, and, most awesome of all, the Christlike power of
resurrection: he brings dead flowers and then himself back to life. Moreover, like a deity, E.T. has an instinctive rapport with children, and adults
must become as little children to understand and love him. With his heartlight and his magic finger, E.T. represents the divinity as creator and
healer. By the end, he has healed Elliott's broken home, united the children
of a fragmented suburban development in their crusade to save him, and
united scientist and layperson, adult and child, in common awe of a miraculous creature beyond their understanding. The film thus blends fairy
tale with religious fable.

Except for the spoken words "miracle" and "believe," the religious
undertones are conveyed visually, iconographically: E.T. clad in a white
robe, heartlight glowing, resembling a Christ figure. One advertisement
emphasized his long, glowing finger, reaching like the hand of God touching Adam in Michelangelo's painting on the Sistine Chapel. *E.T.*, says
the critic Hugh Ruppersburg, gives us "the image of the good-hearted,
kind, loving alien, the cosmic incarnation of Christian myth and doctrine.
The film succeeds by stimulating religious emotions in camouflaged form
and by its vision of a cosmos where the individual has a cosy and secure
place." [14]

E.T. and Elliott

The religious qualities of E.T. as child god do not exhaust his significance,
as he is what psychoanalysts would call an "overdetermined" figure. E.T.

is filled with psychological meaning for both Elliott and the audience—which further accounts for the film's profound emotional impact.

Elliott is a neglected, friendless boy, abandoned by his father, and with a mother too distracted by her own grief to be of much help. He is a middle child squeezed between an older brother who relates mostly to his peers (who disdain Elliott) and a little sister too young to understand the family problems. For Elliott, E.T. functions like an "imaginary companion" who substitutes for an entire family: father, mother, sibling, and pet all rolled into one. If E.T. is the fairy-tale elf, then Elliott is the fairy-tale child: lonely, ignored, ridiculed, clumsy, but still possessing hidden powers of intelligence, resourcefulness, bravery, and love, qualities that will be revealed at the proper time. The coming of E.T. liberates Elliott's heroic potential.

Talking about the genesis of the film, Spielberg says: "I remember wishing one night that I had a friend. It was like, when you were a kid and had grown out of dolls or Teddy bears or Winnie the Pooh, you just wanted a little voice in your mind to talk to. . . . To me, Elliott was always the Nowhere Man from the Beatles song. I was drawing from my own feelings when I was a kid and didn't have that many friends."[15]

"Transitional objects" such as the teddy bear Spielberg mentions mediate between the infantile self and the mother: they are neither self nor nonself, but something in between, transitional in the creation of a self.[16] Imaginary companions are more sophisticated; they are created at a later, Oedipal stage of development: Linus's blanket in *Peanuts* is a transitional object, while Calvin's tiger friend, Hobbes, in *Calvin and Hobbes* is an imaginary companion.

Yale psychology professor Jerome Singer, commenting on the appeal of E.T., mentions that children often need imaginary playmates to "help them make sense in their switch from their parents to the outside world."[17] Many psychiatric commentators see the imaginary companion as a precursor to the ego-ideal or superego—that is, to the psychic function that approximates the role of the parents.[18] The psychiatrist Wayne A. Myers finds that imaginary companions are created in response to "narcissistic blows" such as "abandonment by one or both parents,"[19] which is the case with Elliott (and also with his creator, Spielberg). By splitting the self, one creates a double, compensating for loss. Anna Freud claims that an imaginary animal companion helps its creator to avoid painful realities by denial: "Thus the 'evil' father becomes in phantasy a protective animal, while the helpless child becomes the master of powerful father-substitutes."[20] S. Bach sees the imaginary companion as "an envied and idealized [introjected paternal] phallus . . . used defensively to perpetuate a regressive, narcissistic solution of the oedipus conflict."[21] Myers agrees that the companion serves "as an idealized phallic self-representation" for a child who thinks of himself as castrated.[22]

The notion of E.T. as imaginary companion helps to explain some of his complex and sometimes contradictory functions: as Elliott's double, as father substitute, and as walking phallus. First, as doubles, their names are similar (E.T. and Elliott), and they seem part of the same character, working together like an inseparable pair linked by telepathic empathy: "a little voice in your mind to talk to," as Spielberg says. E.T. is a magical double who completes the boy, which is why the separation of the two at the end is so wrenching for the audience. E.T. represents the part of himself that Elliott has split off or disavowed: the pain, loneliness, and feeling of being abandoned he has been suppressing since his father left. As the psychologist John F. McDermott Jr. puts it, "E.T. looks like Elliott feels. He seems to express Elliott's own bottled-up loneliness as he gradually succumbs to the trauma of separation from a familiar milieu. E.T. is Elliott's alter ego. E.T. and Elliott are really one. They simply split into rescuer and victim as we move back and forth between them."[23] Elliott is able to project his own problems onto E.T., a creature who needs rescuing even more than Elliott does.[24]

As double or alter ego, E.T. also represents the previously repressed, animal side of Elliott and helps him grow up by liberating his libido. (We tend to forget the lascivious nature of Pan, the demigod from whom Peter Pan derives his name.) Kael notes that "the telepathic communication he develops with E.T. eases his cautious, locked-up worries, and he begins to act on his impulses."[25] When E.T. gets drunk, Elliott starts acting silly in the classroom, frees the frogs, and emulates John Wayne in *The Quiet Man* (1952) by sweeping a pretty girl into a rapturous embrace. This liberation is part of Spielberg's strategy: "How many kids, in their Walter Mitty imaginations, would love to save the frogs or kiss the prettiest girl in class? That's every boy's childhood fantasy."[26] Besides being the boy's double, as an imaginary animal companion E.T. is a powerful father substitute the boy can master. As the critic Paul Joannides notes, *E.T.* is a "fantasy of maturation" that "plays on the child's dream of omnipotence—the friend who is equipped with superhuman powers, but who remains dependent."[27] Even as Elliott fathers E.T., so E.T. replaces the missing father. Another critic, Maria Heung, claims that "Elliott and E.T. offer each other the solace of a surrogate family to replace the one each has lost." When E.T. dresses in a bathrobe, drinks beer, and watches TV, he stands in for the father, and when he listens in with Elliott as the mother reads a bedtime story to Gertie, he completes the family circle.[28] Phyllis Deutsch, a feminist critic, writes, "When E.T. is not a clinging infant, making mothers of us all, he is the flipside of the fantasy: the ultimate patriarch who has come to mend the fractured family and restore order in the kingdom."[29] Nevertheless, as a childlike, asexual alien, E.T. is an unthreatening authority figure, a patriarch who needs fathering, the father without the phallus.

Paradoxically, E.T. does not need the phallus because his entire body is a phallic symbol. His asexual, childlike qualities defend against the sexuality he unconsciously represents. The imaginary companion, after all, has been considered as an idealized phallic self-representation, a way of overcoming fears of castration. In Bettelheim's interpretation, the frog king (a kind of imaginary animal companion to a girl) expresses the child's changing attitudes toward sexuality: at first the frog (phallus) looks repugnant, but then it is transformed into a handsome prince (290). Like a frog, E.T. is small, wrinkled, and ugly. But when he is excited, his neck extends in a kind of erection. Elliott hides him in his bedroom, keeping him a secret from his mother but bragging about him to his siblings and peers. He calls his older brother Michael "penis breath," suggesting, perhaps, Elliott's sense of weakness in relation to older males, but once he gains possession of E.T., he tells Michael, "I have absolute power." E.T. inspires the boy to intoxicating feats of virility. And there is no need to mention how Freud would interpret dreams of flying!

If E.T. is Elliott's budding manhood, then the latter part of the film could be interpreted as a nightmare of castration anxiety: male authorities pursue him, circling ever closer, and finally invade his home to sever Elliott from his E.T. But Elliott outsmarts them and finds a satisfactory resolution of the Oedipal crisis. E.T. plays dead and then comes back to life, but Elliott returns him to the womb of the mother ship, where he will be safe from harm.

E.T. ends, like *Close Encounters,* with a retreat from the dangers of masculine assertion, back to the womb of mother ship and Mother Night. Yet *E.T.* does not seem as narcissistic and regressive in its resolution, perhaps because of *E.T.*'s child hero and also because of the successful splitting the film enacts through its double hero. Even as E.T. is being returned to the womb, Elliott escapes from one: he walks out of the plastic sheathing that encloses his house, and when he pulls the pins on the plastic tunnel trailing behind the truck, he symbolically cuts the cord. In contrast, at the end of *Close Encounters,* Barry is reunited with his mother while Neary fuses ecstatically with the alien mother ship. *Poltergeist* reverses the end of *Close Encounters,* emphasizing the potentially terrifying consequences of the retreat, the fear of being reabsorbed by a monster mother. As Andrew Sarris notes, "the most harrowing effects in *Poltergeist* tend to be return-to-the-womb rather than phallocentric." [30]

Conclusion: We Are E.T.

I still have not really answered my initial question: Why do millions weep at the death of E.T.? Why does it move me every time I see it? Why did the little Cambodian boy cry even though he didn't understand a word of the dialogue? I suspect it is because the film operates through the powerfully emotive, irrational imagery of childhood, dreams, and fairy tales. From the beginning its visual style encourages us to identify strongly, first with the alien as underdog, and then with the boy. They can be seen as representatives of our best qualities. This identification is more profound than that effected by other Spielberg films because it is not undercut by irony or distancing (think, for example, of how we are distanced from the aliens for most of *Close Encounters*). The bond between Elliott and E.T. is so strong that we become enmeshed in it. E.T. is such a positive creation and such a suggestive figure on so many possible levels, both conscious and unconscious—as loving mother, innocent child, Christ figure, the child's double or imaginary companion, kindly father, best friend, or even beloved pet (*E.T.* is modeled in part on such boy-and-animal films as *The Yearling* [1946], *Old Yeller* [1957], and *The Black Stallion* [1979])—that viewers will almost certainly respond deeply to one or more of these.

And at the most fundamental level, the film arouses and successfully overcomes the universal human anxiety over separation, thus offering tremendous reassurance. After E.T. dies and is reborn, we are willing to release him, for the creature wants only what we all want: to go back home. And he will remain behind in Elliott's mind, which he touches, saying, "I'll be right here." We can take this as the promise of the parent whose memory will remain to guide us or as the promise of the god who will never abandon us (E.T.'s ship leaves behind the rainbow sign).

So why do I cry when I watch *E.T.?* I'm still not sure; I'm too close to my own feelings to be able to entirely understand their sources. But although I have never met the little Cambodian boy, I think he was crying first from fear and sadness and finally from relief. I suspect something like this was going through his mind:

> *I am E.T.* A little refugee chased from his home by bad men. I don't understand the language or the people in this strange land. I don't look like them. I don't belong here. My country is very far away. I miss my home so much but I may never see it again.
>
> But here is this nice little American boy. He takes me into his home, he protects me, he risks everything for me. He cannot be apart from me. He loves me so much that we become one. Then I die, so sick for home, and he cries over me. But I do not really die. I come back to him. I cannot die as long as he loves me. With his help I will get back home. But we will never be apart because we are really one.

None of the interpretations I have suggested is complete or entirely exhausts the possible meanings of *E.T.* Like a fairy tale, it is a maturational fantasy that recapitulates certain stages of human psychological development, encompassing both our past and our present and suggesting clues about our future. Richard Stoves, a clinical instructor in psychiatry at the Downstate Medical Center of the State University of New York, who interviewed children aged eight to twelve immediately after they saw the film, reports that "*E.T.* is a fairy tale for the preadolescent child."[31] But clearly the film, one of the most popular in movie history, appeals to a far broader audience. Interview a sample audience of a different age and you will come up with different answers. With its abandoned alien who is both omnipotent and dependent, its double hero, its wise children, its thrilling rescue and happy ending, this space age fairy tale appeals on a number of levels. Each viewer will resonate to it on a slightly different psychological chord. For children, *E.T.* is a voyage of emotional discovery; for adults, a rediscovery of feelings we thought we had lost or outgrown. A five-year-old of my acquaintance summed it up very well: "It's a story about love." Like another filmic fairy tale, *The Wizard of Oz, E.T.* shows the extraordinary journey we all must take to return to the place at our heart's core: "Home."

Notes

1. Andrew Gordon, "*Close Encounters:* The Gospel According to Steven Spielberg," *Literature/Film Quarterly* 8.3 (1980): 156–64.

2. Paul Joannides, "Luminous/Numinous," *London Review of Books,* January 20–February 3, 1982, 16.

3. Among the critics who note the E.T.–Peter Pan connection are Andrew Sarris, "Spielberg's Sand Castles," *Village Voice,* June 15, 1982, 59; Charles Michener and Katrine Ames, "A Summer Double Punch," *Newsweek,* May 31, 1982, 64; and Richard Corliss, "Steve's Summer Magic," *Time,* May 31, 1982, 56.

4. See Alex Eisenstein, "The Forerunners of CE3K," *Fantastic Films,* April 1978, 28.

5. "The Frog-King, or Iron Henry," in *The Complete Grimm's Fairy Tales,* trans. James Stern (New York: Pantheon, 1972), 18.

6. Corliss, 56.

7. Bruno Bettelheim, *The Uses of Enchantment: The Meaning and Importance of Fairy Tales* (New York: Knopf, 1977), 12, 26. Later page references in the text are to this edition.

8. Pauline Kael, "The Pure and the Impure," *New Yorker,* June 14, 1982, 124.

9. Amid the almost universal chorus of superlatives for *E.T.,* Andrew Sarris sounds a dissenting note that is worth considering: "Spielberg (and Lucas) may be creating fairy tales that serve not so much as rites of passage as pleas for a permanent childhood" (59). And Richard Grenier, a right-wing critic, objects to "the message of *E.T.* . . . that except for us [Americans], it is a benign universe" (*Commentary,* August 1982, 66).

10. Cited in Michener and Ames, 64.

11. Vivian Sobchack, *Screening Space: The American Science-Fiction Film* (New York: Ungar, 1987), 293.

12. Cited in Michael Sragow, "A Conversation with Steven Spielberg," *Rolling Stone,* July 22, 1982, 26.

13. Roger Neustadter, "Phone Home: The Transformation of Childhood in Contemporary Science Fiction Films," *Youth and Society* 20.3 (1989): 238.

14. Hugh Ruppersburg, "The Alien Messiah in Recent Science Fiction Films," *Journal of Popular Film and Television* 14.4 (1987): 166.

15. Sragow, 26.

16. See D. W. Winnicott, *Playing and Reality* (London: Tavistock, 1971).

17. Cited in Bryce Nelson, "*E.T.* Speaks to Children—but Not via Telephone," *New York Times* News Service, reprinted in the *Gainesville (Fla.) Sun,* December 21, 1982, B6.

18. See, for example, Selma Fraiberg, *The Magic Years* (New York: Scribner's, 1959); O. F. Sperling, "An Imaginary Companion Representing a Prestage of the Supergeo," in *The Psychoanalytic Study of the Child,* vol. 9 (New York: International Universities Press, 1984), 252–58; Humberto Nagera, "The Imaginary Companion: Its Significance for Ego Development and Conflict Solution," in *The Psychoanalytic Study of the Child,* vol. 24 (New York: In-

ternational Universities Press, 1969), 165–96; and S. Bach, "Notes on Some Imaginary Companions," in *The Psychoanalytic Study of the Child,* vol. 26 (New York: Quadrangle Books, 1971), 159–71.

19. Wayne A. Myers, "Imaginary Companions, Fantasy Twins, Mirror Dreams and Depersonalization," *Psychoanalytic Quarterly* 45 (1976): 513.

20. Anna Freud, *The Ego and the Mechanisms of Defense* (New York: International Universities Press, 1946), 85.

21. Bach, 160.

22. Myers, 313.

23. John F. McDermott Jr., "*E.T.*: A Story of Separation" (unpublished essay).

24. Jeffrey Drezner, "*E.T.*: An Odyssey of Loss," *Psychoanalytic Review* 70 (1983): 271.

25. Kael, 119.

26. Cited in Sragow, 26.

27. Joannides, 16.

28. Maria Heung, "Why E.T. Must Go Home: The New Family in American Cinema," *Journal of Popular Film and Television* 11.2 (1983): 84.

29. Phyllis Deutsch, "E.T.: The Ultimate Patriarch," *Jump Cut* 28 (1983): 13.

30. Sarris, 59.

31. Nelson, B6.

Part 3

The Children of Fantasy and Horror

Child Vision in the Fantasy of George MacDonald

Gay Barton

In *Victorian Fantasy,* Stephen Prickett traces a divergent "counter-tradition" that developed in addition to the prevailing realism of the nineteenth century. This secondary tradition sprang most immediately from early nineteenth-century romanticism, although its origins reach as far back as Plato and Dante.[1] Yet only in the Victorian period did the fantasy genre emerge as a truly new kind of literature. Two streams fed this development: what Prickett calls "phantasmagoria," with its "wild and chaotic flux," and allegory, "the most tightly disciplined of literary kinds" (33). Prickett sees in Victorian fantasies a tension between the two, with one represented by Edward Lear's "unconscious" nonsense writing and the other by the "consciously worked-out mathematical structures" of Lewis Carroll (10). During this period, fantasy was developing into a genre able to integrate unconscious flux and conscious, structured meaning. The writer Prickett sees as pivotal in this development is George MacDonald:

> It is only with the works of George MacDonald, possibly the greatest fantasy-writer of that (or any other) period, that something like a fully balanced artistic theory emerges. Before him we are always aware of . . . an unresolved tension in the writer. With MacDonald, and those who follow him, the tension is not removed, but sublimated into a framework of rich and complicated symbolism—at once literary and theological. (10)

Other critics agree. Richard Reis notes that although Edmund Spenser's verse " 'founded' the symbolic fantasy for adults" in the English language, "MacDonald's *Phantastes* is the earliest such work in English prose."[2]

131

Reis sees MacDonald's influence in the works of C. S. Lewis, J. R. R. Tolkien, Mervyn Peake, and even Franz Kafka. C. N. Manlove cites MacDonald as being a direct influence on Ursula K. Le Guin.[3] Understanding MacDonald's importance to the development of modern fantasy as a nonallegorical but symbolic genre, we can turn to MacDonald's treatment of the child figure. Although the child is a multifaceted symbol in his works, MacDonald most prominently represents childhood as a superior mode of wisdom and vision. Furthermore, he elevates the fantasy genre itself as an essentially childlike, and hence superior, mode of writing.[4]

Children are highly visible in MacDonald's fantasy. In addition to Princess Irene and Curdie, which I examine below, he created little Diamond of *At the Back of the North Wind;* Mossy and Tangle of "The Golden Key"; and Lona and her forest companions, the Little Ones, of *Lilith.* Even the protagonist of *Phantastes,* an adult, must undergo various trials in Fairy Land to become more childlike. The ubiquity of childhood in these works is not simply due to the usual Victorian delegation of fantasy to the nursery. MacDonald wrote *Phantastes* and *Lilith,* in fact, specifically for adults. In an 1893 preface to a story collection, MacDonald insists, "I do not write for children, but for the childlike, whether five, or fifty, or seventy-five."[5] MacDonald's interest in childhood included not only the child characters in his stories, but the "child" present, sometimes sleeping, within his reader.

MacDonald's view of the child, at once literary, philosophical, and religious, grew out of seemingly contradictory forces in his own life.[6] His childhood in Scotland was haunted both by John Knox's Calvinism and by Celtic legends and a love for Scotland's wild natural landscape. It was an uneasy blend. Young MacDonald was devoted to the Scriptures and to the concept of being a child of the Father God; he was even a Congregational preacher for a time. Yet he disliked the harsher tenets of Calvinism, especially its view of human nature as essentially depraved, and he sought a theology more consistent with his instinctive mysticism, a kind of inborn Neoplatonism. The force most influential in shaping his new theology was his discovery, during his university years, of the English and German romantics—William Wordsworth, Samuel Taylor Coleridge, Johann Goethe, Friedrich von Schiller, E. T. A. Hoffmann, and Novalis.[7] Central to these writers' works is the view that humans are innately good, not essentially depraved, but are corrupted by society's twisted restraints. In the simple, primitive, and undilutedly natural—in the child—lies goodness.

To MacDonald, the romantics were a fresh wave of Neoplatonism breaking against the dike of eighteenth-century materialism. The English romantic poets sought to enhance humans' ability to see the spiritual or ideal within the immediate physical object. MacDonald regarded Wordsworth as the "high priest" of this "Christian pantheism," and viewed his "Intimations Ode," with its elevation of the special wisdom and vision of the child, as the "grandest ode that has ever been written."[8] Wordsworth's characterization of child vision as a "celestial light," a "glory" that originally clothes all things but then, as Boy grows into Man, fades "into the common light of day," MacDonald considered to be parallel to Jesus' teachings about children. MacDonald's religious essays particularly emphasize Christ's call to "turn and become like children" (Matthew 18:3). One essay interprets a story from the Gospel of Mark in which Jesus silences his followers' arguments over who is the greatest by standing a child in their midst and saying, "Whoever welcomes one of these little children in my name [that is, says MacDonald, as Christ's representative] welcomes me and . . . the one who sent me" (Mark 9:37). What Jesus was teaching, MacDonald insists, is that in the very childishness of the child we find the essential nature of Christ and God. His argument culminates, "God is child-like. . . . Childhood belongs to the divine nature."[9] Thus MacDonald fused his personal theology with his affinity for the writings of Wordsworth and the other romantics.

Reinforcing this romantic/Christian view of childhood was MacDonald's admiration for the seventeenth-century Metaphysical poets. Leah Marcus notes that in these poets' reaction against the Renaissance and Reformation we find a reverence for childhood similar to that of the nineteenth-century romantics. In both eras, a return to the simplicity of childhood was offered as an antidote to the overemphasis on rationalism during the preceding period.[10]

Of the six Metaphysical poets Marcus cites as emphasizing childhood, Henry Vaughan and George Herbert had the greatest impact on MacDonald, whose survey of English poetry, *England's Antiphon,* devotes a separate chapter to each of these poets. The Vaughan poem of most interest to MacDonald is "The Retreate." He points out the "remarkable" resemblance between that poem and Wordsworth's "Intimations Ode," and places several sets of lines from the two poems side by side. In "The Retreate," Vaughan depicts his days of "angel-infancy," before he learned the lessons of the world, as a time of particularly clear vision, a time when he could not only look back and see God, but, as in Wordsworth's poem, could also look on Nature, on "some gilded cloud or flower," and "in those weaker glories spy / Some shadows of eternity."[11] For Vaughan, as for Wordsworth, the physical world reveals the spiritual world—but only to those with the uncorrupted vision of childhood.

MacDonald's praise for Herbert conveys a second characteristic of childhood that he valued. Instead of celebrating childlike vision, Herbert explores his own childlike and trusting relationship with his God. MacDonald writes, "No writer before him has shown such a love to God, such a childlike confidence in him."[12]

From these diverse sources—the romantics, the Metaphysicals, and the Bible—MacDonald gleaned his belief in childhood as a superior state with two special characteristics: *vision*—an ability to see the eternally real Platonic Forms in and behind transient physical appearances, and *trust*—a faith that MacDonald felt demonstrated itself in unquestioning obedience to the one trusted. He also felt that the qualities were interrelated: proper vision produces trust, and trust strong enough to be acted on is necessary for real vision or understanding. He argues, "In respect of great truths investigation goes for little, speculation for nothing; if a man would know them, he must obey them."[13]

To illustrate these two interrelated qualities of childhood, I will examine *The Princess and the Goblin,* probably MacDonald's best fantasy for children, and the beginning of its sequel, *The Princess and Curdie.* In the first story, the child princess Irene can see a spiritual reality that others cannot, a vision that produces knowledge and, with it, trust. Unlike Irene, the miner boy Curdie cannot at first believe in a reality beyond the physical, and thus lacks Irene's perception. At the end of the story and the beginning of the sequel, Curdie learns to trust a divine caretaker he previously could not see and, by obeying her, gains a gift of marvelous perception. Both children display a pattern of imaginative vision that produces trust, and trust that yields vision.

When Princess Irene is introduced, she is described as one who, like Wordsworth's child "trailing clouds of glory," intuitively remembers whence she came. She has "eyes like two bits of night sky, each with a star dissolved in the blue. Those eyes you would have thought must have known they came from there, so often were they turned up in that direction."[14] Irene has retained her original innocence and thus can see spiritual realities invisible to adults. This is shown by her ability to see her fairy great-great-grandmother, whom she discovers one day spinning in a room high in the castle, secluded among winding passages and multiplied stairs. This magical ancient woman, also named Irene, is presented as a divine parent figure who gave the child her own name and has been living in the house watching over the princess since the day the child arrived. This supernatural grandmother is visible only to a special kind of soul. Rolland Hein argues, "The theme of this fantasy is that one must have a certain inner quality—a keen sensibility and childlike naiveté—in order to discern the spiritual nature of the universe and to maintain a trusting, joy-giving contact with higher spiritual powers that work for the good of man." [15]

Operating as a foil to Irene's innocent child vision is the skepticism of Lootie, her nurse. When Irene returns to the nursery after her first encounter with the ancient queen, she excitedly tells this human caretaker about it. Lootie responds simply, "What nonsense you are talking, princess!" (19). That which is not available to the physical sense is, to this adult empiricist, "nonsense." Although Irene argues with Lootie, the nurse's disbelief plants a seed of doubt, which is nurtured the next day by her own inability to find her way back to the grandmother's room. Ultimately, Irene's wavering faith in the grandmother is put completely to sleep; adult rationalism has temporarily ousted childlike faith and vision.

One night, however, the grandmother renews contact with Irene. The child wakes in the night with a pain in her injured thumb, and "suddenly a great longing woke up in her heart to try once more whether she could not find the old lady with the silvery hair" (85). Seeking her grandmother out of her own longing, not from a desire to prove her existence to Lootie, Irene succeeds. She goes straight to the narrow tower stair leading to the queen's room as if she knew every step. Irene's first question is, "Why couldn't I find you before, great-great-grandmother?" The lady answers that Irene would have found her sooner "if you hadn't come to think I was a dream" (86). A failure of trust produced a failure of vision. On this visit, Irene is allowed to enter the queen's bedroom, whose dominant feature is a lamp hanging from the center of the ceiling "as round as a ball, shining as if with the brightest moonlight" (89). The lady tells Irene a secret about her "moon": "[I]f that light were to go out you would fancy yourself lying in a bare garret, on a heap of old straw, and would not see one of the pleasant things round about you all the time" (91). For Hein, the lamp represents "the light of the pure, childlike imagination" necessary for the princess to see the queen. [16]

The miner boy Curdie Peterson provides a parallel to and contrast with Irene. MacDonald's first description of Curdie hints at both similarities and differences: while Irene's eyes are "two bits of night sky, each with a star dissolved in the blue," Curdie's are "as dark as the mines in which he worked and as sparkling as the crystals in their rocks" (36–36). Curdie's eyes and soul are as pure and deep and shining as the princess's, but while her eyes are of the heavens, his are of the earth. This prepares the reader to discover as their stories merge that Curdie does not share Irene's keen vision of spiritual truth. Instead, he must grow in trust and vision in order to fully realize his childhood.

While Irene is having adventures with her grandmother, Curdie's adventures are among the goblins, or "cobs." As he explores the dark maze of goblin tunnels, he carries a large ball of fine string, the end attached to the pickax he leaves at the opening into the human mines, unrolling it as he goes out, and gathering it back in as he returns. One night, however, he tries to return to his entrance hole but finds that the cobs' "animals" have carried his ax to an unknown part of the tunnels, and he is hopelessly lost. The cobs capture him and imprison him in a small cave. Curdie's string, which symbolizes his mode of knowing and the basis of his assurance, is explicitly contrasted with Irene's, inasmuch as MacDonald names the chapter about the string "Curdie's Clue" while a succeeding chapter is named "Irene's Clue." Irene's clue is a magic thread attached to a special ring spun of spiderweb by the queen in the light of the moon. It is a guide that usually cannot be seen, only felt, and its anchor is the divine lady herself. Curdie's clue is a physical string that he trusts because he can see it and because its anchor is his own trusty pickax; but he discovers that his physical guide misleads him and its anchor is mutable.

The morning after Curdie gets lost and is captured, Irene wakes to the terrifying noise of animals snarling and hissing all about her room. Irene's trust has grown to the point that she immediately obeys the lady's instructions about how to respond to danger. Putting the ring under her pillow, she begins to follow its thread with her finger. She expects it to lead up the old stairway to her grandmother's room, but instead it goes off in the opposite direction: down to the kitchen, out a back door, and up the mountainside. Yet Irene's trust is now sure, and she obediently follows, even when the thread leads her through a black hole into the wall of the mountain. Because she trusts her divine guardian, Irene's perception of the magical thread never fails.

At length the thread leads Irene to the cave where Curdie is imprisoned. She sets him free, but to Curdie's dismay, she insists that they continue following the thread back into the hole from which he has just been liberated.

Unbelieving, yet without a choice, he follows her deeper and deeper into this crack in the mountain's rock. Curdie's words throughout this journey that defies all reason recall Lootie's skepticism: "What nonsense the child talks! . . . I can't understand it. . . . [H]ow she should [know the way] passes my comprehension" (162–63). Unsurprisingly, when Irene asks him to feel the thread for himself, he feels nothing. To perceive spiritual truth, he needs a childlike willingness to believe such truth to be possible. When the two children emerge into the sunlight of Irene's garden, the gossamer thread shimmering before them, Curdie insists again, "I don't see anything," but Irene admonishes him, "Then you must believe without seeing" (170).

Troubled by his failure to believe her, Irene takes Curdie to see the ancient lady; but Curdie sees no grandmother, no bed, no moonlike light, only what the queen had earlier said would appear if the lamp went out: "I see a big, bare garret-room . . . a tub, and a heap of musty straw, and a withered apple" (175). After he leaves, the queen explains to Irene that she did not allow Curdie to see her because he was not yet able to believe. When Curdie tells his parents of the incident, his mother suggests, "Perhaps some people can see things other people can't see" (184–85). Chastened by her words, he regrets treating Irene so rudely and hopes for an opportunity to make amends. Now that he is more open to faith, Curdie is allowed glimpses of spiritual sight. One night he is visited by the grandmother, though only in a dream. The next day, in a moment of danger and confusion, he is given the ability to feel Irene's magic thread. He has now gained enough trust to follow it, even though it leads in a direction contrary to his own reason.

As *The Princess and the Goblin* ends, the story of Curdie's blossoming trust and perception is just beginning. In the sequel, *The Princess and Curdie,* the grandmother summons him to her tower room, where his emergent trust is keenly tested. She is about to send him on a difficult mission, and both his childlike trust and his spiritual perception must be secure before he begins. When he opens her door, to his astonishment he finds no room, only the sky above, a wheel of fire in front of him, and darkness beneath him. "Come in," an unseen voice calls, but Curdie says he is not sure he is at her door because he cannot see her room. The queen answers, "That is all right, Curdie. Come in." [17] At her bidding he steps forward. Hein notes that, as with Irene, Curdie's momentary distrust threatens his ability to see the queen; but when he acts in faith, stepping out into what appears to be a void, he is sustained in her presence.[18] His foot finds the floor, and the wheel of fire becomes the grandmother's spinning wheel.

On the hearth, "a great fire was burning, and the fire was a huge heap of roses, and yet it was a fire" (68–69).[19] The queen asks Curdie if he is prepared for a harder test, one that "needs only trust and obedience," and then she commands him, "Go and thrust both your hands into that fire." Daring not to stop and think, lest thought and fear should hinder trusting obedience, Curdie rushes to the fire and thrusts both hands into the middle of the heap of roses. The pain almost overwhelms him. At last the burning subsides, and the queen tells Curdie to look at his hands. They are not charred, but white and smooth, and she reveals the gift he has gained from the fire of roses: "[I]t has made your hands so knowing and wise, it has brought your real hands so near the outside of your flesh gloves, that you will henceforth be able to know at once the hand of a man who is growing into a beast" (73). By purifying Curdie's hands, by burning away all that is not their innate, childlike essence, the fire has made them able directly to perceive truths "unseen by unimaginative eyes."[20]

During the adventure that unfolds in The Princess and Curdie, Curdie's gift proves invaluable in "seeing" truth hidden by appearances. By grasping the hands of various men and women, he discovers the hooves and paws of the beasts they have turned themselves into—oxen, donkeys, pigs, dogs, or even viler creatures. In one man's hand Curdie feels "the belly of a creeping thing" (150). In contrast to these beast-humans is Lina, appointed by the queen to be Curdie's companion and helper. Lina's body is a "horrible mass of incongruities," a cross between a dog and an elephant, a bear and a snake. Yet Lina's hideous exterior masks a pure soul. When Curdie takes her paw, his perceptive hands feel not a dog's paw but "the soft, neat little hand of a child" (76).

As I noted above, MacDonald wrote his fantasies for the "childlike" of all ages. He appropriately designates the childlike as the ideal readers for these works because his symbolic fantasy is uniquely suited to his view of the child—in this case, the child within each of his perceptive readers. What MacDonald saw as the child's vision of the world, its Neoplatonic awareness of ideal Form behind and within all things material, is echoed in the essentially Platonic nature of the fantasy genre. A number of critics have commented on this inherent Platonism. In her argument for reading fantasy "as literature," Charlotte Spivack makes the point that whereas the dominant nineteenth-century tradition of realism is essentially Aristotelian, with its emphasis on art as mimesis of material reality, the counter-tradition of fantasy "is based on an imitation of an Idea, not of a phenomenal object," and is thus essentially Platonic.[21] Ann Swinfen offers a similar "defense" of modern fantasy as a serious genre. Contrary to the attitude she attributes to most modern critics, that "the so-called 'realist' mode of writing is somehow more profound, . . . more involved with 'real' human concerns" than is the literature of the marvelous, Swinfen points to the long tradition of Platonic thought in Western literature: "[W]hat is now regarded as the 'real' world—that is, the world of empirical experience—was for many centuries regarded as the world of 'appearances.' . . . [T]he ultimately real lay in spiritual otherworlds. It is with the reality of such otherworlds that fantasy very largely deals."[22]

In the *Princess* books, the mystical queen, her moon-lamp, Irene's magic thread, and Curdie's knowing hands are all aspects of a spiritual dimension that common adults cannot perceive, but which Irene and Curdie, when their childhood is perfected, are able to easily see. MacDonald believed that fantasy could help his childlike readers see these spiritual realities as well, to "remember"—in the Platonic and Wordsworthian sense—the world of spirit from which they have become estranged. In his introduction to an edition of MacDonald's short stories, Glenn Sadler writes, "[T]here is not a writer in the English language who has beatified the intrinsic worth of the common child better than did George MacDonald." His tales offer the reader "the one thing better than words, the fairy-tale event that we all, adults or children, desire and long for most . . . the 'child-nature' in us restored."[23]

Notes

1. Stephen Prickett, *Victorian Fantasy* (Bloomington: Indiana University Press, 1979), xiii–xv. Later page references in the text are to this edition.
2. Richard H. Reis, *George MacDonald* (New York: Twayne, 1972), 87.
3. C. N. Manlove, *The Impulse of Fantasy Literature* (Kent, Ohio: Kent State University Press, 1983), 38.
4. For additional critical analysis of MacDonald's fantasy, see *For the Childlike: George MacDonald's Fantasies for Children,* ed. Roderick McGillis (Metuchen, N.J.: Children's Literature Association/Scarecrow, 1992); *The Gold Thread: Essays on George MacDonald,* ed. William Raeper (Edinburgh: Edinburgh University Press, 1990); and David S. Robb, *George MacDonald* (Edinburgh: Edinburgh University Press, 1987).

5. George MacDonald, "The Fantastic Imagination," in *The Gifts of the Child Christ: Fairytales and Stories for the Childlike,* vol. 1, ed. Glenn Edward Sadler (Grand Rapids: Eerdmans, 1973), 25; first published as the preface to *The Light Princess and Other Fairy Tales.*

6. For biographical information, see Kathy Triggs, *The Stars and the Stillness: A Portrait of George MacDonald* (Cambridge: Lutterworth Press, 1986); and William Raeper, *George MacDonald* (Batavia, Ill.: Lion, 1987).

7. Raeper, *George MacDonald,* 49, 107.

8. George MacDonald, "Wordsworth's Poetry," in *The Imagination and Other Essays* (Boston: Lothrop, 1883), 246–47, 256.

9. George MacDonald, "The Child in the Midst," in *Creation in Christ,* edited by Rolland Hein from the three volumes of *Unspoken Sermons* (1870, 1885, 1891) (Wheaton, Ill.: Harold Shaw, 1976), 33.

10. Leah Sinanoglou Marcus, *Childhood and Cultural Despair: A Theme and Variations in Seventeenth-Century Literature* (Pittsburgh: University of Pittsburgh Press, 1978), 89–90.

11. Quoted in George MacDonald, *England's Antiphon* (London: Macmillan, 1874), 254–56.

12. MacDonald, *England's Antiphon,* 178. Herbert's elevation of childhood is best seen in "H. Baptisme (II)," in which he plays with the idea that children's smallness makes them better able to pass through the "narrow way and little gate" to God. Another example is "The Collar," in which the persona relinquishes rebellion and acquiesces in trusting obedience when God calls him "Child!" MacDonald admired this poem and included it in *England's Antiphon.*

13. George MacDonald, "A Sketch of Individual Development," in *The Imagination and Other Essays,* 72.

14. George MacDonald, *The Princess and the Goblin* (1872; Harmondsworth, England: Penguin-Puffin, 1996), 2. Later page references in the text are to this edition.

15. Rolland Hein, *The Harmony Within: The Spiritual Vision of George MacDonald* (Grand Rapids: Eerdmans, 1982), 34.

16. Hein, 36.

17. George MacDonald, *The Princess and Curdie* (1882; Harmondsworth, England: Penguin-Puffin, 1994), 65. Later page references in the text are to this edition.

18. Hein, 39.

19. Hein suggests that this image of the flaming roses is comparable to the "consuming fire" of God that MacDonald writes about in many sermonic essays. This fire purges and refines, burning up all that is not a part of man's essential nature so that he may become more godlike—that is to say, more childlike (32–33, 40).

20. C. N. Manlove, *Modern Fantasy: Five Studies* (Cambridge: Cambridge University Press, 1975), 73.

21. Charlotte Spivack, "The Perilous Realm: Phantasy as Literature," *Centennial Review* 25 (1981): 134.

22. Ann Swinfen, *In Defense of Fantasy: A Study of the Genre in English and American Literature since 1945* (London: Routledge and Kegan Paul, 1984), 10–11.

23. Glenn Edward Sadler, Introduction to *The Gifts of the Child Christ*, 20, 21.

If Not Today, Then Tomorrow: Fact, Faith, and Fantasy in Isaac Bashevis Singer's Autobiographical Writings

Alida Allison

> Many grownups have made up their minds that there is no purpose in asking questions and that one should accept the facts as they are. But the child is often a philosopher and a seeker of God.
> —Isaac Bashevis Singer, *Stories for Children*

Although clearly useful as characters or symbols, children are rarely essential components in fantasy aimed at mature audiences. Many fantasies barely mention children. But fantasy that aims to include children in its readership always involves children of some sort, whether they are humans, animals, or innocent aliens. The child protagonist usually lives in the real world but has consciously to operate in another world sometimes at very great odds with it. The abundant examples include Sebastian in Michael Erde's *The Neverending Story,* who reads his way in and out of a real fairy tale, and John in Russell Hoban's *Monsters,* whose therapeutic crayon drawing of a monster comes to life and eats the psychiatrist his parents hired to "cure" him. The fantasy world experiences of both characters are entirely distinct from, or even antagonistic to, the world in which they live with their parents.

Kathryn Hume calls these worlds "contrastive."[1] That term is useful because the ways the child character learns first to recognize the contrast, and then to negotiate it, are often central to the story. In Susan Cooper's

The Dark Is Rising, the young hero, Will, mediates between a modern Welsh world and a distinctly medieval one concurrent with it. In Philippa Pearce's time-travel fantasy *Tom's Midnight Garden,* the two worlds merge at the conclusion, but only as a secret between the child protagonist and one special adult.

As in similar adult books, the tension in fantasy written for children plays on knowledge of the margin between fact and fantasy. Take that very sane Victorian, Alice: she can recognize—and readers can revel in—the fantasy because as toddlers we all went to generic human development school and (presumably) we all learned reality. Part of the popularity of fantasies is that they evoke a nostalgia for that prelapsarian state in which Reality and reality? are still fluid concepts.

In "Growing Up," Isaac Bashevis Singer describes the sometimes uneasy transfer from fantasy to fact and illustrates a child's consciousness of the movement from one world to the other:

> In my fantasy I envisioned the city of Jerusalem and the Holy Temple. The Messiah had come and the Resurrection had taken place. . . . King David again occupied his royal throne, and his son Solomon learned the language of lions, tigers, eagles, and the woodcock. . . . All my ancestors, going back to Adam and Eve, had risen from their graves. There was no more death or injustice, only happiness and divine revelation.
>
> At the same time I knew full well that this was all just in my head. Actually, I was in Warsaw, my father was a poor neighborhood rabbi, The Land of Israel belonged to the Turks, the Temple lay in ruins. David, Solomon, Bathsheba, and the Queen of Sheba were all dead. My friend was not a prince in the Kingdom of Israel but Black Feivel, whose father was a porter . . . and whose mother sold crockery in the marketplace.[2]

A large part of growing up, after all, is precisely the process of being domesticated into agreement with the adult world about what Hume calls "consensual reality."[3] Adults may be insignificant in literary fantasies for children, but in real life, those who do the domesticating largely determine what the child consents to believe. Whatever that reality turns out to be, the child will eventually define, experience, and exercise fantasy against it. Singer, who was about ten years old when he experienced his fantasy, has a firm grasp of the difference between fantasy and fact.

Instead of discussing the child as a character or symbol in adult or children's fantasies, I will provide examples of Singer's richly detailed, often humorous portrayals of himself as a child sorting through the insistent claims of contrastive realities. Why Singer? Simply because of all major authors, he is unique in having made his experience with fact and fantasy the key drama in dozens of his childhood and children's stories. As Thomas Riggio writes, Singer "creates stories that deal with the first stages of belief in life, the period during which the child depends on intuition and cultural norms for guidance."[4] This is the period Bud Foote refers to in his essay in this volume, noting the correlation between fantasy as a literary genre and early childhood.

For many nonsecular people, the categories "fact" and "fantasy" are sufficiently comprehensive. Fantasy is measured against fact. Fantasy is aware of itself, voluntary, and playful in the sense of being time out of fact. But there is another mode of perception—the mode of faith. With faith, as with fact, once one accepts the premises, everything else logically follows. Since faith satisfies many adults, it figures prominently in the reality training of many children; it certainly figured in Singer's childhood and in the shtetls (villages) of his eastern European Jewish culture. An example is described in *A Little Boy in Search of God:*

> In Bilgoraj, my mother's home town, there was a ritual slaughterer, Avromele, on whose window the evil spirit had been beating for weeks on end. Every evening the whole population of the town gathered to listen to the invisible force knock on the pane. One could discourse with it. One asked it questions and it tapped out answers—mostly "yes" or "no" but occasionally entire words. . . . The town *nachalnik* . . . was apparently an enlightened man who didn't believe in evil spirits. He sent the police and soldiers to search the entire house . . . to discover the source of the noises, but they found nothing.[5]

A faith mode such as this sees divine forces at work in the world. The fact mode sees natural forces at work. The fantasy mode sees conscious forces at work because a conscious agreement to suspend fact mode is required. Naturally, faith mode sees itself as fact mode, and fact mode sees faith mode as fantasy mode. All children, unless they are incapable, learn these modes, although definitions and expectations can change over a lifetime. Such is the case with Singer.

In his panoramic, multivolume autobiographies of his early years in Poland, Singer portrays little Isaac growing up in a family in which debate over the nature of reality was a nearly nightly event. Singer describes his family in his 1978 Nobel Prize acceptance speech:

My father's home on Krochmalna Street in Warsaw was a study house, a court of justice, a house of prayer, of storytelling. . . . As a child I had heard from my older brother and master, I. J. Singer, who later wrote *The Brothers Ashkenazi,* all the arguments that the rationalists . . . brought out against religion. I have heard from my father and mother all the answers that faith in God could offer to those who doubt and search for the truth. In our home . . . the eternal questions were more actual than the latest news in the Yiddish newspapers.[6]

Fifteen years earlier, in 1963, he noted that "our house was always filled with problems, doubts, and unrest."[7]

Of all these controversies Singer writes, "Although later in my life I read a great deal of philosophy, I never found more compelling arguments than those that came up in my own kitchen."[8]

And the child was no fool. Listening to his "hero" (his much older brother Israel Joshua) disdain a life spent studying the Torah, watching him discard his ritual dress, Singer recalls, "Every word which he said to me was a bomb, a real spiritual kind of explosion. And my parents were not really able to answer him. Because sooner or later my father began to scream, You Unbeliever, you wicked man. The fact that he screamed proved he couldn't answer."[9]

In a scene from "Growing Up," another memoir, Joshua's secularist hackles are raised by a storytelling visitor:

"How did Warsaw become Warsaw? [The guest asks rhetorically.] First they built one house, then another, and gradually a city emerged. Everything grows. Even stones grow."

"Stones don't grow, Reb Wolf Bear," my brother, Joshua, interjected.

"No? Well, so be it." [The guest goes on to describe the gateway to Gehenna, or Hell:]

"The earth is hollow there. There are caves underground and cities and who knows what else."

"The earth isn't hollow," my brother, Joshua, said.

"Why not? Everything is possible. . . . In Lublin [continues the undaunted guest] there was a wonder child, a Yenuka, and at the age of three he sprouted a beard. At five he gave a sermon in the synagogue. . . . He was married at seven. When he reached nine, his beard turned white as snow and he died."

"Did you see this Yenuka with your own eyes?" Joshua asked.

"See him? No. But the whole world knows about it."

My father arched the brows over his blue eyes and his red beard glowed like fire. "Joshua, don't contradict!"

"It isn't true," Joshua said. He turned pale and his blue eyes reflected scorn.

"Have you been everywhere and do you know the truth?" Father asked.

"The world is full of wonders. Only God the Almighty knows what goes on down here."

Young Isaac's reaction? He leaves the room in tears, unable to contain the turmoil engendered by the contrastive world conflicts: "It was all one great mystery. I went into my parents' bedroom and lay down in the dark" (229).

But the influences on Singer were not limited simply to belief and non-belief. Even between his parents there was fundamental disagreement. Before Joshua Singer died young from a heart attack, he left his own memoir, *Of a World That Is No More,* in which he wrote about the "mismatch" between his parents: "[M]y mother and my father . . . would have been a well-mated couple if she had been the husband and he had been the wife. . . . They were as different in spirit as in physique." [10] The Singers' ecstatic Hasidic father believed in miracles, believed the world was *tref,* or unclean; their mother was equally pious but more fretful and cerebral, a well-read, frustrated intellectual and the daughter of a famous Orthodox rabbi.

In "Why the Geese Shrieked," a wistful story first published in *A Day of Pleasure,* Isaac Singer remembers a long-ago day that altered his life. Most of us can remember a similar moment when fact and faith collided, when the vectoring of our own personal belief systems was set, and the side we rooted for perhaps did not win. As the rabbi for the tenement block where the family lived, Singer's father was often called on to judge lawsuits, divorces, and questions of dietary law. One day when Singer was eight, a woman entered the tiny apartment, her eyes full of fear. She laid two dead geese on the kitchen table and said, "Rabbi, I have a very unusual problem." [11] Her problem? The geese, although ritually slaughtered, shrieked in unholy voices, and the woman feared they were possessed. Singer's father paled, and the child Isaac felt himself fill with dread. This could be proof that the world of spirits really did exist: a sign from Heaven that Singer's father was a gifted rabbi elected to perform an exorcism—or it could be a sign from Hell. Singer's mother, however, "came from a family of rationalists and was by nature a skeptic."

"Slaughtered geese don't shriek," she said.

But these geese did. Alhough "headless, disemboweled—in short, ordinary dead geese," these geese, when the woman struck one against the other, emitted such a mournful and otherworldly sound that Singer himself shrieked and sought shelter in the maternal skirt. Two times the woman demonstrated the unearthly phenomenon. The eyes of Singer's father showed a mixture of "fear and vindication." "My father's voice became hoarse," the author remembers, and "broken by sobs" as he said, "'Well, can anyone still doubt that there *is* a creator?' Angrily, he looked at his wife and demanded, 'And what do you say now, eh?'" (41–42).

"'I cannot understand what is going on here,' she said, with a certain resentment. . . . 'I want to hear it again.' Her words were half pleading, half commanding."

For the third time the woman smacked the geese together, and for the third time the geese shrieked. "Suddenly my mother laughed. . . . 'Did you remove the windpipe?' . . . Mother took hold of one of the geese . . . and with all her might pulled out the thin tube. . . . I stood trembling. . . . Her hands had become bloodied. On her face could be seen the wrath of the rationalist whom someone has tried to frighten in broad daylight." And Singer's father's face? "He knew what had happened here: logic, cold logic, was again tearing down faith, mocking it" (43–44).

One more time, and this time with faith or fact hanging in the balance, the goose woman prepared to slap the birds against each other. The child's hope? "Although I was afraid I prayed inwardly the geese *would* shriek, shriek so loud that people in the street would hear." But the windpipeless fowl no longer shrieked.

Victoriously announcing, "That's all it was!" and, "there is always an explanation," the mother returned to the kitchen. Father and son sat together; suddenly the father spoke to Isaac "as if I were an adult. 'Your mother takes after your grandfather, the rabbi of Bilgoray. He is a great scholar, but a cold-blooded rationalist. People warned me before our betrothal'" (44–45).

You might think that the intelligent child Singer would have sided squarely with his mother, eschewing the more extreme tenets of fundamentalist Judaism; or that he would have joined his brother in becoming emancipated, worldly, and scientific. If you have read Singer, however, you know that didn't happen. As an adult writing for children, he often described children's fantasies and reveries, especially his own. The child Singer knew the difference between fact and fantasy and had witnessed the dethroning of faith by fact. Nonetheless, strange though it may be to say about a writer known for tales of demon possession and witches, Singer as an adult was not interested in fantasy. He did not merely write about ghosts or playfully imagine them: he actively sought them out. Dorothea Straus, Singer's friend and translator, and the wife of one of his publishers, tells of a day he visited their country home. The first thing Singer asked was, "Where is the ghost room?" He had heard Straus recount the tale of a haunted room in the house. Singer spent the day there and didn't find anything, but told his hosts, "You know that it is usually those who scoff at the existence of spirits who will most probably meet one. All my life I have searched for them, but so far, I have had no success."¹²

The key phrase in that statement is "so far." That is the language of faith. After all the kitchen controversies over contrastive realities that he heard in his youth, for Singer, faith was no fantasy. He believed, simply, that all the facts were not yet in: "[T]he supernatural is only a word for things whose existence we can't yet prove," he once said, noting that three hundred years ago no one believed in the existence of microbes. He continued, "I knew even as a child that the world which we see is not the whole world. Whether you call them demons or angels or some other name, I knew then, and I know now, that there are entities of whom we have no idea, and they do exist. . . . I also use them as symbols in my writing. . . . But it is not only a literary method, it is connected to a belief that the world is full of powers that we don't know."¹³

Singer put his mature, well-considered, conscious choice between faith, fact, and fantasy into literary form through the words of Reb Zebulun, a fictional storyteller whom the village children love. The Reb sounds a good deal like the dinnertime guest who so infuriated Joshua in "Growing Up." Actually, the Reb expresses only one of the consensual attitudes I have discussed: faith, the mode that Singer clearly grew to share. The Reb says: "The brain is created by God, and human thoughts and fantasies are also God's works. Even dreams are from God. If a thing doesn't happen today, it might easily happen tomorrow."¹⁴

Notes

1. Kathryn Hume, *Fantasy and Mimesis: Responses to Reality in Western Literature* (New York: Methuen, 1984), 83.
2. Isaac Bashevis Singer, "Growing Up," in *Stories for Children* (New York: Farrar, Straus and Giroux, 1984), 218. Page references in the text are to this edition.

3. Hume, 22.

4. Thomas Riggio, "Symbols of Faith: Isaac Bashevis Singer's Children's Books," in *Recovering the Canon: Essays on Isaac Bashevis Singer* (Leiden: Brill, 1986), 135.

5. Isaac Bashevis Singer, *A Little Boy in Search of God: Mysticism in a Personal Light* (New York: Doubleday, 1975), 36.

6. Cited in Dorothea Straus, *Under the Canopy* (New York: Braziller, 1982), 68.

7. Isaac Bashevis Singer, *A Day of Pleasure* (New York: Farrar, Straus and Giroux, 1963), 52.

8. Isaac Bashevis Singer, *In My Father's Court* (New York: Farrar, Straus and Giroux, 1962), 211.

9. Cited in Clive Sinclair, "A Conversation with Isaac Bashevis Singer," *Encounter* 52.2 (1979): 22.

10. Joshua Singer, *Of a World That Is No More* (New York: Vanguard, 1970), 30.

11. Isaac Bashevis Singer, "Why the Geese Shrieked," in *Stories for Children*, 41. Page references in the text are to this edition.

12. Cited in Straus, 23.

13. Richard Burgin and Isaac Bashevis Singer, *Conversations with Isaac Bashevis Singer* (New York: Doubleday, 1985), 105, 107.

14. I. B. Singer, *Stories*, 172.

A Real-World Source for the "Little People":
A Comparison of Fairies to
Individuals with Williams Syndrome

Howard M. Lenhoff

I would like to add a new wrinkle to some ideas concerning the origin of the forever young characters of folklore: the pixies, elves, and other fairies. Some historians, including Eugen Weber of UCLA, believe that a good deal of folklore is based on real-life situations.[1] Weber suggests, for example, that the story of Hansel and Gretel may have originated in times of famine when parents sacrificed children to improve their own chance of survival. Robert Gorlin, in "Facial Folklore," states, "In European folklore, physically deformed or mentally retarded children were often regarded as offspring of fairies, elves, or other subhuman beings." Supposedly these mentally and/or physically deformed "changelings" were substituted for normal children stolen by fairies.[2]

As my wrinkle, I suggest that some of the lore regarding the "wee people" developed from people's reactions to little understood mental and physical abnormalities found in a small percentage of newborns worldwide. I focus on a relatively newly described condition, Williams syndrome, sometimes called elfin facies syndrome.

During the late 1950s, some physicians in New Zealand, one of them J. C. P. Williams, encountered a number of infants having in common a specific heart problem, varying degrees of mental retardation, and certain facial features resembling those often ascribed to pixies of folklore.[3] Other physicians soon noticed similar features.[4] Still others observed that some of these infants had high levels of calcium in their blood.[5] It is now estimated that Williams syndrome affects about one in twenty thousand newborns, including currently some six thousand individuals in the United States and Great Britain.[6]

Individuals with Williams syndrome lack a small segment in one of their chromosomes, a segment containing the gene that controls the synthesis of the contractile protein elastin.[7] Lack of the gene for making elastin may account for only some of the characteristics of Williams syndrome, however; about twenty genes are missing, with about ten identified.

While reviewing the characteristics of Williams syndrome in 1986, Dr. J. Burn wrote: "Whether or not these children have elfin facies is difficult to establish, for while examples of the syndrome are common, this author has never seen an elf."[8] Burn's statement was contested by Mr. Gordon Biescar, former president of the Williams Syndrome Association, a parent support group. At a national meeting of the association held in Boston in 1990, Mr. Biescar said, "Of course Dr. Burn has seen elves before, because he has seen our Williams syndrome children." Biescar went on to suggest that Williams syndrome individuals have existed for ages, but storytellers unable to fathom the cause of their unique features referred to them as elves, pixies, brownies, and other such names, and thus the folk tales regarding the "good people" or "little people" began.

In this essay, I describe the facial features of individuals with Williams syndrome as compared with artists' renderings of elves and pixies, the distribution of a number of fairy legends and of Williams syndrome support groups, and similarities in behavioral and physical characteristics attributed to fairies and those observed in individuals with Williams syndrome.

Facial Features of Individuals with Williams Syndrome

Individuals having Williams syndrome tend to look more like each other than they do their parents. The two children shown in Figure 1 bear a striking resemblance, although they are not related. Their eyes have a slight squint, appear to be puffy, and are relatively close together. There is a depressed nasal bridge with a small, upturned "pug" nose. Each child has a wide mouth with full lips and a small chin with receding jaw.

Although authors and artists have depicted elves and pixies in various forms, certain features reappear frequently, including small stature and an upturned nose. N. Arrowsmith speaks of pixies with "turned up noses,"

Figure 1. Two unrelated children with Williams syndrome: Alexander "Alex" Biescar of Texas (L) at age 3 and Daniel Patrick Smith of California (R) at age 4. Photo of Alex Biescar: Houston Chronicle. Photo of Daniel Smith: Kristine Recalde Photography.

Figure 2. Detail from *Wood Elves Hiding and Watching a Lady* by Richard Doyle. From *Richard Doyle and His Family,* catalog from an exhibition held at the Victoria and Albert Museum, 30 November 1983–26 February 1984 (London: Victoria and Albert Museum, 1983).

Figure 3. Garden ornament of a cross-legged pixie, designed by H. Simeon and produced by Royal Doulton, c1920. Photograph taken from A. Packer, S. Beddoe, and L. Jarrett, *Fairies in Legend and the Arts* (London: Cameron and Taylor, 1980), 18.

and of brownies as having "no real noses, just two nostrils."[9] K. M. Briggs gives similar descriptions of the nose of brownies.[10] Figure 2 shows an elf drawn more than one hundred years ago by British artist Richard Doyle in his *Wood Elves Hiding and Watching a Lady,* and Figure 3 shows a garden ornament depicting a pixie. Both characters have a remarkable resemblance to individuals with Williams syndrome. Notice that the ears of the pixie in Figure 3 are pointed and relatively large. This feature, often seen in artists' drawings of fairy folk and regularly mentioned in descriptions, may represent the sensitivity of those mythical individuals to sound and music, characteristics exhibited to a high degree by many individuals with Williams syndrome.[11] It may also be an artistic exaggeration of the prominent earlobes often observed in Williams syndrome individuals.[12]

Distribution of Tales of Fairies and of Individuals with Williams Syndrome

The concept and lore of fairies, the "good people" and "little people," occur in cultures worldwide. Great Britain has fairies, elves, brownies, sprites, and Puck; Scandinavia has the trolls (Arrowsmith 198); Germany, the kobolds and hinzelmännchens (Arrowsmith 135, 248); and Italy, the fates or fatas (Arrowsmith 252–55).[13] Arab literature describes jinnis (jan, geni) and mubarakin; Hawaii and Polynesia have menehunes; China has the Hsien, and Japan, the flower fairy; among some North American Indians we find the pukwudjies; and among some Africans, the yumboes.[14]

Williams syndrome also has a widespread distribution. Parent support groups exist in Australia, Belgium, Canada, Chile, England, France, Germany, Ireland, Israel, Japan, Malta, Mexico, New Zealand, Norway, Portugal, Sweden, and the United States.[15] There is little doubt that as awareness of Williams syndrome spreads, individuals with the syndrome will be found in much of the world. In the United States and Great Britain, Williams syndrome is known to occur in families of African and East Indian descent. I recently met in Israel a young woman with Williams syndrome whose family came from Yemen.

Comparing the "Fairy Syndrome" with Williams Syndrome

The term *syndrome* is generally used to refer to a group of signs or symptoms that characterize a particular condition. Individuals with Williams syndrome have many symptoms in common, but each does not necessarily display all of the symptoms to the same degree. For purposes of comparison, I have assembled descriptions of many of the characteristics ascribed to fairies of folk tales to define the "fairy syndrome." Searching through anthologies and secondary literature sources dealing with fairies, I found a number of recurring physical and behavioral characteristics remarkably similar to those of individuals with Williams syndrome. I also found a number of less frequently mentioned idiosyncrasies of fairies similar to attributes common among those with Williams syndrome. Aside from the facial features already noted, I found seven key characteristics: stature; kindness; sensitivity; love of music, song, and dance; hyperacusis; fascination with circles and spinning objects; and orderliness and concern for the future.

Stature   The "little people" are known for their small stature. Fairies have been described to be as tall as five feet and as small as the size of a thumb. The descriptions of size often seem to be exaggerated, some tales even suggesting that fairies grow smaller the longer one looks at them. Individuals with Williams syndrome are usually short; the average height for males is five to five and one-half feet, and for females, four to five feet, although there may be exceptions.[16] Their overall height may be determined by their digestive problems during infancy and, in the case of females, the relatively early puberty.[17] Some fairies have been described as misshapen, as having an unusual gait, a groove along their backs, or both (Arrowsmith 26, 55, 192, 201). Individuals with Williams syndrome have an unusual gait, often walking on their toes as infants, and have to varying degrees a curvature of the spine known as kyphosis and lordosis.[18]

Kindness   Most frequently referred to as the "good people," fairies are said to be kind and gentle-hearted. Likewise, individuals with Williams syndrome are characterized by their loving, trusting, and caring nature and extreme sensitivity to the feelings of others.[19] The kindheartedness of some fairies is especially evident in their attitude toward children. According to some legends, fairies may steal children and substitute "changelings" (i.e., physically or mentally disabled children) for them.[20] Williams syndrome individuals, especially young adults, are attracted to babies and make a great fuss over them, and the infants usually sense their warmth and reciprocate. Williams syndrome individuals also seem to have an uncanny way of befriending animals, a characteristic also shared by the fairies of folk literature.

Sensitivity   Although fairies are considered good-natured, they are also mischievous and sensitive to ridicule. Arrowsmith says that elves "should be treated with respect, and never insulted or mocked" (74). L. C. Jones writes, "Getting along with little people takes a certain amount of patience and understanding, and a knowledge of the actions which annoy and anger them. They are a touchy lot and many are the sources of their irritation." He also states that one must either use "most carefully ordered compliments or [not] speak to them at all."[21] A similar sensitivity is common among individuals with Williams syndrome. They become upset when criticized or ridiculed and seem to need constant approval, especially from adults. They retain this childlike sensitivity to criticism throughout much of their adult lives.[22]

Love of Music, Song, and Dance   Another recurring attribute of fairies is their passion for music, song, and dance. Briggs says that "they dance and love music."[23] The hinzelmännchen of German legend are said to love "to repeat songs they have heard."[24] Elves and sirens are reported to sing melodies that "enchant" humans" (Arrowsmith 169, 237). Jones writes that "fairies are people who sing instead of talking,"[25] and Arrowsmith claims that "their music without compare, [is] a joy to listen to" and their "favorite occupation is dancing" (20, 25). Some legends tell of the dancing of fairies making the "crops grow better" (Arrowsmith 179, 190). There is growing evidence that individuals with Williams syndrome have a great love and talent for music.[26] Although not yet fully documented, this unique feature has been discussed a great deal at recent meetings of Williams syndrome support groups worldwide. It appears that a high percentage of individuals with Williams syndrome have perfect pitch, are able to retain the words and melodies of a remarkable number of songs, have great recall of melodies and lyrics, have a facility with foreign language and accents, and enjoy song and dance. Some play musical instruments proficiently, learning by ear. For a large number, music is a major outlet.

At this point I need to describe our forty-three-year-old daughter, Gloria. She has exhibited many of the characteristics common to children with Williams syndrome since infancy, but when she was born in 1955, the syndrome had not yet been recognized. My wife and I did not realize that she had Williams syndrome until the spring of 1988 when we received a number of letters and phone calls following the broadcast of a television special about her. That program, titled *Bravo Gloria,*[27] described her life as a mentally disabled adult and her particular talent for singing and playing the accordion. She sings in twenty-five languages, chats in about a dozen tongues, and has a repertoire of more than two thousand songs. She has perfect pitch and an operatic lyric soprano voice, and she plays popular, folk, rock, blues, and classical music on the piano accordion.

We thought that Gloria might be unusual among Williams syndrome individuals; however, when she performed at functions sponsored by Williams syndrome support groups, we soon noticed that many Williams syndrome children and adults showed similar talents with the organ, piano, keyboard, guitar, saxophone, or other instruments. The Williams Syndrome Association and Foundation sponsor a week-long music and arts summer camp for Williams syndrome individuals at Belvoir Terrace in Lenox, Massachusetts, adjacent to the Tanglewood Music Center. A current goal of the Williams Syndrome Foundation is to develop several residential academies of the musical arts for musically gifted mentally asymmetric individuals.

Hyperacusis   Their talent for music may be related to the special characteristic common to Williams syndrome individuals known as hyperacusis, an extreme sensitivity to sound, often to the point of its being painful.[28] Their hyperacusis may also account, at least in part, for the unusually rich vocabulary and remarkable storytelling abilities of adolescent and older Williams syndrome individuals.[29] Although I could not find many examples of fairies being hypersensitive to sounds, there are a number of related stories. For example, "Two things the Knockers despise most are whistling and swearing; whistling sends them into fits of rage" (Arrowsmith 39–40). Arrowsmith also writes about the Tomtrå and Nissen of Sweden: "All loud noises and irregularities are forbidden" (53).

Possibly related to hyperacusis is the ability to detect and awaken to slight noises. Williams syndrome children are notoriously restless, and it may be years before they begin to sleep through an entire night on a regular basis. Even the adults detect the slightest sounds at night, and in an almost ghostlike fashion will quietly appear to check on any minor disturbance. So it is with many fairies, who are active at night when everyone else is sleeping. There are many stories from England, for example, of the brownies who clean homes and do their good deeds in the nighttime and disappear at daybreak.[30] In fact, it is this trait of the brownies that led Robert Baden-Powell of England, the founder of the scouting movement, to use that name for young Girl Scouts "who like to be useful as well as to play."[31]

Fascination with Circles and Spinning Objects   Another feature fairies and individuals with Williams syndrome have in common is their attraction to circles and spinning objects. Fairy tales tied to spinning wheels and fortune-telling spinning women (e.g., the Three Fates), are common. When fairies dance, they always dance in circles, never in squares or lines. For example, Hecate, in *Macbeth,* says, "Like elves and fairies in a ring, enchanting all that you put in."[32] Some tales describe how spinning objects can be used to distract elves; for example, "[to] distract tree elves, bring something to spin and something to eat" and say, "Eat and spin and forget my child" (Arrowsmith 18). Individuals with Williams syndrome also have a special fascination with spinning. They will watch spinning objects, whether these be tops, record turntables, mechanical toys, or washing machines and dryers, for hours.

Orderliness and Concern for the Future   Another recurring theme in stories about fairies that reflects behavioral characteristics of individuals with Williams syndrome is a concern for order and the future. Briggs refers to fairies as "greatly concerned with order and cleanliness."[33] The Will 'o the Wisp, "[b]ecause of their insecurity . . . are worried about the future" (Arrowsmith 34).

The Tomtrå and Nissen of Sweden are said to have a rigid feeding schedule (Arrowsmith 165); likewise, the "Rusalkies are tied to a rigid schedule" (Arrowsmith 189). The same appears to hold true for individuals with Williams syndrome. Every day has a routine that is followed religiously. Any change in their daily routine throws them off balance. Most work best when the day's events proceed as planned. They also enjoy planning ahead. No matter how exciting a day may be, once its events are over, their minds and conversations move immediately toward the future and what it will bring.

In reviewing the physical and behavioral characteristics shared by the fairies of legend and individuals with Williams syndrome, I find the similarities too striking to be merely coincidental. There is no doubt that authors of oral and written folk tales in earlier times encountered dwarfs and other individuals whose physical and mental handicaps set them apart from the main population. Their lack of understanding of genetics and human embryology led them to invent magical and mystical explanations to account for these unusual people and their behaviors. In this essay I provide evidence to support the hypothesis that some of those legends evolved from encounters with individuals having Williams syndrome.

Analyzing Shakespeare's treatment of fairies, Thomas Keightly in 1850 wrote: "His Fairies agree with [the descriptions of elves] . . . in their diminutive stature . . . fondness for dancing, their love of cleanliness, and their child-abstracting propensities."[34] In those words Keightly could just as well have been describing individuals with Williams syndrome.

Notes

I thank George Slusser, William Lillyman, Eric Rabkin, and Howard Hendrix for their encouragement and suggestions; Sylvia G. Lenhoff and Bernie Lenhoff for their editorial suggestions; the Williams Syndrome Foundation–USA for information on Williams syndrome, help in acquiring the photographs of the children with Williams syndrome, and permissions; the librarians of the J. Lloyd Eaton Collection at the University of California, Riverside; Eddie Yeghiayan and Lorelei Tanji of the University of California, Irvine, library; Martha Gallegos of the Girl Scout Council of Orange County; and, last but not least, my daughter Gloria, who was born with Williams syndrome, and who has entertained audiences over the world with her remarkable talents as an accordionist and soprano. (At the end of the original presentation of this paper, Gloria sang two numbers: the Chinese folk song "Hwa Fay Hwa" and both parts of "Sound the Trumpet," a duet for sopranos by Purcell. As did the fairies of yore, Gloria enchanted the conferees with her music.)

1. Eugen Weber, *My France: Politics, Culture, Myth* (Cambridge: Harvard University Press, 1991), 77.

2. Robert J. Gorlin, "Facial Folklore," in *Developmental Medicine and Neonatal Genetics,* Mead Johnson Symposium on Perinatal and Developmental Medicine No. 22 (Evansville, Ind.: 1984), 43–44; no editors listed, but members of the advisory board for the series were Joseph B. Warshaw, Ronald S. Bloom, and John C. Sinclair.

3. See J. C. P. Williams, B. G. Barratt-Boyes, and J. B. Lowe, "Supravalvular Aortic Stenosis," *Circulation* 24 (1961): 1311–18; K. L. Jones and D. W. Smith, "The Williams Elfin Facies Syndrome: A New Perspective," *Pediatrics* 86 (1975): 718–23. Supravalvular aortic stenosis is a significant narrowing of large elastic arteries, especially of the large ascending aorta.

As will become clear, individuals with Williams syndrome do not fit typical definitions of mental retardation. Although most are deficient in the ability to solve simple arithmetic problems, they may have exceptional abilities in language and music. Hence, the board of trustees of the Williams Syndrome Foundation recommends that the term *mental asymmetry* be used to describe the mental capacities of individuals with Williams syndrome.

4. A. J. Beuren, J. Apitz, and D. Harmjanz, "Supravalvular Aortic Stenosis in Association with Mental Retardation and Certain Facial Appearance," *Circulation* 26 (1962): 1235–40.

5. See J. A. Black and R. E. Bonham Carter, "Association between Aortic Stenosis and Facies of Severe Infantile Hypercalcaemia," *Lancet* 2 (1963): 745–49.

6. The Williams Syndrome Association in America has a membership of 4,000 families; another 1,800 belong to the Williams Syndrome Foundation of the United Kingdom. Others are known to exist worldwide.

7. See A. Ewart, C. Morris, M. Keating, M. Leppert, K. Sternes, P. Spallone, and A. Stock, "Hemizygosity at the Elastin Locus in a Developmental Disorder, Williams Syndrome," *Nature Genetics* 5 (September 1993): 11–16. This gene is apparently lost by a microdeletion of a number 7 chromosome that occurs in the sperm or egg just before fertilization. Hence, neither parent lacks those genes, but there is one chance in two that offspring with Williams syndrome will pass on the chromosome with the microdeletion to their children. If that chromosome is passed on, the next generation will also show the characteristics of Williams syndrome.

8. J. Burn, "Williams Syndrome," *Journal of Medical Genetics* 23 (1986): 389–95.

9. N. Arrowsmith, *A Field Guide to the Little People* (London: Macmillan, 1977), 134, 193–94. Later page references in the text are to this edition.

10. K. M. Briggs, *The Anatomy of Puck* (London: Routledge and Kegan Paul, 1959), 186.

11. As Howard V. Hendrix suggested after this talk was presented at the 1993 Eaton Conference.

12. For example, see Ewart et al., fn. 11.

13. See Briggs, 21.

14. *Encyclopaedia Britannica,* 11th ed. (New York: Encyclopaedia Britannica, 1911), 10:134–35. K. Luomala, *The Menehune of Polynesia and Other Mythical Little People of Oceania* (New York: Kraus, 1976); G. Jobes, *Dictionary of Mythology, Folklore and Symbols* (New York: Scarecrow, 1961–62); *World Book Encyclopedia* (Chicago: Field Corp., 1962), 6:13; Jobes, 1300; T. Keightley, *The Fairy Mythology* (1850; New York: Haskell House, 1968), 495.

15. Information supplied by Williams Syndrome Association, P.O. Box 297, Clawson, MI 48017-0297.

16. C. A. Morris, C. O. Leonard, C. Dilts, and S. A. Demsey, "Adults with Williams Syndrome," *American Journal of Medical Genetics,* suppl. 6 (1990): 102–7.

17. C. A. Morris, S. A. Demsey, C. O. Leonard, C. Dilts, and B. L. Blackburn, "Natural History of Williams Syndrome: Physical Characteristics," *Journal of Pediatrics* 113 (1988): 318–26.

18. Morris et al., 1988.

19. J. Reilly, E. S. Klima, and U. Bellugi, "Once More with Feeling: Affect of Language in Atypical Populations," *Development and Psychopathology* 2 (1992): 367–91.

20. Gorlin, 43–44.

21. L. C. Jones, "The Little People," *New York Folklore Quarterly* 13 (1962): 243–64.

22. O. Udwin and W. Yule, *Williams Syndrome: Guidelines for Parents* (Tonbridge, Kent: Williams Syndrome Association, 1998), 31 pp.

23. Briggs, 14.

24. *World Book Encyclopedia,* 6:14.

25. Jones, 248.

26. Howard Lenhoff, "Musical Ability of a Williams Syndrome Adult: A Case Study," *Williams Syndrome Professional Symposium, Abstracts* (1990), 31; Howard M. Lenhoff, "Insights into the Musical Potential of Cognitively Impaired People Diagnosed with Williams Syndrome," *Music Theory Perspectives* 16 (1998): 33–36.

27. Produced by J. Maas, Cornell University; directed by Arlene Alda. Released by Public Broadcasting System, May 1988. The program was funded by the MacArthur Foundation and is available in two thousand public libraries in the United States as part of the MacArthur Foundation Mental Health Series.

28. A. J. Klein, B. L. Armstrong, M. K. Greer, and F. R. Brown, "Hyperacusis and Otitis Media in Individuals with Williams Syndrome," *Journal of Speech and Hearing Disorders* 55 (1990): 339–44.

29. Reilly et al.; H. M. Lenhoff, P. P. Wang, F. Greenberg, and U. Bellagi, "Williams Syndrome and the Brain," *Scientific American* 277 (1997): 42–47.

30. G. Edwards, *Hobgoblin and Sweet Puck* (London: Geoffrey Bles, 1974), 103–4.

31. R. Mitchell, *Brownie Scout Handbook* (New York: Girl Scouts of the United States of America, 1951), 9.

32. William Shakespeare, *The Tragedy of Macbeth* (1623), act 4, scene 1, lines 42–44.

33. Briggs, 14.

34. Keightly, *Fairy Mythology,* 325.

Coming of Age in Fantasyland: The Self-Parenting Child in Walt Disney Animated Films

Lynne Lundquist and Gary Westfahl

Recent studies of children's literature commonly assert that a certain work is "subversive" in one way or another, so this once-alarming claim may have lost all capacity to shock or surprise. Unless, perhaps, the charge is aimed at a body of works that are universally regarded as extremely conservative and conventional in every way: the Walt Disney animated films. Indeed, someone in search of entertainment that affirms "traditional family values" would probably look first to Disney, since no other company has so vigorously promoted itself as a purveyor of wholesome, family-oriented movies. Yet if we examine the best known and most popular Disney films—the full-length animated features—we discover one curious feature. In these films about family values, *there are no families,* at least in the way that they are typically defined: a mother and father, often accompanied by siblings, grandparents, or other relatives, who both nurture and control a child. Instead, we find children who are separated or estranged from their families, or children living in various types of shattered or dysfunctional families. This in itself suggests that these apparently innocuous and unthreatening films may conceal a troubling and subversive subtext.

Examining first the major human characters in these animated films, we notice numerous children who lack parents: Pinocchio (*Pinocchio,* 1939), magically brought to life by the Blue Fairy without genuine parents; Peter Pan (*Peter Pan,* 1953), of course; Arthur in *The Sword in the Stone* (1963); Mowgli in *The Jungle Book* (1966); Penny in *The Rescuers*

(1976); Taran in *The Black Cauldron* (1984); Prince Eric in *The Little Mermaid* (1989); and Aladdin (*Aladdin,* 1992).

Next are children with single parents. Strangely—a point to study later—there is only one child with a single mother, Cody in *The Rescuers Down Under* (1990), although two adaptations of famous fairy tales (*Snow White and the Seven Dwarfs,* 1937; and *Cinderella,* 1950) feature daughters with single stepmothers. There are boys or young men with single fathers (Prince Charming in *Cinderella;* and Prince Phillip in *Sleeping Beauty,* 1958), boys with single foster fathers (such as Pinocchio; and Quasimodo in *The Hunchback of Notre Dame,* 1996), and daughters with single fathers (such as Ariel in *The Little Mermaid;* Belle in *Beauty and the Beast,* 1991; Princess Jasmine in *Aladdin;* and Pocahontas in *Pocahontas,* 1995).

Finally, there are children with parents who appear distant or uninvolved. The parents of Wendy, John, and Michael of *Peter Pan* seem loving and devoted, but they do regularly leave their children in the care of a dog, and they leave the children alone and unprotected on an evening when a visit from a mysterious stranger seems imminent. Alice in *Alice in Wonderland* (1950) has a normal set of parents, we assume, but we never see them; we only see Alice being supervised by an older sister. The parents of Princess Aurora of *Sleeping Beauty* agree to let three fairies take their infant daughter and raise her until the age of sixteen, so they are voluntarily not part of her young life. And the parents of the girl in *Oliver and Company* (1988) have gone on an extended trip—something they do habitually—leaving her in the care of servants.[1]

Confronted with this pattern of absent or broken families, one could respond with two explanations. First, perhaps Disney writers and animators are simply controlled by their source materials, which often stipulate unusual situations, so the reason for these odd families must be sought in the original texts, not the film adaptations. In some cases, this is surely true; it is hard to imagine, for example, how one might adapt *Cinderella* or *Peter Pan* so as to provide the title characters with a normal set of parents. But in other cases that explanation does not hold: a few films, such as *Oliver and Company* and *The Rescuers Down Under,* are basically original creations,[2] and the source materials of other films do not demand an unusual family structure. The story "Sleeping Beauty" does not state that the princess grows up separated from her parents, and neither Hans Christian Andersen's "The Little Mermaid" nor the histories of Pocahontas stipulate that the heroine lacks a mother. Most striking of all is

Aladdin. While all other versions of the story include Aladdin's mother as an active character, the Disney version removes her from the scene; far from being forced to rely on a story about an orphan, here the animators contradicted their source material and deliberately made their protagonist an orphan. Also, any number of familiar fairy tales feature more conventional families—including "Rumpelstiltskin," "The Elves and the Shoemaker," "The Princess and the Pea," and "King Thrushbeard"—but the Disney company has not used them, as if there were some desire to avoid depicting normal families.

A second explanation is that these absent or shattered families are presented to evoke a sense of pathos; young characters quickly earn the audience's sympathy because they lack normal parents. Again, there is some truth in this response; but also again it is not wholly satisfactory, for there are other devices for separating children from parents—misunderstandings, accidents, or criminal activities—involving no permanent disruption of the family unit. The characteristic strategy of Disney animated films is final or injurious separation. How funny would *Home Alone* have been if Kevin's parents had died or had deliberately left him alone? However, such permanent or willful parental absence is exactly the sort of situation that often confronts a child at the start of a Disney film.

We are driven, then, to this hypothesis: the premise preferred by the writers and animators who create these films is the destroyed or shattered family, and the characteristic problem confronting their young characters is the need to compensate for their irremediable lack of one or both parents.

Children and young people in Disney animated films employ two strategies to replace their absent or inadequate families. The first could be described as a reconciliation with nature: without nurturing support from parents, the young person turns to the natural world, to sympathetic and often anthropomorphic animals who can provide that support. Thus, after fleeing through a stormy forest, Snow White is surrounded by forest animals who comfort her. When the Blue Fairy brings *Pinocchio* to life, she appoints an insect named Jiminy Cricket as his mentor and companion. Arthur of *The Sword in the Stone* is supervised by a talking owl when he travels to London. Mowgli of *The Jungle Book,* of course, is raised by wolves and later guided by a bear and a panther. Penny of *The Rescuers* is helped by two mice, Bernard and Miss Bianca, from the Rescue Aid Society. King Triton of *The Little Mermaid* appoints the crab Sebastian to serve as his daughter's guardian. Cody of *The Rescuers Down Under* bonds with a mighty mother eagle, and is later rescued by Bernard and Miss Bianca.[3] (Animals in other Disney films also provide support, but they are more like friends than parents: Princess Aurora of *Sleeping Beauty* frolics with some forest animals; the girl in *Oliver and Company* turns to the kitten Oliver for companionship; Ariel, of *The Little Mermaid,* has a flounder and seagull as her friends; Aladdin has a pet monkey, Abu, and Princess Jasmine has a protective pet tiger named Rajah; and Pocahontas has a rambunctious pet raccoon.)

The other strategy is to seek out or find a surrogate parent—a friendly adult, typically a magical being who can provide the support and guidance of a parent. Snow White finds seven dwarfs to protect her from the Queen, Pinocchio is adopted by the woodcutter Geppetto, and Cinderella finds a fairy godmother. Peter Pan enjoys the help of the adult Tinker Bell, who saves him from Captain Hook. Aurora of *Sleeping Beauty* is raised by motherly fairies. Arthur of *The Sword in the Stone* is taken in by Merlin the Magician; Taran in *The Black Cauldron* finds a sorcerer to serve as a father figure; Aladdin stumbles on a friendly genie to help him woo Princess Jasmine; and Pocahontas obtains advice and guidance from an ancient talking tree, Grandmother Willow.

All these developments might serve a transitional function, temporarily helping children deal with an unpleasant situation until the normal family can be restored, or until a new normal family can be created. And some of the films in which human characters are subordinate to animal characters—such as *The Rescuers, Oliver and Company,* and *The Rescuers Down Under*—do move to this kind of conclusion: after being helped by Bernard and Miss Bianca, Penny is adopted by two loving parents; after the crisis provoked by her pet cat, the girl in *Oliver and Company* is reunited with her parents; and although Cody in *The Rescuers Down Under* is last seen as the triumphant master of his natural realm, riding the mighty eagle to America, we assume he will soon be reunited with his mother.

In other Disney animated films, however, something different happens: the children's mentors do not give way to true parents and do not retain the role of surrogate parents. Instead there occurs a role reversal: although animals and magical adults first appear in parental roles, the children later assume the parental roles, with the animals and adults recast as their children. In effect, children manage to construct their own families, with themselves as parents.

The pattern is twice enacted in the first Disney animated film, *Snow*

White and the Seven Dwarfs. When they first appear, the forest animals comfort Snow White as she is sadly crying in the forest; but after she pulls herself together and becomes a little more cheerful, she takes charge of the animals and issues commands as they clean up the dwarfs' cottage. Snow White initially appeals to the dwarfs for protection against the Queen, but then she begins to act like their mother—cooking their meals, scolding them to wash their hands before eating, and kissing them good-bye as they go off to work.

The ostensible child who functions as a parent also appears in the second Disney animated film, *Pinocchio.* Although Jiminy is assigned to be Pinocchio's conscience, the puppet-boy completely ignores him, never asks for advice, and goes where he pleases, leaving the cricket to literally and figuratively play the role of Pinocchio's follower throughout the film. Pinocchio twice disobeys Geppetto by abandoning school to join Stromboli's puppet show, and by going to Pleasure Island; and he decides to rescue the drowning Geppetto even though the woodcutter tells him not to do so. From the beginning to the end of the film, Pinocchio is completely in control of his own actions, and Jiminy Cricket and Geppetto are little more than his puppets.

Similar role reversals occur in other animated films. Despite their careful parenting, the fairies in *Sleeping Beauty* cannot prevent Aurora from falling in love with a handsome stranger. Baloo the bear and Bagheera the panther of *The Jungle Book* are powerless to keep Mowgli from doing what he wants; Ariel does what she pleases, despite the advice of her aquatic friends; Aladdin soon learns how to manipulate and control his genie; and Pocahontas becomes an assertive voice for peace in her tribe. The most extreme such case is *The Sword in the Stone:* when young Arthur announces that he is going to London against Merlin's wishes, the magician angrily vanishes, abandoning his parental role and leaving Arthur completely in control of his own actions; the owl Archimedes tries to replace Merlin as tutor and guide but remains subordinate to Arthur; and Arthur then pulls the sword from the stone and becomes king of England—making himself the ultimate parental figure.

A variation of this pattern occurs in *Cinderella* and *Peter Pan.* Here, the child is already in a position of dominance when first seen; that is, while Cinderella may have initially turned to the household animals to console her in her times of unhappiness, by the time the movie begins she, like Snow White, has established herself as their parent, feeding, dressing, and fussing over them. Similarly, Peter Pan was no doubt a rather helpless figure when he first came to Neverland, but at the start of the film he is the leader of the Lost Boys and Tinker Bell's master. In these films, the crucial action is a crisis that temporarily returns the child-parent to the status of a child, so that animals and magical beings must temporarily resume the role of parents. When Cinderella is reduced to despair because she has no dress for the ball, the mice and birds come to her rescue by crafting a beautiful dress for her; and when Peter Pan naïvely opens the deadly present from Captain Hook, Tinker Bell rushes to save him, like a good mother. Once the crisis has passed, however, Cinderella and Peter Pan return to their parental roles; indeed, it is interesting that in the one major change from J. M. Barrie's original story, the Disney version of *Peter Pan* has the Lost Boys stay behind with Peter in Neverland so that he can remain a dominant parental figure.

Far from affirming "traditional family values," then, these animated films directly argue against them. Their message is that parents are not an important element in childhood: children can prosper without true parents or effective parents, and when they encounter parentlike figures, they can learn how to dominate and control those potential surrogate parents. In effect, children in Disney animated films create their own families and make themselves the parents.[4]

Some readers may not accept our thesis that these classic and beloved films are a functional assault on American family values. The true test of a model is how well it explains otherwise puzzling aspects of its subject, and we can employ this model to propose solutions to a few problems raised by the Disney animated films.

We have already alluded to the first problem: the peculiar and conspicuous absence of mothers in these films. This is crucial, for while fathers were once traditionally allowed to periodically leave the home or be absent for extended periods, the established role of the mother was to always be at home, nurturing the children and keeping the family functioning as a unit. Thus, removing the mother rather than the father—the usual preference in these films—is the strongest device for attacking the family. Yet these films rarely lack a strong female figure. A key transformation occurs, however: the mother figure is recast as a powerful villainess.

The transformation is transparent in *Snow White and the Seven Dwarfs* and *Cinderella,* in which the evil woman is a *step*mother, not a true mother, but other films have domineering, malevolent women who are less obviously mothers in disguise—the Red Queen of *Alice in Wonderland,* the fairy Maleficent in *Sleeping Beauty,* Madame Mim in *The Sword* *in the Stone,* Madame Medusa in *The Rescuers,* and Ursula in *The Little Mermaid.* Watching boys and girls without mothers struggling to free themselves from the evil machinations of powerful older women, we witness an enactment of children struggling to free themselves from their families, as personified by the figures who most strongly hold those families together, the mothers. In contrast, the early Disney films feature relatively few male villains, the prominent exceptions being Stromboli and the Coachman in *Pinocchio* and Captain Hook in *Peter Pan,* who in that film, as in the play, is a version of the children's father, Mr. Darling (on the stage, the same actor plays both roles, and in the Disney film, Hans Conreid provided the voice for both roles).

Yet, an odd shift has occurred in recent Disney animated films: except for *The Little Mermaid,* these films focus on powerful male villains who are warped transformations of the father figure: the Horned King in *The Black Cauldron,* Bill Sykes in *Oliver and Company,* McHeath in *The Rescuers Down Under,* Gaston in *Beauty and the Beast,* the Grand Vizier of *Aladdin,* the English colonialist of *Pocahontas,* Frollo of *The Hunchback of Notre Dame,* and Hades in *Hercules* (1997).[5] After relying on villainous women in its previous films, why has Disney suddenly shifted, in the last ten years, to an emphasis on villainous men?

Our answer is this: the idealized image of the family has radically changed in recent times. Modern fathers are not supposed to be distant or absent, leaving mothers to care for and unite the family; instead, fathers are supposed to be intimately involved in all aspects of family life, participating as equals in nurturing children and maintaining the family. In other words, at the very moment when the father assumed a new prominence as an avatar of family values, Disney animated films gave new prominence to the evil, domineering male villain. This cannot be coincidental; it must represent a recognition that a modern attack on family values must focus on the father as well as on the mother.

Our model may also offer some insight regarding what must be regarded as the strangest and most problematic of the Disney animated films, *Alice in Wonderland.* Based on a popular children's classic, the film features, as most critics agree, many colorful and entertaining characters, some brilliantly creative animation, and a soundtrack filled with memorable songs. Thus, *Alice in Wonderland* should have been highly successful. However, it is widely viewed as Disney's most spectacular failure: it is one of the few animated features that lost money on its initial release, the first Disney animated film to be shown on television (as early as 1954), and one of the few films that has never been rereleased to theaters. What is wrong with this movie?

Although other explanations have been offered, our model provides the answer: overly constrained by very familiar source material, Disney writers and animators could not make *Alice in Wonderland* fit the pattern of the family-creating, self-parenting child, so the film lacked appeal both to its creators and to its audiences.

At the start of the film, we see Alice as a young girl who wishes to follow in the footsteps of other Disney children. The first song she sings, "In a World of My Own," may be the purest expression of the impulse that drives these independent youths:

> Cats and rabbits
> Would reside in fancy little houses
> And be dressed in shoes and fancy trousers
> In a world of my own.
> All the flowers
> Would have very extra-special powers;
> I would sit and talk to them for hours
> When I'm lonely in a world of my own. . . .
> I would listen to a babbling brook
> And hear a song that I could understand.
> I keep hoping it could be that way,
> because my world would be a Wonderland.

Like other Disney children, Alice is ready to abandon her family, at least temporarily, to establish rapport with anthropomorphic animals and make herself a parent in her own world.

Unfortunately, Alice cannot accomplish these goals. She tries to establish sympathetic contact with the natural world, but the animals she encounters—the White Rabbit, the talking flowers, the caterpillar, and the Cheshire Cat—are either hostile or enigmatic. She encounters adults who might serve as surrogate parents—Tweedledum and Tweedledee, the Mad Hatter, and the Red Queen—but these people are also unhelpful and sometimes maddening. Unable to dominate the animals or the magical adults, or even to connect with them, Alice cannot begin to construct her own family with herself as a parent. Late in the film, at a time when other Disney children have established themselves as the centers of their own families, we see Alice sitting alone in the forest, crying her heart out, in a scene not found in Carroll's books that is an exact analogue to the forest scene in *Snow White and the Seven Dwarfs*. As she cries, various baffling creatures surround her and cry sympathetic tears. But, in contrast to *Snow White,* the creatures do not approach her, and Alice cannot parent them. Instead, they vanish, and she must travel by herself to another unsettling adventure. Unable to commune with or control her Wonderland, Alice must ultimately retreat, returning to her old life under the guidance of her older sister and finding, reassuringly, that Wonderland was only a dream.

The odd thing is that *Alice in Wonderland* is also the one Disney film that offers a traditional message: "there's no place like home." To be happy, Alice must remain at home, in what we presume is a normal family; if she goes away from home, she will get in trouble, find no worthwhile friends, and feel lost and confused. This is, presumably, the message that parents would want their children to hear; and it is surprising to find it only in a Disney movie that most critics and viewers despise.

Twentieth-century children are more independent and more rebellious to their parents than previous generations were, and one posited explanation has been the influence of disreputable literature. Vigorous crusades have been mounted to keep children away from pulp magazines, comic books, violent cartoons, and video games, all seen as causes of undesirable childhood or adolescent behavior. And during all these periods of alarm, Disney animated films have been cast as wholesome, desirable alternatives to these despised examples of children's subliterature. We suggest here that these films have, in fact, conveyed a subversive message of their own; and parents who insist on blaming outside influences for their children's bad conduct now have a new, and surprising, candidate for their concern and condemnation.

Notes

1. Because we are interested in how the movies affect young viewers, we consider only human characters; animals, no matter how anthropomorphic, are unlikely to be influential role models. Yet Disney's animal characters do display irregular family structures: *Dumbo* (1941) has no father and is separated from his mother; *Bambi* (1942) loses his mother and sees his father only sporadically; *The Aristocats* (1970) are a single mother cat and her kittens; the mouse in *The Great Mouse Detective* (1986) helps a little girl mouse find her single father; the cat in *Oliver and Company* is an orphan; and the eagle in *The Rescuers Down Under* is a single mother. These movies differ, though, in that the animals frequently not only marry—a typical conclusion in many

Disney films—but also go on to have children and establish their own normal families, as in *Lady and the Tramp* (1954) *101 Dalmatians* (1961), and *The Lion King* (1994).

2. *Oliver and Company* is derived, very loosely, from Charles Dickens's *Oliver Twist.*

3. A variation in this pattern occurs in two films featuring artificial structures: *Beauty and the Beast,* largely set in the Beast's mansion, and *The Hunchback of Notre Dame,* largely set in the cathedral. Here the protagonist establishes rapport not with creatures from the natural world but with man-made objects from the civilized world: a talking candlestick, clock, teapot, cup, and wardrobe for Belle; and three statues of gargoyles for Quasimodo.

4. Some may argue that these films are not truly "subversive." All children like pretending to be parents, and films appeal to that desire by depicting such situations. What's subversive about that? Just as children playing house must eventually return to their roles as children, however, films in which youths act as adults usually end with the characters returned to their previous status. Only the animated films lack such humbling or restorative endings; the child becomes not a temporary parent but a permanent parent. (Eric S. Rabkin suggested in conversation that audiences may find it easier to observe drastic role reversals when animated characters are involved.)

5. *Hercules,* released after our original research was completed, does violate the pattern noted here in one key respect: the goddess Hera, formerly portrayed as Hercules' vengeful, antagonistic stepmother, is recast as a loving mother, making this one case in which Disney animators altered source material to strengthen a maternal relationship. Perhaps this was done to differentiate the film from the television series *Hercules, the Legendary Journeys,* in which an offstage Hera is a recurring villainess; or perhaps complaints about the absence of sympathetic mothers in Disney films engendered this response.

Nasty Boys, Feminine Longing, and Mourning the Mother in J. M. Barrie's *Peter Pan* and Anne Rice's *The Witching Hour*

Stephanie Barbé Hammer

> The PPS chauvinism is, in some ways, more lethal than the standard blatant variety. The braggart doesn't hide the fact that he believes in two sets of rules. . . . [T]he PPS victim, on the other hand, is a master of deception.
> —Dan Kiley, *The Peter Pan Syndrome*

> Nasty boys don't ever change.
> —Janet Jackson, "Nasty" (1986)

In this essay I examine two authors who skew standard usage of the boy child as hero, yoking a supernatural juvenile male explicitly to young female desirers and entering into an increasingly critical revisionist dialogue with the male centering of the Oedipus complex.[1] But my analysis will be skewed as well, to the girl-desirers rather than the boy-objects, to perform two different sorts of interpretation: a rereading of a well-known canonical work (normally classified as juvenile literature), and a preliminary approach to an ambitious recent text. J. M. Barrie's drama-turned-narrative *Peter Pan* and Anne Rice's magnum opus *The Witching Hour* are among the twentieth century's most resonant childhood fantasies. What do these seemingly disparate works have in common? Both Peter Pan and his twentieth-century son Lasher form strange, shifting variations on the heterosexual couple with girl-mothers, and their power lies in their ability to infinitely repeat the coupling process. In this sense, Peter Pan and Lasher are supernatural, infantile Don Juans encased in fictional formats that seem themselves capable of infinite repetition in the mass media—as the many Peter Pan adaptations and Rice's sequels testify.

Both males are obsessed with the mother—a typical Oedipal drive—although not in the usual sense. Peter Pan's mythic resonance lies in perpetuating an act that is both erotically charged and (practically speaking) erotically empty—a paradox marked by the oppositions in his name: Peter, ascetic apostle of Christianity, and Pan, the sexual male satyr of pagan mythology. True to his contradictory nomenclature, Pan is the virgin boy who courts without sex, able to seduce generations of girl children to be his mother. In Rice's intensified rewriting of the scenario, the demon Lasher is a capricious male being of uncertain ontological status, often likened to a willful child who must be taught proper behavior and etiquette. He also repeats acts of seduction on generations of mothers and daughters to find the perfect vessel to be born from. Like Pan, Lasher would be a son completely on his own terms.

Both Barrie and Rice seem to invoke these supernatural male partners as desirable alternatives, from a feminine viewpoint, to the limited negotiations that female heroes can make within a society dominated by men, Barrie overtly, Rice covertly. Consequently, both characterize human adulthood by all the features of gendered capitalism and its concomitant woes: money plays an important role in both works, as do marriage and power struggles within the extended family. But for all the attractive "otherness" Pan and Lasher promise precisely because they are *not* biological men, their own fictions undercut their desirability. These constructions of the supernatural boy foreground the limitations of adult society while revealing how these characters are both formed by that ideology and inseparable from it. The limitations of gender and the problems of power cannot be overcome by magic; they are actually intensified, rather than bypassed, through the magical opportunities offered by what turn out to be profoundly nasty boys.

The giddy adaptations of *Peter Pan* that permeate American pop culture often deflect us from the original 1911 novel (based on the 1904 play), so that such critics as Martin Green extol the "charm" of Barrie over the better-known Disney animated film.[2] But much of the oddness of later adaptations, from Disney's sanitized sexuality to the covertly homoerotic Mary Martin musical, derives from the more conspicuous oddness of the original work. Although I am not the first to notice this, it is significant that critics ranging from Jack Zipes to Jacqueline Rose have invoked *Peter Pan*'s curious quality while being unable to name the source of its strangeness.[3]

Part of that strangeness stems from *Peter Pan*'s ability to travesty without reenacting fairy-tale romance. This romantic travesty (along with the gender trouble the term implies) aligns Barrie, in turn, with such tech-noir narratives as *The Terminator,* which *Peter Pan*—unlikely as it seems—resembles in certain key respects: most importantly in their similar anxieties about history as eternal repeatability and their similar plots. In both, perverse rivalries between abnormal male antagonists take place for possession of a potential mother. Stylistically the novel is also similar to the James Cameron film: for all its neoromantic theatrics, *Peter Pan* is, like *The Terminator,* a profoundly ugly story, powerful for us *because* of—not despite—that ugliness; it is a narrative whose whimsy veils but does not conceal a host of unspeakable, negative emotions: anger, frustration, guilt, envy, as well as forbidden desires of several sorts.

Read superficially, Barrie's novel offers a vicarious escape from the adult workaday world, and *Peter Pan*'s opening pages demand that we recognize the advantages of ephemeral, ahistorical Neverland over material, chronological London in a cutesified version of Plato's ideal/real dichotomy. At first, the difference seems enormous. Unlike the dreamy island "where children at play are forever beaching their coracles,"[4] Barrie's apparently sweet portrayal of the Darlings (the ideal family we should all aspire to) depicts all the grim realities of the Victorian household we encounter in Dickens and later in Freud—notably the bourgeois division of labor in which father fights the good fight at the office while mother functions as domestic angel.[5] In fact, the entire introductory scenery is so grotesquely unpleasant that the opening of *Peter Pan* should probably be read as satire. Power is strictly in the hands of the father, despite his utter silliness, and an anxious frugality governs the proceedings—one that acts with special force on females. In one creepy scene, Mr. Darling tots up child-care expenses in an account book, with a cold calculation reminiscent of Jonathan Swift's *A Modest Proposal,* while a respectful, just barely postpartum Mrs. Darling gazes up anxiously from her bed, wondering if she will be permitted to keep her baby. Elsewhere in the household, bourgeois appearances are kept up while costs are cut by engaging a ten-year-old girl as housekeeper and a female dog as nanny. And what Barbara Ehrenreich calls the middle-class "fear of falling" is always prevalent, for

Mr. Darling declares that if he does not attend the dinner party, he will lose his job and the entire family will be thrown into the street.

The parents have no sexual, emotional, or indeed personal relationship, and Barrie coyly indicates the sterility of their marriage: "Her romantic mind was like the tiny boxes, one within the other, that come from the puzzling east, however many you discover there is always one more, and her sweet mocking mouth had one kiss on it that Wendy could never get. . . . [Mr. Darling] got all of her except the innermost box and the kiss. He never knew about the box, and in time he gave up trying for the kiss" (2). Faced with these constricted possibilities, small wonder that Wendy decides to fly away, with a boy apparently very different from her father and brothers, to a place where she can run her own household and win the "respect" of an otherwise entirely male group (31)—the promise that seduces her to go in the first place.

But Wendy is really choosing between false opposites: Neverland proves to be, appropriately, rather like its almost namesake Disneyland, where one goes to a great deal of trouble and expense to acquire an illusion of total freedom, leisure, and "innocent" pleasure while the space one visits really mimics and reinscribes all the values of the place one sought to escape (as shown by the outrageous—though now corrected—sexual politics of the "Pirates of the Caribbean" ride). The fantasy is carefully constructed so the visitor is never exposed to any desire or pleasure not sanctified by Western capitalism; she never truly "leaves" the world she knows and is considerably poorer when she walks out than when she walked in.

So it is with Wendy in Neverland. The building of Wendy's house is a key moment in Barrie's narrative. The house is potentially a symbol of idealized feminine domesticity to contrast with the fallen materialistic Darling household; yet Wendy's house is symbolically and literally empty: no one really dwells in this feminine construction. Instead she must spend most of her time underground, laboring for her boys in the womblike cavern that is their real "home" but where, curiously, it is Peter, not Wendy, who presides. In this feminine space dominated by the masculine, Wendy's faint role of pretend mother has even less agency than that of Mrs. Darling, for she must fill Nana's and Liza's functions as well (mother, nanny, housekeeper). The curious result is that Wendy falls into the working class: she becomes a household drudge, and like all servants, she cleans and cooks for children who really are not hers (so she cannot even revel in the process or fact of their production) and for a master who is not her husband.

Wendy's life in Neverland, then, ironically exaggerates her mother's home life and incarnates the very "fear of falling" that her parents are struggling to avoid. Both the misguided patriarchal authority and the false economy of the Darling household are reproduced in intensified fashion, as another cutely horrid scene testifies:[6] "The cooking, I can tell you, kept her nose to the pot. Their chief food was roasted breadfruit, yams, coconuts, baked pig . . . but you never exactly knew whether there would be a real meal or just a make-believe, it all depended on Peter's whim. . . . [O]f course it was trying, but you simply had to follow his lead and if you could prove to him that you were getting loose for your tree [i.e, that you were getting too thin] he let you stodge [eat]" (71). Peter's power to starve his household if he pleases and his cavalier inclination to make them prove physical diminution (inferiority to the child-father) to obtain needed nourishment dramatizes the real powerlessness of Wendy in the Neverland household as it foregrounds two things: the gratuitous cruelty that informs many of Peter's parental actions, and the degree to which the entire underground space reproduces the kind of dysfunctional working-poor nightmare (abusive father, overworked and exhausted mother, hordes of hungry, wild children) common to nineteenth-century bourgeois novels— the criminal antifamily in the quintessential lost-boy story *Oliver Twist* being perhaps *Peter Pan*'s most resonant forerunner.

Thus, Barrie affirms the magical island's atemporality—its "neverness" and consequent freedom from history, adulthood, decay, sex, and death— primarily in terms of an idealized domesticity; but this "neverness" has nothing transcendental about it. "Nothing happens" at home because of the nature of household maintenance and the repetitive chores that form the "work" in housework; atemporality here is not endless adventure, but rather the tortured and tortuous monotony of housekeeping—worse, even, than factory work.[7] In this way, the domestic geography of Neverland reinscribes gender/class enslavement, so that Wendy's escape from workaday London backfires with a proletariat-flavored vengeance in the infantile, patriarchal Neverland. Work becomes Wendy's only play, and wherever she goes, the pattern tellingly repeats. After all, the pirates want her to be *their* mother as well, ostensibly to make their ship as cozy as Peter's cave—a state of affairs suggesting that Peter Pan and Captain Hook bear a striking psychological resemblance, as Dan Kiley astutely notes.[8]

Clearly, then, Peter Pan is a dangerous creature (especially where little girls are concerned) who combines infantile petulance with shrewd powers of manipulation. Disdainful of real mothers—he detests Mrs. Darling, and the author/narrator openly shares this evaluation—he longs for a little girl–mother whom he can transform into an unpaid housekeeper, a border guard of his own precarious masculinity. In short, Wendy is not Peter's mother, wife, lover, or friend; she is literally an organ of production for the next surrogate mother and the next, as well as for Pan's followers, the ubiquitous Lost Boys. Deludedly thinking that Peter Pan will serve her, Wendy is inveigled into serving him—and how: making pockets, telling stories, cleaning, and dispensing medicine.

Wendy's daughters always fall for Peter's line, too, but they never stay with him very long (suggesting another understanding of the "never" in Neverland), and their decisions to return home betray that they know this arrangement to be a very raw deal. Each girl must eventually resign herself to the real patriarchal world of London, where if she is fortunate she can count on three square meals a day; but this is the best she can hope for.[9]

While Barrie thus articulates the ways that feminine longing is thwarted and overdetermined from the outset, his portrayal is far from sympathetic; rather it seems to take a peculiar, sadistic pleasure in making this failure come about, as George Blake sensed in the 1950s.[10] This textual gratification in creating and then inviting us to share scenes of pain and suffering culminates in a deeply misogynistic, antimaternal moment near the end of the book:

> [Mrs. Darling] had no proper spirit. I had meant to say extraordinarily nice things about her but I despise her, and not one of them will I say now. . . . All the beds are aired, and she never leaves the house, and observe, the window is open. For all the use we are to her, we might go back to the ship. However, as we are here we may as well stay and look on. That is all we are, lookers-on. Nobody really wants us. So let us watch and say jaggy things, in the hope that some of them will hurt. (49–50)

While *Peter Pan* may be read as a deeply closeted homosexual and pedophiliac fantasy (as Rose argues), underneath that fantasy of deviant pleasure lies even more deviance. Behind Peter Pan's hatred of the adult mother lurk two kinds of grief: his sadness that he cannot actually become the mother and thereby replace her (give birth himself to the Lost Boys), and the longing for the mother herself—a longing the novel reveals so heartbreakingly even and especially when it is at its absolute meanest—made manifest at that strange instant when Peter Pan looks through the window, "forever barred," we are told, from embracing Mrs. Darling (156).[11]

Peter Pan unwillingly enunciates in its interstices the tragic awareness that the mother *is* a mystery, *is* elusive; that no one, not even the omniscient, omnipotent narrator, can get (back?) into her innermost box (which clearly has symbolic connections to the womb); and that in the Freudian *fort/da* game of absence and return that every child plays, it is *fort*—away—that ultimately prevails.[12] So the mourning of one's lost childhood—usually seen as the theme of *Peter Pan* by critics as William Blackburn—masks another act of mourning: the real, inevitable loss of the mother, and with that a deferred recognition of the force of the maternal, the feminine: "I find I won't be able to say nasty things about her after all. . . . The corner of her mouth . . . is almost withered up. Her hand moves restlessly on her breast as if there were a pain there. Some like Peter best and some like Wendy best, but *I like her best*" (151, my italics).[13] But that grief, along with the subversive, potentially feminist recognition that accompanies it, denies itself even at the moment of its articulation, becoming an infantile rage that radiates out and invades everything it touches: an act of grief turned hateful narrative that delights in creating discomfort and outright pain for its characters—the jaggy things that hurt—which it then regrets, only to start all over again. And this is why *Peter Pan* remains so powerful: it performs a clever repressive trick, by which the mother can be eradicated and her power denied, while at the same time venting the emotions of the loss and fetishizing the elusive fairy son who appears to but does not subvert the patriarchal (bourgeois) order. One shudders to consider the effects of this icon in the United States, especially its influence on overachieving "baby-boomers."

Viewed from this perspective, Peter Pan has different antecedents and descendants than those normally cited: he resembles Rumpelstiltskin—who hates the mother but would usurp her function by robbing her of her baby—and the other problematic Victorian child seducer, the Pied Piper of Hamelin. Lizzie Francke notes another relationship: "Described throughout the novel as a child with gnashing milk-white teeth, a greedy look in his eye and a detachable shadow, he seems to have an ominous connection with that other *fin-de-siècle* specter, the vampire. He feeds on emotional sustenance from the countless Wendys he transports to Neverland where they tell him 'stories about himself to which he listens eagerly.'"[14] Peter's sons in science fiction and horror are not Parzivalian boy heroes like Luke Skywalker and Robert A. Heinlein's Stranger, but rather the almost coeval/coevil Dorian Gray, the little-boy tyrant of *The Twilight Zone*'s "It's a *Good* Life"; William Gibson's self-destructive, physicality-hating *Count Zero;* and a cavalcade of boy vampires: the insidious tyke in Stephen King's "Poppy"; the adult-hating, little-girl-craving androgyne of Kathryn Bigelow's film *Near Dark;* the teenage vampires of *The Lost Boys;* and the regressive Armand of Rice's *The Vampire Lestat* (to which *Interview with the Vampire*'s Claudia is a subversive feminist corrective). Rice's most recent incarnation of Peter Pan thus has a long legacy.

Barrie uses feminine desire for the supernatural boy in a half-knowing critique of the later Victorian era, and this critique also haltingly articulates desires unaccommodated by heterosexuality. In contrast, feminist and eroticist Rice provides a more unflinching picture of feminine desire at the service of the demonic. A feminist parable about the dangers of phallic womanhood (the woman who would be just like a man)—an interest already implicit in her vampire novel *The Queen of the Damned*— *The Witching Hour* also evocatively explores the different, subtle ways women are imprisoned by/in our culture, primarily through the gendered constructions of desire, maternity, and childhood.

The Witching Hour is a daunting work because of its length and its complicated intertextual relations with a variety of literary and cinematic works, so I will note only one important connection. The novel may be understood as a revision of Goethe's *Faust.* Although Rice later refers to this classic in *The Body Thief, Witching Hour* provides an even more interesting rewriting of that text: here the occult scientist's victim, innocent Marguerite, is herself transformed into the Faustian necromancer—a passionate, idealistic seeker of knowledge. Rice's demonic Lasher conflates the urbane, dangerous Mephisto (Goethe's Satan) with Homunculus, that strange test-tube fetus from *Faust II,* who would give all to obtain carnal existence through self-annihilating union with the goddess Galatea. Not coincidentally, both sections of *Faust* evoke anxiety about maternity and the business of birth, although it is alleviated in the end by that profoundly annoying vision of the eternal feminine.

But a female Faust perforce marshals different imaginative strategies than does the explicitly masculine framework of the original, and rather than appealing to God the father at the beginning, as Goethe does, Rice invokes the figure of the mother, like Barrie, as the source-site of all the action. Rice gives us a triptych of masculine responses to two different contemporized images of the *mater dolorosa* (suffering mother). One is classically Oedipal: the young boy Michael who watches his beautiful mother—tricked into marrying a man she does not love—languish in ladylike alcoholism while he resolutely denies that there is anything wrong with her or that anything can be done to help her. The other is the central picture the novel obsessively returns to: the figure of Deirdre Mayfair sitting motionless, heavily drugged, in a rocking chair on the rotting porch of a New Orleans mansion so dilapidated as to make Miss Havisham's look like a Florida condo. This figure is evocative because it is so heavily freighted with negative female iconography that a brief tabulation will suffice: the hysteric, the madwoman, the drug addict, the single mother, the unfit mother, the bad mother, the whore, the witch. These epithets are all assigned to Deirdre, the mother of heroine Rowan Mayfair, in the opening pages of the book.

In alternating chapters the family's medical doctor and parish priest look in on Deirdre, but their opposing wisdoms and the power of their knowledge do not inspire them to alleviate her obvious suffering. Rather their "expertise" serves as an excuse to avoid taking part in the sinister reality of her existence. The doctor wants to stop her massive Thorazine doses out of professional curiosity, only to retreat from the scene when the experiment fails. Such willful denial is even more heartbreakingly demonstrated in a flashback when Father Mattingly remembers the child Deirdre's confession that she is possessed. This is Rice at her most powerful, when she speaks not for the child but *as* a child, specifically as a little girl:

> Aunt Carl says it's a mortal sin even to think of him or think of his name. It makes him come immediately, if you say his name! . . . [T]he worst part is when he comes through and scares her. And she threatens him! She says if he doesn't leave me alone, she'll hurt me! . . . But all the time, Father, even when I'm alone, or even at Mass with everybody there, I know he's right beside me. I can feel him. I can hear him crying and it makes me cry too.[15]

This report eerily echoes Wendy's first question to Peter: "Boy, why are you crying?" Like his predecessor, Lasher seduces girl-mothers through appeals to their compassion—an emotion that, as Martha Nussbaum argues, is our first important social feeling, the ground for all our subsequent good conduct, and the basis for justice.[16] But Lasher uses Deirdre's pity against her, as he has done with the Mayfair women for generations—we later learn—forcing her to a psychic impasse: in order to have feelings she must contend with Lasher, who thrives on them, or else she must renounce emotions altogether, like the masculinized Aunt Carl and to an extent Rowan herself. And while Mattingly feels the resonance of Deirdre's claim, his knowledge prevents him from recognizing and acting on it, because Deirdre is a child and a girl, and finally because she is a "bad" girl.

These therapeutically impotent and yet socially powerful epistemologies—medical and religious—contrast dramatically with the different sort of knowing embodied by Deirdre's girlfriend Rita Mae. But Rita's intuitive knowledge of Deirdre's goodness, for all its accuracy, cannot help either Deirdre or herself, because both women are already trapped in a set of false alternatives, as Rita's memory of seeing Deirdre and Lasher together at the convent testifies:

> But late that night when she lay in bed, Rita repeated those words: *My beloved. Only want to make you happy, my beloved.* Oh, to think that a man would say such things to Deirdre.
>
> All Rita had ever known were boys who wanted to "feel you up" if they got a chance. Clumsy, stupid guys like her boyfriend Terry from Holy Cross, who said, "You know, I think I like you a lot Rita." Sure, sure. 'Cause I let you "feel me up." You ox.
>
> "You tramp!" Rita's father had said. "You are going to boarding school, that's where you're going. . . ."
>
> "*My beloved.*" It made her think of beautiful music, of elegant gentlemen in old movies she saw on late night television. Of voices from another time, soft and distinct, the very words like kisses. And he was so handsome too. . . . Rita would have met him in the garden . . . Rita would have done anything with him. (137)

Through the reminiscences of Rita Mae, Rice delineates the narrow field within which feminine aspirations are permitted to move: the real world ruled by masculine desire (Rita Mae's boyfriend) and masculine law (her father), and the demonic world of Lasher, who allows the articulation of feminine desire and promises pleasure but really is only another, more glamorous face culled from the same power. Rice later underlines this fact by revealing that while Lasher was first called forth by a woman, it was a man (another expert—a witch judge) who showed her how to do it (292).

Yet the novel also demonstrates that the patent falseness of Lasher's appeal cannot be easily counteracted. More so than *Peter Pan, The Witching Hour* depicts the tragedy of feminine repetition, as thirteen generations of Mayfair women attempt to harness Lasher and are themselves undone by him. Arguably, if the pop psychology intertext to *Peter Pan* is *The Peter Pan Syndrome, The Witching Hour*'s equivalent might be *My Mother, Myself,* for that book suggests that the mother's limitations and psychic wounds trap her daughter through love and a false sense of superiority into perpetuating her mistakes. But Rice makes it clear that this is not where the main trouble lies. Unlike Peter Pan, Lasher is dangerous precisely because he is adept at keeping his promises. Like Mephisto he can provide the Mayfair women with the financial wherewithal to obtain social status and independence. More important, he offers himself to the girl witches as their imaginary servant and familiar when they are children (appearing to them in their bedrooms and other private, romantically charged locations), while his apparently unconditional, selfless, literally "spiritual" love also functions as an ironic corrective for that of the real mother—ironic because the Mayfair women are usually orphans. Lasher almost always finds a way to get rid of the individual mother as soon as she has served her biological purpose, so that the Mayfairs become the feminine equivalents of Barrie's Lost Boys. And having won the trust of his charges when they are children, Lasher shifts with increasing ease into a more adult service when they grow up—providing them with unsurpassed sexual pleasure on demand. In this way, Lasher pretends to fill the function of the entire Oedipal triangle. The wannabe son becomes a male mother who in turn becomes the lover of the mother and the father to himself.

And this is, of course, the big problem, for if sexual desire is the question that cannot even be asked in *Peter Pan,* it is the reality of sexual pleasure that cannot be answered in *The Witching Hour.* Erotics battles politics in the second half of the novel and at least temporarily triumphs over both intelligence and love. Even gorgeous Michael Curry, the modern, sensitive hero—an emotional, psychically gifted, slightly mad lover of houses—cannot compete with his future demonic son for Rowan's attention. For her part, Rowan is no Wendy; she is a liberated woman cut off from her mother and thus supposedly incapable of the mistakes made by the generations of confused Mayfair women who preceded her. An ambitious, brilliant doctor who "mans" her own yacht, executes her unfaithful adopted father, and fears nothing, Rowan gains access to the complete Mayfair history and possesses the most valuable weapon of all: knowledge. But like both Faust and Frankenstein, she is a scientist, and her ability to interpret the information she receives is skewed by a false sense of objectivity and an inability to recognize her own deepest emotional-sexual needs. Rowan's failure to understand her own recurring dream about a fetal operation—which warns her in no uncertain terms of what Lasher plans—testifies to the failure of her imagination, and on another level to a failure of nerve to know (and love) herself. Possessed by fellow feeling for others, Rowan censors her own emotions so thoroughly that, for all her genius, she does not know what she wants, needs, or fears until it is possibly too late.

Knowing the enemy, the novel devastatingly shows, is not enough, and Rice makes her readers experience the danger viscerally through vivid sexual encounters between Rowan and Lasher with sadomasochistic resonances reminiscent of the neo-Sadian dynamics of her earlier *Beauty* erotica. For the Mayfair women to rid themselves of Lasher—for women at large to escape the false alternatives of masculine desire and masculine-determined feminine fantasy (which Lasher clearly is—the ghostly Don Giovanni no woman can hold)—they must learn to feel otherwise, to desire differently.

But can they? Significantly, *The Witching Hour* resists closure on this crucial point and looks beyond the limits of its own story to a possible future utopian resolution. In a visionary monologue at the end of the book the abandoned Michael, the man left at home waiting for the questing woman, dreams that Rowan may yet defeat Lasher, that perhaps she will break the chain of dependence on and tutelage to him, that she will one day defeat the nasty boy once and for all. As in *Peter Pan,* feminine longing proves catastrophic, but *The Witching Hour* allows this desire to speak itself through a multiplicity of female voices—related, yet distinct—and empowers readers to simultaneously grieve for its unfulfillment and both hope and act for change: "I refuse to judge Rowan. . . . And I choose of my own free will to stay here, waiting for her, and believing in her. . . . [N]o matter how enormous and intricate this web of events seems, no matter how much it is like all the patterns of flags and balustrades and repetitive cast iron that dominate this little plot of earth, I maintain my credo" (963).

Can this mother do what her own mothers could not? Can Rowan control her son-lover without either destroying or surrendering to him? Masculine literature's pictures of desiring mothers have veered consistently and obsessively between just those two destructive and self-destructive poles: *Medea* and *Phaedra, The Grifters* and *Rosemary's Baby.* And today, it remains a dilemma that J. M. Barrie did not wish to, and Anne Rice could not—in the novel—resolve.

Notes

1. The ideas in this essay were enhanced by conversations with Martha Nussbaum and by exposure to her work on the emotions.

2. Martin Green, "The Charm of Peter Pan," *Children's Literature* 9 (1981): 19–27.

3. Jack Zipes, "Negating History and Male Fantasies through Psychoanalytic Criticism," *Children's Literature* 18 (1990): 141–43; Jacqueline Rose, *The Case of Peter Pan: Of the Impossibility of Children's Fiction* (London: Macmillan, 1984).

4. J. M. Barrie, *Peter Pan* (1911; New York: Bantam Books, 1985), 6. Later page references in the text are to this edition.

5. As discussed by Sandra M. Gilbert and Susan Gubar in *The Madwoman in the Attic* (New Haven: Yale University Press, 1984).

6. Interestingly, Steven Spielberg's film *Hook* reinvokes this particular scene—explicitly without Wendy—to establish the fertility (read maternity) of the adult Peter's imaginative powers.

7. "Few tasks are more like the torture of Sisyphus than housework, with its endless repetition . . . the years . . . lie spread out ahead, gray and identical" (Simone de Beauvoir, *The Second Sex,* trans. H. M. Parshley [New York: Bantam Books, 1970], 425).

8. Dan Kiley, *The Peter Pan Syndrome* (New York: Dodd, Mead, 1983), 32.

9. If Wendy and her daughters are Persephone figures, as Lois Ruach Gibson maintains in "Beyond the Apron: Archetypes, Stereotypes, and Alternative Portrayals of Mothers in Children's Literature," *Children's Literature Association Quarterly* 13.4 (1988): 177–81, then it is in a completely ironized and desexualized manner, for that powerful erotic/seasonal icon is recast in terms of Victorian, bourgeois sexual politics.

10. "You never know where you are with Barrie. . . . For all his reputation for the understanding of women and children, we have to deal here with what seems to be a case of refined sadism" (George Blake, *Barrie and the Kailyard School,* cited in Andrew Birkin, *J. M. Barrie and the Lost Boys* [London: Constable, 1979], 37).

11. Thus I disagree with Richard Rotert ("The Kiss in a Box," *Children's Literature* 18 [1990]: 114–23), who sees Peter Pan's banishment as a reaction of fatherliness. It's not the father he wants—or wants to be.

12. Such an understanding (on the part of both the child and Freud) is implicit in Freud's observation that the child often plays the *fort* part of the *fort/da* game

by itself. See Sigmund Freud, "Beyond the Pleasure Principle," in *A General Selection from the Works of Sigmund Freud,* ed. John Rickman (New York: Anchor, 1989), 146–47.

13. See William Blackburn, "Mirror in the Sea: *Treasure Island* and the Internalization of Juvenile Romance," *Children's Literature Association Quarterly* 8.3 (1983): 7–12; and Howard Kissel's discussion of Barrie's obsession with his mother in "Peter Pan," *Horizon* 22 (December 1979): 19–24.

14. Lizzie Francke, "Boys and Girls Come Out to Play," *Sight and Sound* 1 (April 1992): 17.

15. Anne Rice, *The Witching Hour* (New York: Knopf, 1990), 82. Later page references in the text are to this edition.

16. Martha Nussbaum, *Love's Knowledge: Essays on Philosophy and Literature* (New York: Oxford University Press, 1990), 209.

Unsealing Sense in *The Turn of the Screw*

Susan J. Navarette

> If we look merely into the book of nature, death appears an inscrutible [*sic*] mystery, a strange and unaccountable anomaly among the arrangements of Providence; but if we look into the book of God's word, we find a satisfactory explanation of the phenomenon.
> —W. B. Clark, *Asleep in Jesus* (1856)

> 'Twas like a Maelstrom, with a notch,
> That nearer, every Day,
> Kept narrowing its boiling Wheel . . .
> —Emily Dickinson (c. 1862)

Although the narrator of *The Turn of the Screw* (1898) avers that without "a few words of prologue" a "proper intelligence" of the governess's manuscript is impossible, nothing he can relate concerning Douglas's prefatory warning that the story is "beyond everything" for "general uncanny ugliness and horror and pain" adequately prepares the reader for the verbal assault leveled in and through Miles's deathbed cry: "Peter Quint— you devil! . . . *Where?*"[1] True, what James referred to in his notebook as the "strangely gruesome effect" of the governess's story builds from the earliest stages of its telling: from her receipt of the letter hinting that Miles's may have been a contaminating presence at his boarding school, to her growing certainty that there are "depths, depths!" (121) that are penetrated with each turn of the screw—with the steady accretion, that is, of rumors possessed (to her) of terrible implications.[2] In this sense James's story is an ironic exemplar of the romance as Hawthorne defined it—its

185

"high truth . . . never any truer, and seldom any more evident, at the last page than at the first."[3] The governess's narrative begins at the moment when Miles's heart (and, by extension, her experience at Bly) is "stopped"; yet nothing in the preceding pages sufficiently braces the careful reader for the shock that Miles's death delivers.

His final cryptic cry may be said to embody what James described in one letter as "'Terror' *peut bien en être*":[4] "the dear old sacred terror" that the "new type" of ghost story, to his mind, failed miserably to convey, so that the story that contains it, in turn, may be thought of as constituting James's "lament for a beautiful lost form" ("Preface" 169).[5] True to his manner, however, James subjects to "cold artistic calculation" ("Preface" 172) not only the literary form whose loss he laments, but also the cultural traditions and attitudes that facilitated its emergence. In other words, the Gothic tradition, the Victorian *ars moriendi,* and the cult of the child are invoked, inverted, and reconstituted in the climactic death scene, the final turn of the screw that transforms James's story from "a fairy-tale pure and simple" into an "excursion into chaos": a hybridized *"amusette"* whose charm is reserved for "the jaded, the disillusioned, the fastidious"—in short, for "the distracted modern mind" ("Preface" 171–72).

Douglas fires his audience's imagination with several stock performative strategies, exercising a "quiet art" that assures the "triumph" of his delivery. He hedges and hunts for words, interrupting himself or weighing one word against another, and then rejecting both. He heightens his listeners' curiosity by avoiding the actual telling of the story of which he has afforded only tantalizing glimpses ("He turned round to the fire, gave a kick to a log, watched it an instant. Then as he faced us again: 'I can't begin.'" [82]). The bait that attracts his audience, however, is the subject of his story: "a visitation" that had "fallen on a child" (81). Douglas acknowledges the obvious appeal of his subject—a "little boy, at so tender an age, adds a particular touch . . . [and] gives the effect another turn of the screw" (81)—and when he asks what effect *two* children give to a ghost story, his audience readily answers: "two turns!" (81). They need little prompting, versed as they are in Gothic conventions and in the Victorian celebration of childhood.

The mock Gothic is at work throughout Douglas's story (and, by extension, throughout James's story, which from its outset—"The story held us, round the fire, sufficiently breathless" [81]—puts to ironic uses the very Gothic traditions to which James draws mock-affectionate attention in his preface). With "immense effect" Douglas commences reading to the "hushed little circle" (85) several days after striking the spark of his audience's imagination with the information that he possesses a manuscript telling a story "quite too horrible" (82). Their ready responses—" 'Oh, how delicious,' cried one of the women" (82)—bespeak their recognition that theirs is the role of percipient listener—consumed by "a rage of curiosity" (85), hungry to decode hints and partial revelations, but also confident that the story will impart what James calls the sense of "the terrible 'pleasant'" ("Preface" 169–70), the vaguely erotic but finally nonthreatening feeling that James's disciple M. R. James would later describe as "pleasantly uncomfortable."[6]

When *The Turn of the Screw* made its first appearance, both audiences—the fictive and the actual—were familiar with the conventions governing the Victorian cult of childhood. Although it accorded with their belief in the perfectibility of man, the tendency to sentimentalize and idealize childhood did not, of course, originate with the Victorians, for the influence of the French *philosophes* and the German Romantics had already begun to shape cultural attitudes during the preceding century. Rousseau's insistence in *Émile* (1762) that "nothing is more foolish than to try and substitute our ways" for a child's way "of seeing, thinking, and feeling" anticipated what would later become a commonplace: that children represented a different, and even a higher, order of being and consciousness.[7] Blake associated childhood with divinity, while Schopenhauer, some years later, associated it with genius. Thomas Jefferson Hogg reminds us of the stroll during which Percy Shelley sought to prove that infants retain memories of another world that fade away as they grow older. Catching hold of a several-weeks-old infant, he asked its mother, "Will your baby tell us anything about pre-existence, Madam?" When she demurred, Shelley insisted that the baby *could* "speak if he [would], for he is only a few weeks old": "He may fancy perhaps that he cannot, but it is only a silly whim; he cannot have forgotten entirely the use of speech in so short a time; the thing is absolutely impossible."[8] By the mid–nineteenth century, both child and mother were thought of as mediating figures retaining intuitive powers as well as a natural vitality and a natural (if untutored) piety. H. G. Wells's characterization of the Eloi may owe something to the growing conviction that human evolution would reveal itself in neoteny—in the juvenilization evinced as an evolutionary progression within a species.[9] Seeking biological evidence to show that "the child is really the 'father of the man,' for the modern man is becoming more and more a child," Alexander Francis Chamberlain argued in

1906 that within an individual lifetime "upward zoological evolution" is most pronounced in infancy, whereas, with maturation, humankind forfeits "the comparatively ultra-human character of . . . early childhood": "the 'Fall,' if there be one for the race, is in the descent from the high promise of childhood to the comparative barrenness of senility."[10] To die as a child, then, is to avoid the "falls" (biological and spiritual) that lie in wait for humankind—or such is the message contained in the Victorian comfort books that are the subject of a study by Judith Plotz. "Since the loveliness of childhood is obliterated by maturation into adulthood," she writes, "the child who dies remains quintessentially childlike—indeed, he is the only lasting child."[11] The Victorians believed the dead child to be twice blessed—granted everlasting life in the memories of those left behind, and more likely than those who reached adulthood to secure eternal bliss. They would have remembered the words of Matthew: "Except ye be converted, and become as little children, ye shall not enter into the kingdom of heaven" (Matt. 18:3).

If the living child was understood to be a figure of authority, how much more so the dying innocent, who sinks into the visionary state of grace in which, in the words of one nineteenth-century minister, "hovering as it were midway between earth and heaven, he catches a glimpse of the spiritual world, before he leaves the material."[12] The ardor with which the Victorians celebrated childhood was matched only by the fervor with which they celebrated the hour of death, and the intersection of the two— the cult of childhood and *ars moriendi*—provided for some of the most affective deathbed scenes in Victorian literature. As John Kucich reminds us in his analysis of Little Nell's death in Dickens's *The Old Curiosity Shop* (1841), the Victorians—viewing death as "the most important event of an individual lifetime"—"made the etiquette of mourning and burial into an elaborate catechism."[13] Dickens provides us with one version of this ritualized performance in the chapter of *Dombey and Son* (1848) in which Paul Dombey learns "What the Waves Were Always Saying." Lying "tranquilly" in his bed, Paul studies the sunbeams that dance on the walls of his bedroom like "golden water," and that, as he grows weaker, he associates with "the dark dark river [that rolls] towards the sea in spite of him."[14] Visitors drift in and out of his flickering consciousness: old Mrs. Pipchin becomes Miss Tox, who becomes Louisa Chick. As his death approaches, he makes various requests: asking, for example, that his father remember Walter Gay, for Paul is "fond of Walter" (224). Locked in the arms of his sister, he can at last hear what the waves are saying: "tell them that the print upon the stairs at school, is not Divine enough. The light about the head is shining on me as I go!" (225). The scene largely adheres to conventional deathbed rituals: Paul is surrounded by mourning relatives, to whom he makes his final farewells, and his spoken behests are followed by less intelligible murmurings that suggest that, for him, the pall of mortality is being lifted.

Such theatrical performances were not limited to Victorian fiction. Margarete Holubetz notes that "the ritual celebration of death . . . was the ideal to which people on their death-beds aspired." [15] Excerpts from memoirs, journals, and letters indicate that most people had absorbed and were prepared to enact the rites of death. Thus, the mother of the American child-poet Frances (Fannie) Lavinia Michener records that just as her daughter's "sweet disposition manifested itself in the patience with which she bore her sufferings," her purity and state of grace were evident at the hour of her death.[16] Like Paul Dombey, Fannie bid a tender adieu to her relatives and exacted promises from them, telling some "to take care of mother, and her father to meet her in heaven." Her final statement, duly recorded, attests to her love for her mother and to her belief that her "sins are all washed away in the blood of the Lamb" (12). Her closing comments are followed by a feverish (and, it is implied, an unpremeditated and unedited) recital of her vision of the hereafter:

> Presently she said, "Please turn up the light, for it is growing dark"; and a moment later, "The light has gone down." On being told it was still burning, she replied, "The light is all right, but it is still dark, and I know why; but it is all right. I'm not afraid to die. I'm growing cold." Gazing through the darkness, she said, "I can see you all yet," and each name for the last time lingered lovingly on her lips,—"Mother—best—of—all next to Jesus." Then as if gazing beyond, "It is all light now. Good-by—good-by. I'm going home—home—home—forever and forever more."
>
> Again her lips moved faintly, but the last word was inaudible, and with perhaps the word "Mother" or "Jesus" she had passed through the darkness beyond the shadow into the light of the blessed. (13)

Although obviously romanticized in order to fulfill the expectations of Fannie's mourning readers, the report of her death does not differ dramatically in content, form, and ideology from those recorded in diaries and personal correspondence that would not have enjoyed the same wide circulation as the memoirs of a famous child-poet's mother. In a 1784 letter, for example, John Choate of Ipswich, Massachusetts, draws on what were becoming the stock accoutrements of bereavement as a means of comforting himself and his brother, in whose care his daughter Hannah had died:

> I received your Letter of June 7 sometime Since, giveing the very Melancholly and heavy news of the Death of my Dear Daughter Hannah—I should have wrote you before but Want of Opportunity and the discumposure of mind underso Great a Tryall will I hope plead my excuse—although we had no rational Grounds to expect Hannah would continue any considerable lenth of time when my wife left her, yet Death came unexpected, and my wife and Children as well as my Self are greatly Affected with the Loss, and, Oh, Brother I doubt not but you and Sister were sencibly tutch't with the Loss of one who (perhaps not without good reason) you expected much comfort from—but the agreeable Account you give of the Frame and temper of her mind—her calm Composedness, her Resignation to the Divine will, her beautifull expressions to her mourning friends around her; her firm faith in the Blessed Jesus—and her happy prospect of the Heavenly Canaan at the near Approach of Death and wile actually passing thr° the Gloomy Vale and engag,d with the King of Terror, alth° very affecting, yet dos administer unspeakable comfort to her surviving friends—who do not mourn as those who have no hope—but have the fullest evidence to conclude that Our Sweet Child is now in Yonder Glory Celebrating Redeeming Love—I most Heartily Joine you in Adoring the Riches of Gods free Grace in the Wonderfull Plan of Salvation wrought out by our Blessed Jesus, and in perticular for his Communicating his Grace in so wonderfull a manner to my Dear Departed Child—[17]

Aside from the "high degree of cultural shaping," as Michael Wheeler calls it, that is evinced in the shared vocabulary and structure of such deathbed scenes, what links them is the implication that the moment of death is a revelatory one, for both the living and the deceased.[18] The latter struggles to describe divinations or "communications of grace." The former cherish the dying visionary's final statement as a text laden with intimations of immortality and prophetic or homiletic inscriptions. Choate can speak with confidence of having divined "the Wonderfull Plan of Salvation wrought out by our Blessed Jesus" because his faith is anchored in a culturally sanctioned belief that death occurs at the authorizing moment when, as Elisabeth Bronfen puts it, "an inherent though invisible truth could apotheotically be fulfilled, where an otherwise incommunicable secret could be made visible."[19]

In focusing on the experience of the dying child, the deathbed scenes featured in Choate's letter or A.E.M.'s memoir recast the child as hero. Debarred because of their youth or frailty from other forms of public achievement, such "child heroes" achieve, as Plotz suggests, "a kind of grandeur in their death." [20] Children are memorable figures in death not only because they show pietistic fortitude in extremis, however, but also because they have not yet "fallen" into adulthood, and so retain visions of preexistence (however inarticulable) that enhance those of eternity that are intensified at the hour of death. In his comfort book for bereaved parents, Reverend W. B. Clark speculates that, suspended at such a transformative moment in "a state of vastly increased activity," the "believer" espies "the glories of paradise" that "are partially disclosed to his view" while "the distant tones of its hymns of sweetest melody burst upon his ravished ear." [21]

Such beliefs were still widespread in the early twentieth century, although they became less overtly Christian. Wells's "The Door in the Wall" (1911), for example, describes one such vividly portentous experience. The adult Lionel Wallace, Wells's protagonist, admits to a friend that he is haunted by the memory "of a beauty and a happiness that filled his heart with insatiable longings that made all the interests and spectacle of worldly life seem dull and tedious and vain to him." [22] The memory concerns an excursion, undertaken in childhood, through a green door in a white wall that led to a garden "full of the quality and promise of heart's desire" (10). Although fragmentary in nature, his memory conveys "an impression of delightful rightness" (10). That his was an early excursion into an otherworldly domain seems clear by the story's end, when, determined never again to forgo an opportunity that has several times presented itself to him over the course of his ambitious adulthood, he passes through a door—and falls to his death in a deep excavation. His friend speculates that although by "our daylight standard he walked out of security into darkness, danger and death," viewed from Wallace's childlike perspective, the door provided "a secret and peculiar passage of escape into another and altogether more beautiful world" (24).

Wallace's adult world seems dull and common, whereas his vision revealed a realm infused with an "indescribable quality of translucent reality" (13)—a reality starkly at odds with that hinted at in the desperate cry with which James's story concludes: "Peter Quint—you devil! . . . *Where?*" Miles's dying pronouncement proves horrific in part because it conveys a truth—if it can be said to convey *anything* definitive—grossly antithetical to those expressed by the dying innocents of Victorian literature. In an essay on vulgarity in literature, Aldous Huxley claims that "the suffering and death of children raise the problem of evil in its most unanswerable form."[23] His suggestion is that such a circumstance calls into question the beneficence of the divinity who could sap the vitality of such precious beings and simultaneously beggar those whose hopes for the future resided in them, forcing a confrontation with what Kucich calls "the abyss of negativity."[24] The form that Miles's unexpected death takes complicates our reading of Huxley's statement: what happens when, demon-inspired, the child becomes the medium through whom we confront the *abîme,* the child in such a context functioning not as an innocent victim but as an active participant in the transmission of evil? What happens, in other words, when the dying child espies not grace and sanctification but damnation and demon-madness? Douglas admits that the piquancy of his tale derives from the fact that the "visitation had fallen on a child" (81). The "visitation" that falls on Miles and Flora (the governess applies the epithet "visitant" both to Peter Quint and to Miss Jessel) resembles those biblical visitations that have their genesis in abominations (Jer. 8:12) that deliver desolation and days of recompense (Hos. 9:7).

Miles's cry proves destabilizing in other ways as well. Just as nothing in Douglas's opening comments would have prepared James's late Victorian audience for the shock, so nothing in Victorian deathbed fiction would have prepared them to interpret it. Although hieroglyphic in the sense that its language reflects the transcendence of the moment, the conventional deathbed utterance was understood to contain a truth that, if carefully scrutinized, could serve as a signpost on the path to righteousness for those left behind. The life that draws to a close assumes most strikingly in its concluding hours the quality and texture of a narrative. In his near-death experience, for example, Wells's Lionel Wallace meets a "sombre dark woman, with a grave, pale face and dreamy eyes," who carries a book "in the living pages" of which he sees the "harsh reality" of his life: "it was a story about myself, and in it were all the things that had happened to me since ever I was born" (11–12). At such a supercharged moment the dying speaker is, as Bronfen suggests, imbued with an " 'authority,' arising from the aporia of speaking or writing in the shadow of death and against it, that lies at the origin of all narratives. Death is the sanction for all that a storyteller might relate."[25] Not merely sanctioning what the storyteller has to tell, death mimics the narrative that contains it so that, as Garrett Stewart argues, death and fiction become "two controlling frameworks within which story and mortality interrogate and exchange with each other." [26]

Miles's final statement, however, constitutes a text from which we cannot extract precise meaning; nothing in our training and experience has taught us to *how* to read it. The ultimate solipsistic text, it creates not meaning but a series of unanswerable questions: Why does Miles call out "Peter Quint"? Is he admitting to an unholy association? Does he seek Quint's help in extremis? Does he suspect that the dead man has become the governess's idée fixe, and does he hurl his name at her as a final condemnation? Who is the "you" referred to in "you devil"? Quint, whose friendship has damned Miles? The governess, whose ministrations have damned him? Like so much in the story, the statement is cryptic; we are left only with questions whose answers are locked deep in the heart of the narrative—and in the heart of the reader touched by the horrors thus unveiled.

James's readers have been no more successful in reading Miles's final statement than in reading Miles himself. Precursor death scenes had taught the Victorians that the victim's body could serve as a signifier of inward as well as past and future states. In the deathbed scene that concludes his *Nana* (1880), Émile Zola substitutes a mountain of foundering, suppurating flesh for the body of the once resplendent but consummately corrupt "blond Venus." Alternatively, in the deathbed scene that dampened many Victorian handkerchiefs, Little Nell's marmoreal body is encased in a beauty that testifies to her incorruptibility in life and her sanctity in death. "Peace and perfect happiness were . . . imaged in her tranquil beauty and profound repose." [27] Her face is set in "the same mild look" by which we shall "know the angels in their majesty, after death" (654). We "read" Little Nell's body and discover that in death it received the seal of salvation. Dickens establishes a correlation between the physical and the metaphysical, for at Nell's grave "all outward things and inward thoughts teem with assurances of immortality" (659). In *The Turn of the Screw*, however, childhood beauty is at best misleading and is perhaps a signifier of damnation rather than the state of grace it would seem to embody. Miles and Flora are repeatedly described as nothing short of seraphic in their beauty. The governess suffers no "uneasiness in a connection with anything so beatific as the radiant image of [her] little girl," who possesses "the deep, sweet serenity . . . of one of Raphael's holy infants" (91). "Incredibly beautiful," Miles radiates "something divine" that the governess has "never found to the same degree in any child—his indescribable little air of knowing nothing in the world but love" (98). Because "it would have been impossible to carry a bad name with a greater sweetness of innocence" (98), the governess knows that to attach such a name to such innocence would be merely to confess the "guilty . . . cynicism" (126) of a "fallen" adult.

The children's beauty, however, so far from merely *carrying* a bad name, comes to *name* the very opposite of beatific innocence, and to occasion it: "For what else—when he's so clever and beautiful and perfect" could Miles be indicted, she eventually demands to know, but "for wickedness" (162)? The governess is forced to finesse her interpretive procedure in order to accommodate her growing recognition that "their more than earthly beauty, their absolutely unnatural goodness" are in fact "a game, . . . a policy and a fraud!" (145). The beauty and apparently innocent intuition seem, in the end, to signal contrivance and to carry with them not the fragrance of purity but an odor of corruption powerful enough to penetrate the surrounding environs, so that the term "shrouded" in the passage "the white curtain draping . . . the head of Flora's little bed, shrouded . . . the perfection of childish rest" (133) is a hint that the innocence that had once lain there is (to the governess's imagination) transforming itself into something ominous.

The shock with which James's late Victorian audience would have witnessed the unceremonious destruction of cherished conventions would have been matched by that sustained in its encounter with Bram Stoker's *Dracula* (1897).[28] In the broadest sense, both texts draw for their fund of horror from the exploding of certain set expectations—among them the high Victorian conviction that, as Bronfen puts it, "'the good death,' is that of a virtuous and preferably innocent person: of children or virgins."[29] As *The Turn of the Screw* offers an equation in which juvenile beauty may exist in direct proportion to the evil it embodies, so *Dracula* (as many critics have noted) equates the beauty of women—formerly the visible sign of their salvific powers—with predatory allure and mobile sexual desire. Where the very fact of her being "so fair to look upon"— like "a creature fresh from the hand of God, and waiting for the breath of life" (652)—indicates that Dickens's Little Nell has gone to dwell in glory, Lucy Westenra's apparent immunity from corporeal corruption is a sign of her spiritual degradation. Under the tutelage of Van Helsing, a seasoned physiognomist and metaphysician, John Seward, Lucy's disappointed suitor, learns to be suspicious of the bloom of feminine beauty in general, and to understand that postmortem pulchritude "means" evil: "If ever a face meant death—," Dr. Seward announces, "if looks could kill—we saw it at that moment."[30]

Just as full-blown feminine beauty serves as so clear a determinant of uncleanness that Van Helsing rejoices to find the infected Mina Harker looking "pale and thin and weak" (477), so the governess despairs to consider that little Flora's "extraordinary childish grace" (130) and "child's sincerity" (179) are explicable only if read as the dissembling typical of "an old, old woman" (172). The governess increasingly portrays herself as being practiced on by scheming children, so that Miles, for example, with a "charming exhibition of tact, of magnanimity," exercises an influence that leaves her with "a strange sense of having literally slept at my post" (168). "What surpassed everything," she marvels, "was that there was a little boy in the world who could have for the inferior age, sex, and intelligence so fine a consideration" (132). This "consideration" she later identifies as the coefficient of "his small strange genius" (190), although what she comprehends by this culturally weighted term is starkly at odds with the conditions that occasion its use. Miles's genius betrays itself in the sort of precocity that, according to the nineteenth-century Italian criminologist Cesare Lombroso, "is morbid and atavistic," "common to genius and to insanity," and observable "among all savages."[31] Thus, the governess slights the success that Quint and Miss Jessel appear to have enjoyed in making the children "still cleverer even than nature did," their achievement diminished, to her mind, by their having had, in the first place, "wondrous material to play on!" (180). Miles's cleverness, delicacy, and "discrimination" (190) are all attributable, the governess informs us, to the "outbreak in him of the little natural man" (130) ("natural" having its old Calvinist meaning here rather than the romantic one), just as Van Helsing recognizes Dracula's cunning as the fledgling expression of "that so great child-brain of his" (390).

One of Van Helsing's greatest challenges is to convince his associates that "there are things old and new which must not be contemplate [*sic*] by men's eyes, because they know—or think they know—some things which other men have told them" (246). The brutal discrediting in *The Turn of the Screw* of things that "other men have told" complicates a text that would have been unnerving even had James not produced one last excruciating turn of the screw precisely at the moment of Miles's death. James's treatment of childhood innocence—and of insight at the moment of death—being less reductive than Stoker's treatment of feminine beauty, we confront in *The Turn of the Screw* something more complex than the mere inversion of the equation plotted by Wilde's Miss Prism ("The good end happily, and the bad unhappily. That is what Fiction means").[32] Miles may, in fact, have been as stainless spiritually as he is physically: moments before she witnesses his death, the governess acknowledges that qualifying her pity is "the appalling alarm" of Miles's being "perhaps innocent" (196). Discernment, vision, obscurity, what cannot or must not be "contemplate by men's eyes": these concerns—at least as pressing in *The Turn of the Screw* as the question of whether or not youthful beauty is an accurate indicator of innocence—are inextricably bound together in a text that explores its own hermeneutics. "*Look* at him" (98) is the governess's antiphonal response to Mrs. Grose's "*look* at her!" (95), each pledging a coded allegiance to the High Victorian belief that truth and beauty are interchangeable, cleanly intersecting within a common ground of established equivalencies. When asked to provide proof of her assertion that Miss Jessel is "a horror of horrors," the governess promptly retorts that she is certain "by the way she looked" (122)—her answer, to her mind, amply definitive and admitting of no ambiguity.

The governess had begun by equating mere looking with clear seeing, and clear seeing with absolute knowing. She learns in time, however, that looking and seeing name two essentially different procedures, as well as two distinct states of awareness, and that one can fathom "the depths of the sinister" (the phrase is James's ["Preface" 175]) only if one's eyes are not "sealed" to evil, a term that she fixes on as she comes to differentiate between the visionary acuities of her companion and her charges and their allied capacity to distill essence from appearance. She fears, for example, that her own "eyes might be sealed just while" those of her charges "were most opened" (149–50). Although she rues Mrs. Grose's blindness—"her eyes were hopelessly sealed" to the sight of Miss Jessel, who looms up before the governess "as big as a blazing fire" (176)—she considers it "prodigious" that, through her efforts, Miles's "sense was sealed" (194) to the haunting pair. Even at the last, the boy can catch "with his sealed eyes the direction" of her words only, his confusion recorded in the punctuated cry that follows his "glaring vainly over the place and missing wholly . . . the wide, overwhelming presence" of Quint (197).

In employing the term as she does, the governess transforms her "dreadful liability to impressions of the order so vividly exemplified" (113) into the authority that sanctions her readings of the texts available to her: Quint's appearance (and the design it embodies), Miles's appearance, or look (and the premature cunning it conceals). In the end, however, she cannot resolve the meaning of Miles's deathbed utterance. Like a purloined letter—available to view but finally unseen—Miles's final enigmatic statement remains for the governess (and by extension, for her readers) a sealed text. In his preface, James applies the term to texts that are "absolutely sealed and beyond test or proof" ("Preface" 162)—texts, such as *The Turn of the Screw,* that will not be "baited by earnest criticism" ("Preface" 169) and that refuse, like the German book of which Poe writes in "The Man of the Crowd" (1840), to allow themselves to be read.[33] His sense of the word echoes that conveyed in a passage from Isaiah: "For the Lord . . . hath closed your eyes: the prophets and your rulers, the seers hath he covered. And the vision of all is become unto you as the words of a book that is sealed, which men deliver to one that is learned, saying, Read this, I pray thee: and he saith, I cannot; for it is sealed" (Isa. 29:10–11).

Dickens could comfort those mourning at the death of Little Nell by reminding them that "in the Destroyer's steps there spring up bright creations that defy his power, and his dark path becomes a way of light to Heaven" (659). Writing in 1840, nearly half a century before James produced his self-obscuring text, Dickens could still insist on the existence of an infinitely wise and beneficent author of all things whose "dispensations" were being defended in the pulpit as "kindly meant, and wisely ordered, . . . however inscrutable they may appear."[34] Miming another order of being and limning another order of experience (hermeneutic and teleological), James offers his late Victorian audience a seraphic child who, following in the Destroyer's steps, is "hurled over an abyss" (198) while he leads his governess "not into clearness, but into a darker obscure" (196).

Notes

1. Henry James, *The Turn of the Screw,* vol. 11 of *The Bodley Head Henry James,* ed. Leon Edel (1898; London: Bodley Head, 1974), 85, 82, 198. Page references in the text are to this edition.

2. Leon Edel and Lyall H. Powers, eds., *The Complete Notebooks of Henry James* (New York: Oxford University Press, 1987), 109.

3. Nathaniel Hawthorne, preface to *The House of the Seven Gables* (1851; Athens: Ohio State University Press, 1971), 1.

4. Edel and Powers, 190.

5. Henry James, preface to *The Aspern Papers*, in *The Art of the Novel* (1934; New York: Scribner's, 1962), 169. Page references in the text are to this edition.

6. M. R. James, cited in Jack Sullivan, "Psychological, Antiquarian, and Cosmic Horror 1872–1919," in *Horror Literature*, ed. Marshall B. Tymn (New York: Bowker, 1981), 251.

7. Jean Jacques Rousseau, *Émile* (1762; London: Dent, 1911), 54.

8. James Sutherland, ed., *The Oxford Book of Literary Anecdotes* (London: Oxford University Press, 1975), 190–91.

9. The evolutionary trail leading from Wells's Eloi to many creatures in contemporary science fiction films is littered with aliens whose superiority is expressed neotenously. The superiority of the beings featured in Stephen Spielberg's *Close Encounters of the Third Kind* (1977) is evidenced in their hairless, exaggerated crania and wide eyes. One of their progeny, who makes its appearance some years later in *E.T.* (1982), bears a striking resemblance to an aged baby. In "A Biological Homage to Mickey Mouse," Stephen Jay Gould describes a similar process of reverse ontogeny—"a true evolutionary transformation," as he calls it—that Mickey Mouse (though his "chronological age never altered") has undergone since his inception roughly seventy years ago (*The Panda's Thumb* [New York: Norton, 1980], 97).

10. Alexander Francis Chamberlain, *The Child: A Study in the Evolution of Man* (London: Walter Scott, 1906), 9, 32.

11. Judith A. Plotz, "A Victorian Comfort Book: Juliana Ewing's *The Story of a Short Life*," in *Romanticism and Children's Literature in Nineteenth-Century England*, ed. James Holt McGavran Jr. (Athens: University of Georgia Press, 1991), 173.

12. W. B. Clark, *Asleep in Jesus; or, Words of Consolation to Bereaved Parents* (Edinburgh: T. Nelson, 1856), 28–29.

13. John Kucich, "Death Worship among the Victorians: *The Old Curiosity Shop*," *PMLA* 95.1 (1980): 59.

14. Charles Dickens, *Dombey and Son* (1848; Oxford: Clarendon Press, 1974), 220, 222. Page references in the text are to this edition.

15. Margarete Holubetz, "Death-Bed Scenes in Victorian Fiction," *English Studies* 67.1 (1986): 16.

16. A. E. Michener, "Memoir," in *The Prose and Poetical Works of Fannie L. Michener* (Philadelphia: Lippincott, 1884), 11. Page references in the text are to this edition.

17. John Choate, "To his Dear Brother," August 7, 1784, in author's private collection. All spelling and punctuation follow the original.

18. Michael Wheeler, *Death and the Future Life in Victorian Literature and Theology* (Cambridge: Cambridge University Press, 1990), 30.

19. Elisabeth Bronfen, *Over Her Dead Body: Death, Femininity, and the Aesthetic* (New York: Routledge, 1992), 77.
20. Plotz, 178.
21. Clark, 28–30.
22. H. G. Wells, "The Door in the Wall," in *The Door in the Wall and Other Stories* (Boston: David R. Godine, 1980), 6. Page references in the text are to this edition.
23. Aldous Huxley, "Vulgarity in Literature," in *Music at Night and Other Essays* (London: Chatto and Windus, 1949), 333–34.
24. Kucich, 59.
25. Bronfen, 80.
26. Garrett Stewart, "Thresholds of the Visible: The Death Scene of Film," *Mosaic* 16.1–2 (1983): 33–34.
27. Charles Dickens, *The Old Curiosity Shop* (1841; Harmondsworth: Penguin Books, 1977), 654. Page references in the text are to this edition.
28. For a fuller treatment of the similarities between James's story and Stoker's novel, see the third chapter of my *The Shape of Fear: Horror and the Fin de Siècle Culture of Decadence* (Lexington: University Press of Kentucky, 1998).
29. Bronfen, 78.
30. Bram Stoker, *Dracula* (1897; Harmondsworth: Penguin Books, 1993), 272.
31. Cesare Lombroso, *The Man of Genius* (1910; New York: Garland, 1984), 15–16.
32. Oscar Wilde, *The Importance of Being Earnest,* in *Oscar Wilde,* ed. Isobel Murray (1895; Oxford: Oxford University Press, 1989), 501.
33. Edgar Allan Poe, "The Man in the Crowd," vol. 2 of *Collected Works of Edgar Allan Poe,* ed. Thomas Ollive Mabbott (Cambridge: Harvard University Press, 1978), 145–46.
34. Clark, 19.

Getting Things in the Right Order:
Stephen King's *The Shining, The Stand,* and *It*

Bud Foote

Any right-thinking person must feel a certain diffidence when writing a paper on Stephen King, particularly one concerned with definition; remember what King himself says in *Danse Macabre:* "It's a trap, this matter of definition, and I can't think of a more boring academic subject. . . . [I]t is really a discussion of how many angels can dance on the head of a pin, and not really interesting unless those involved in the discussion are drunk or graduate students—two states of roughly similar incompetence."[1] On the other hand, in the headnote to *The Tommyknockers,* King says, "If you get mad at critics, you almost always can be sure they are right."[2] That makes me feel a bit better, because I plan to slice up King's horror novels in two ways, thus multiplying divisions, distinctions, and definitions beyond all reason. If King reads this, I hope that he finds it irritating at least, infuriating at best—both much better than boring.

My first division, which I hope relates to the whole business of childhood, is one proposed by King himself in *Danse Macabre;* one cannot, it appears, totally avoid definition, no matter how sober or unacademic one may be. King says that horror fiction—a somewhat confusing term, as we shall see—appeals in descending order of excellence to terror, horror, and the gross-out (4–7, 25).

To take the last first: the gross-out is firmly rooted in reality, not in fantasy, rooted in the knowledge that many products of the human body are less than attractive, that the interior of the human self is best left decently veiled in its skin, and that what is left of us after death is not something the tribe is going to want sitting around the cave for an extended period. We are grossed out *not* by a stake driven into a vampire's heart, but by the predictable results of such an act: the gushers of good old everyday blood, the yelling and screaming any reasonable person might expect, and the somewhat accelerated but perfectly natural process of decomposition.

Further, the gross-out is one of the first things we learn as children, quite likely in the process of being toilet trained. Nursery school humor, as parents know, relies heavily on "ka-ka," "pi-pi," and "do-do," all basic to the vocabulary of the linguistically deprived, followed shortly thereafter by "yuck!" I am persuaded that part of Homer's success as a wandering minstrel lay in his ability to shotgun all parts of his audience, dishing up Odysseus the crafty for the old men, describing the slaughter of the suitors for the young warriors, amusing the women with Penelope's suggestion that the man claiming to be her husband can sleep in the hall his first night home, and targeting the urchins under the table with the description of the pieces of Odysseus's companions showing up in the vomit of the drunken Polyphemus. "Ooooh, gross!" they must have said, as my own children did when I read the passage to them.

What King calls *horror,* however, as opposed to the gross-out, involves the appearance of the Monster, Vampire, Zombie, or Werewolf, and thus tends to be grounded in the fantastic rather than in the everyday. A dead roach mashed on the floor may be gross, but a nine-foot roach scrabbling at the door is horrible. Horror, then, means that the person horrified has drawn a line between the everyday and the fantastic. A scabby, drunken pedophile is scary, right enough, and like as not even gross; but a dead friend standing a floor off the ground at your window and begging admission is horrific. Therefore, horror belongs to a slightly older child than does the gross-out, a child who has learned a bit more about the boundaries of that system we call reality.

Terror, as King defines it, is still more complex and more subtle. Terror is when the door never opens to reveal the Monster, the Werewolf, or the Vampire, and the viewers or readers are left to create the Thing Behind the Door in their own minds. Terror is what Vic in *Cujo* experiences when he feels that there may be something in the closet but never sees it, only confronts it in his mind. Manifestly, terror depends on a mind more developed, an imagination more exercised, than does horror; and therefore, just as the gross-out belongs to the nursery and horror to the young child, so terror typically is the province of later childhood.

King does all three, of course, and at his best he does them very well. Reading *Misery* (1987), I am terrified, when Annie is out of the house and Paul is out of his room, that any minute she will return and catch him; I am horrified when she chops off his foot; and I am grossed out when she makes him drink the mop water. As King says in *Danse Macabre*, "I recognize terror as the finest emotion . . . and so I will try to terrorize the reader. But if I find I cannot terrify him/her, I will try to horrify; and if I find I cannot horrify, I'll go for the gross-out. I'm not proud" (25).

On the most basic level, death is gross. It turns pussycats into road pizzas. Sir Thomas Browne notes that we are not so much afraid of death as we are ashamed of it. It is also horrid: death, Mark Petrie reflects in *'Salem's Lot*, is when the monsters get you.[3] And because nobody knows what is behind death's door, death is terrible. King appeals on all three levels, which means that he appeals to three different levels of our childhoods.

King calls fiction that makes this appeal *horror fiction*, which is in his own terms a bit confusing because he says that it appeals to terror, horror, and the gross-out. However, since we obviously can't call it *terror, horror, and gross-out fiction*, we seem to be stuck with *horror fiction*, even though its most refined and most basic appeals are not to horror but to terror and the gross-out.

In much the same way, we are stuck with term *science fiction*, in spite of the fact that most science fiction has little to do with science and a lot to do with technology and history. Now I am going to abandon King's classification and return to the traditional division of fiction into mainstream (or mimetic, or mundane) fiction, which deals with events that might plausibly happen within our conventional scientific and historical paradigms; science fiction, which deals with events that represent more-or-less reasonable extensions of those paradigms; and fantasy, which deals with events that cannot be so connected. King himself invites us to revisit these categories when, after castigating drunken doctoral definers in *Danse Macabre,* he goes on to define the kind of fiction he creates as a subset of fantasy and then almost immediately notes that horror fiction does not have to be unscientific, citing Curt Siodmak's *Donovan's Brain* as a novel that is "really" a horror novel, however much it may masquerade as science fiction (17–20). He then retells a story most of us remember from oral tradition, the one about the maniac with a hook for a hand who preys on teenage parking couples. But that story is not fantasy, nor is it science fiction; it is mainstream, requiring neither a belief in magic or the supernatural nor an extrapolation from the here and now to make it work. There *are* maniacal murderers among us, worse luck, and some people *do* have hooks instead of hands, and while it may be outrageously coincidental, nothing prevents a driver from settling down in a lover's lane at the very moment that a maniac's hook engages the car's door handle. It is mainstream all the way, but horror beyond any doubt.

So is King's novel *Cujo*. Oh, there are a couple of hints of fantasy in the novel: one little boy has a three-states-away hunch that his dog is in trouble, and another boy thinks he sees a monster in his closet, as later, in a state of great mental agitation, does his father. But surely the most important thing here is the litany of Monster Words that Vic devises to protect his son against the monsters in the closet:

> No vampires, no werewolves, no things that bite,
> You have no business here.
> Nothing will touch Tad, or hurt Tad, all this night.
> You have no business here.[4]

Vic finds the paper on which he wrote this charm at the scene of his son's death. It may have worked against creatures of the imagination; it might even have worked against fantasy vampires or werewolves—charms often do; but it does not work against real-life mainstream *things that bite*. Vampires and werewolves have business in a fantasy context, not in a mimetic novel; but rabid Saint Bernards have as much business in the daily world as you and I do, and that is the horror of *Cujo*.

King's *Misery* is likewise mainstream fiction. As in *Cujo*, the application of the principles of fantasy to the real world is the mistake the characters make at the center of the novel. And because Annie the mad nurse, knowing full well that Misery is a heroine created by the captive Paul, believes her to be—in some sense—real, she goes all unplugged from sanity and reality and inflicts the most terrible punishment on Paul, herself, and the surrounding territory. When Annie is dead, Paul, seduced by his own fictional wisdom of a pagan idol, finds himself believing in her survival until he can begin a new novel, this one realistic, not romantic. Horror then can reside in the mimetic as well as in the fantastic.

But some of King's work *is* straight fantasy, *'Salem's Lot,* for example: devised, he says, in homage to Bram Stoker, it is full of traditional magic. No plausible reason is given for the peculiar psychology of the vampire; that is Anne Rice's business, not King's. No excuse is given for the efficacy of crosses or garlic or rose petals; were these items rationally justified, we would have a science fiction–style vampire, as in Richard Matheson's *I*

Am Legend (1954). In *'Salem's Lot,* as so often in King's work, a major point-of-view character is a young child, not only because death or threatened death or molestation of the young is peculiarly poignant, but also because only the child can see magic with absolute belief and therefore absolute horror.

Christine (1983) is likewise fantasy, though complicated by the fact that it is fantasy in the service of a teenager's dreams. Fantasy revolving around an automobile has to be technological fantasy, and it has never been clear to me whether Christine is a haunted automobile or a Frankenstein's monster or a vampire; furthermore, in dealing with Christine the protagonists have no backlog of traditional weaponry to wield.

How you categorize *Carrie* (1974), *Firestarter* (1980), and *The Dead Zone* (1980) depends on whether you consider parapsychology a young science or old magic in disguise. John W. Campbell Jr. might have seen them as science fiction; for me they are borderline fantasy, *Firestarter* rather more science-fictiony than the others. But about *The Tommyknockers,* on the other hand, there can be little doubt; it is in the old SF tradition, directly descended from H. G. Wells's *The War of the Worlds* (1898), a story about what might have happened had Arthur C. Clarke's Rama decided to act like Robert A. Heinlein's Puppet Masters. In it, Bobbi Anderson points out that the author of *Brain Wave* has her last name (219); the elfish gadgeteering, the dog, and the woodchuck echo Clifford D. Simak's "The Big Front Yard" (1958); and the hatch on the flying saucer irises open (610) in tribute to the famous line in Heinlein's *Beyond This Horizon* (1942, 1948), "the door dilated." King constantly touches base with science fiction here, referring to Wells, *Startling Stories,* Hugo Gernsback, *Return of the Jedi,* and so on. He even allows himself the kind of dumb mistake that fans leap on with delight when it appears in TV sci-fi, inexplicably misplacing our planet and the Milky Way in the Lesser Magellanic Cloud (458). Thus horror, as written by King, appears in the clothing of all three subgenres: mainstream, fantasy, and science fiction.

Now, let me float a hypothesis for you: fantasy is the typical literature of early childhood; science fiction, that of adolescence; and mainstream fiction, that of adulthood. The first is the literature of magical discovery; the second, the literature of anticipation of the future; and the third, the literature of coming to terms with the real past and the real present.

The young child discovers a world in which everything is more or less magical; the difference between the technology necessary for a 747 or TV screen and the magic needed for a crystal ball or witch's broomstick is not immediately obvious. William Wordsworth would have it that the child's world is full of this sense of wonder, forgetting that this sense extends not only to Triton and his wreathed horn but also to the demons and ogres of every schoolyard. (Notice that J. R. R. Tolkien's *The Lord of the Rings* [1954–55] has its beginning in *The Hobbit* [1937], a tale for children.)

The older child, having more or less worked out the line between magic and technology, takes that same sense of wonder and transfers it to science fiction, the literature of a potential future—both his own future and that of the human race. Like the fantasy of the younger child, the science fiction of the older child includes both threat and promise, George Orwell's *1984* (1949) as well as Edward Bellamy's *Looking Backward* (1888), reflecting the threats of adulthood, sexuality, and an unknown future as well as their promise. (Consider, in passing, how much of the science fiction of the Golden Age was aimed at a juvenile audience, and how very good the best of it—for example, Heinlein's *The Star Beast* (1954)—really was; note also, if you will, how often the hero, even in today's adult science fiction, is engaged in the sort of initiation experience typical of the teen years in mainstream fiction.)

Mimetic, or mainstream, or mundane fiction is typically the fiction of the adult attempting to see through the everyday veil into everyday things and attempting to rediscover the wonder in daily-ness that the child finds in the fantastic and the teenager in the science fictional.

I am *not* saying that fantasy is for kids, science fiction is for teens, and hard-assed realism is the only proper fare for adults; if I thought that way, I wouldn't be writing this essay. King himself says that

> [k]ids are bent. They think around corners. But starting at roughly age eight, when childhood's second great era begins, the kinks begin to straighten out, one by one. The boundaries of thought and vision begin to close down to a tunnel as we gear up to get along. . . . The job of the fantasy writer, or the horror writer, is to bust the walls of that tunnel vision wide for a little while. . . . The job of the fantasy-horror writer is to make you, for a little while, a child again. (*Danse Macabre* 407)

All three sorts of fiction, then, appeal to our sense of wonder in different ways, appeal to different parts of us: the child, the young adult, and the adult.

If it is easy to classify *Misery* and *'Salem's Lot* and *The Tommyknockers,* however, three of King's books present us with peculiar problems: *The Shining* (1977), *The Stand* (1978, 1990), and *It* (1986). They won't hold still and let us fit them into neat categories. They zigzag. Some zigzagging is expected and indeed almost necessary: horror fiction intended for adults tends to begin in the mimetic mode. Starting in the fantasy mode is mostly for kids: "Once there were a lion, a witch, and a werewolf who lived together in a house built by the third little pig." You have to really turn yourself into a kid to go for an opening like that.

Furthermore, if the horror story doesn't begin in the real world, something in us tends to giggle. I think of the Bela Lugosi *Dracula,* and my reaction is that anybody driving across Transylvania in a rainstorm who takes shelter in a spooky ruined castle full of cobwebs and is greeted by a sinister caped count, *and doesn't bug out of there immediately,* gets exactly what he deserves. You *expect* vampires in that sort of situation, and the horror somehow just doesn't take. What is horrid is when the nice gray-haired old lady down the street who makes your kids cookies turns out to be a vampire. "I never drink . . . wine" is camp and funny. "Have a cookie, dear," can be horrific, if the sun is down.

As all the world knows, King is superb at drawing the realistic small town in which he begins his horrors. He has it all down cold—the characters, the speech patterns, the signs, the songs, the architecture; he is so good at it that if you were to read only fifty pages into each of his books set in Maine, you might think you were reading an outstanding local colorist. And after the catastrophes are over, he most often returns to a normal realistic world, almost like the pattern of a Shakespeare tragedy in which order is replaced by disruption leading to the slaughter of innocent and guilty alike, followed at the end by Fortinbras or Albany coming in to pick up the pieces and restore order.

But that's not the sort of zigzag I'm talking about in *The Shining, The Stand,* and *It.* In all three, it is as if the writer, halfway or threequarters or almost through the book, decided, "I don't want this to be mainstream, so I'll change it to fantasy"; or "No, science fiction wasn't what I meant, I meant fantasy"; or "Let's see, was I doing fantasy or science fiction? Science fiction, I guess."

The Shining is tricky. Through most of the book, the only unrealistic element we are forced to accept is the possibility of paranormal foreknowledge in both Halloran, the cook, and Danny, the little boy, and of telepathic communication between the two. Even these elements are considerably compromised by Halloran's cautioning Danny, early on, that the flash of foreknowledge doesn't always work; and that moves us comfortably back into reality, where our strangest hunches sometimes work and sometimes don't. From there on until nearly the end of the book, *The Shining* maintains a near-perfect balance, much like that of Henry James's *The Turn of the Screw* (1898). You may read it as fantasy if you like, in which case the hotel really *is* haunted and really *is* taking possession of Danny's father, Jack, and so on; but King has also left us free to read a mainstream story of a near-insane and often-violent alcoholic driven over the edge by isolation and alienation from the world the hotel represents to him, and a story of his impressionable and vulnerable son's seeing monsters in every closet and the emerging monster his father is becoming, and being quite naturally driven over the edge himself in the process.

The Shining is admirably balanced between fantasy and mainstream for 350 pages. Then, all of a sudden, it takes a sharp left turn into fantasy. The hotel seems to find liquor for Jack where there was no liquor before; the hedges move; Grady, whom we could have read as a hallucination, pulls the bolt and lets Jack out of the pantry; and we aren't in Kansas anymore, Toto.

The Stand, by contrast, begins as straightforward near-future science fiction of the postapocalyptic variety. In the book's near future, a government-engineered disease gets loose and takes out more than nine-tenths of the population in good gross-out fashion; both the results of the disease and its symptoms are graphically repellent. After the first 150 pages, people begin to have dreams about a good woman and bad man. When it turns out that these dreams have some relationship to reality, we are shoved into that frontier realm between science fiction and fantasy where telepathy and telekinesis work—the realm of *Firestarter, Carrie,* and most of *The Shining.*

As *The Stand* wears on, however, it becomes increasingly clear that the bad man has paranormal powers and is, indeed, some sort of demon. All of a sudden we are in the world of *'Salem's Lot,* and there we stay until the demon is exorcised with a thermonuclear device and we return to the world of mainstream fiction.

Each novel is quite powerful in its own way, but many readers have been troubled by the shift from one subgenre to another. The books just do not end as satisfactorily as they began. *It,* on the other hand, which also involves such a shift, seems to be very satisfactory indeed. Throughout most of the book the fantastic is constantly intruding on the world of everyday reality, sometimes in the form of a grotesque clown, sometimes in the form of Orwell's Room 101—whatever scares the observer the most, whether it be the Mummy, or the teenage Frankenstein monster, or the Creature from the Black Lagoon. We cannot, however, believe that It is the creation of the observers' minds, because It yanks a little boy's arm out of its socket some fifteen pages into the book.

Early on, we learn that the group of children who confront It have apparently triumphed, lived to grow up, and forgotten almost everything about it. (This group of children, almost all of them losers of one sort or another, who nonetheless combine to make a powerful collective being, strongly echoes the group of misfits in Theodore Sturgeon's *More than Human* [1953].) After maturing, the grown-up children live in an adult world, the world of mimetic fiction, of realistic cause and effect, the world most passionately desired by Stan, the most solidly rational among them. The world of fantasy repels Stan: "[T]here were things that were not supposed to be. They offended any sane person's sense of order. . . . [T]wo and two makes four, the lights in the sky are stars, if there's blood grownups can see it as well as kids, and dead boys stay dead. . . . You can live with fear. . . . It's *offense* you can't live with, because it opens up a crack inside your thinking." [5]

Stan cannot revert from the mundane world to the fantasy world, and so he kills himself. The others in the group can, but interestingly enough, while we see the young group encountering It in purely fantastic terms, complete with silver bullet, the older group goes through much the same encounter in terms that become increasingly science-fictiony. Richie has a vision of It arriving in a spaceship long ages ago "from a place much farther away than another star or another galaxy" (723). Like any malignant SF alien, It lays eggs, which Ben stomps on as he goes (1033). And by the time the adventurers have triumphed and are again released into the mundane world, once again to forget, nearly all of the fantasy terms of the first encounter have been transformed into the more nearly adult terms of science fiction.

In sum, then: the book begins in the mimetic world, as King often does, but the fantastic intrudes on that world almost immediately. We are then set up with two parallel encounters between the group and It, one (that of the children) done in purely fantastic and often fantastic-movie terms, the other (that of the adults) moving from the world of fantasy into the world of science fiction. We conclude back in the world of everyday realism, with even the memories of the encounter fading away.

The book works better than either *The Shining* or *The Stand* in its mixture of subgenres because, first, it is appropriate that the children perceive It in terms of fantasy, and the adults in terms of science fiction; second, science fiction can *explain* fantasy, as fantasy cannot explain science fiction; and third, the progression from fantasy to science fiction to mimetic fiction echoes the progression of childhood to adolescence to adulthood, and we sense its essential correctness. King has put things in the proper sequence.

There; that should be enough definitions and distinctions to infuriate anybody. In fact, I hope that my ideas make some people mad, for as King himself pointed out, that will mean that I am almost certainly right. And who am I to argue with Stephen King?

Notes

1. Stephen King, *Danse Macabre* (1981; New York: Berkley Books, 1983), 16. Page references in the text are to this edition.
2. Stephen King, *The Tommyknockers* (1987; New York: Signet, 1988), [7]. Page references in the text are to this edition.
3. Stephen King, *'Salem's Lot* (1975; New York: Signet, 1976), 139.
4. Stephen King, *Cujo* (1981, New York: Signet, 1982), 60.
5. Stephen King, *It* (1986; New York: Signet, 1987), 411. Page references in the text are to this edition.

Contributors

ALIDA ALLISON is an associate professor in the Department of English and Comparative Literature at San Diego State University. Her *I. B. Singer: Children's Stories and Childhood Memoirs* was published in 1996. Her current book is *Russell Hoban/Forty Years.*

GAY BARTON, a professor of English at Abilene Christian University, wrote her master's thesis on the child image in the fantasies of George MacDonald.

BUD FOOTE, a professor in the School of Literature, Communication, and Culture, Georgia Institute of Technology, has published several articles on science fiction and a study of time travel, *The Connecticut Yankee in the Twentieth Century.*

ANDREW GORDON, an associate professor of English at the University of Florida, is writing a book on the films of Steven Spielberg.

STEPHANIE BARBÉ HAMMER, an associate professor in the Literature and Languages Department of the University of California at Riverside, has published two critical studies: *Satirizing the Satirist* and *The Sublime Crime.*

HOWARD V. HENDRIX is the author of the novels *Lightpaths* and *Standing Wave,* the critical study *The Ecstasy of Catastrophe,* and numerous stories, articles, and reviews.

GARY KERN is a noted translator of Russian and a scholar whose works include *Zamiatin's "We": A Collection of Critical Essays.*

SUSAN KRAY, an assistant professor of radio/TV/film at Indiana State University, Terre Haute, has earned Ph.D. and master of professional writing degrees, and is a 1987 graduate of Clarion West.

HOWARD M. LENHOFF is a professor emeritus of biology at the University of California at Irvine, and currently is investigating music cognition in people with Williams syndrome.

FRANCES DEUTSCH LOUIS, who retired in 1995, is a professor emerita of English, York College, the City University of New York. For a few years, she reviewed science fiction for the *Christian Science Monitor.*

211

LYNNE LUNDQUIST teaches in the Theatre and Dance Department of California State University, Fullerton. She has contributed essays to *Extrapolation* and the Eaton volume *Immortal Engines*.

JOSEPH D. MILLER, an associate professor of pharmacology at Texas Tech University Health Sciences Center and an ex–project director for the Space Shuttle program, is a frequent contributor to the Eaton volumes.

SUSAN J. NAVARETTE is an associate professor of English at the University of North Carolina at Chapel Hill. She has published a book on science and horror in the nineteenth century.

ERIC S. RABKIN, a professor of English at the University of Michigan, is the author or co-editor of more than twenty books on science fiction and fantasy.

GEORGE SLUSSER is a professor of comparative literature at the University of California at Riverside and the curator of the Eaton Collection. He has written or edited numerous books on science fiction and earned the Pilgrim Award from the Science Fiction Research Association for lifetime contributions to the field.

GARY WESTFAHL, who teaches at the University of California at Riverside, has published two critical studies and numerous articles on science fiction and fantasy and co-edited three Eaton volumes.

Index